BALOTELLI

About the author

Luca Caioli is the bestselling author of *Messi, Ronaldo, Torres, Neymar* and *Suárez*. A renowned Italian sports journalist, he lives in Spain.

BALOTELLI

THE REMARKABLE STORY BEHIND
THE SENSATIONAL HEADLINES

LUCA CAIOLI

Translated from the Italian by Laura Bennett

ICON

Published in the UK and USA in 2015 by
Icon Books Ltd, Omnibus Business Centre,
39–41 North Road, London N7 9DP
email: info@iconbooks.com
www.iconbooks.com

Sold in the UK, Europe and Asia
by Faber & Faber Ltd, Bloomsbury House,
74–77 Great Russell Street, London WC1B 3DA or their agents

Distributed in the UK, Europe and Asia
by TBS Ltd, TBS Distribution Centre, Colchester Road
Frating Green, Colchester CO7 7DW

Distributed in Australia and New Zealand
by Allen & Unwin Pty Ltd, PO Box 8500,
83 Alexander Street, Crows Nest, NSW 2065

Distributed in South Africa
by Jonathan Ball, Office B4, The District,
41 Sir Lowry Road, Woodstock 7925

Distributed in India by Penguin Books India,
7th Floor, Infinity Tower – C, DLF Cyber City, Gurgaon 122002, Haryana

Distributed in Canada by Publishers Group Canada,
76 Stafford Street, Unit 300, Toronto, Ontario M6J 2S1

Distributed to the trade in the USA by
Consortium Book Sales and Distribution,
The Keg House, 34 Thirteenth Avenue NE,
Suite 101, Minneapolis, Minnesota 55413-1007

ISBN: 978-184831-913-4

Typeset in New Baskerville by Marie Doherty

Printed and bound in the UK by
Clays Ltd, St Ives plc

Contents

Chapter 1

The Beginning of a Fairy Tale

'I gave him his first start. Me. And it was down to luck. That is how life is. But you want to know the details.'

Of course.

'OK, so I'll tell you everything. Usually when I'm in charge of a team, if they're playing on a Sunday, I get them to play a friendly against a local team on the Thursday before. Amateur non-league teams of different standards. I never make them play against the *Berretti* Under-20 team or the *Allievi* Under-17 team from my club. I send on eleven players for the first half and then another eleven for the second half. In the first half, the reserves play. In the second half, it's more or less the first team.

'I had joined the Lumezzane bench towards the end of the season, for the 27th match. There were only eight games left until the end of the Serie C1 championship. For the first two matches, we managed to find teams that weren't local, but before the sixth, there wasn't a team for us to play our usual practice match against, so they told me we had to play the first half against the Under-20 team and the second against the Under-17s.'

Valter 'Sandro' Salvioni, born in 1953, is a former midfielder with 56 appearances in Serie A, at Foggia and Brescia, and one goal to his name in Italy's top flight. In 1989, he swapped the pitch for the bench and became a manager. He has spent his career looking after Under-20 teams and those in Serie B, C and D in Italy, Switzerland and France. In the spring of 2006, this took him to AC Lumezzane. Sitting in the living room of his terraced house in Gorlago, his home-town in the province of Bergamo, Salvioni has an hour or so to spare before he is due to commentate on the Atalanta match for local TV. With a Bergamasque accent and deliber-ate patience, he recalls those days in late March and early April 2006, days that would change the life of a boy whose surname at that time was Barwuah.

'That Thursday, the non-first team players had to play the first half against the *Berretti* team, boys aged between seven-teen and nineteen. It was a tough test for the reserves. In the second half, the first team played the Under-17s. There I am, on my feet, minding my own business watching the game quietly when I see this kid do a rainbow flick to get past my central defender, a Lumezzane first team player, and speed off down the wing. I watched him for about five minutes, then I went to the Under-17s' coach and said: "Listen, that boy there, he's coming with me tomorrow. I'm going to play him on Sunday."'

Massimo Boninsegna, 47, a former player with Orceana and Forlì and now coach in one of the top amateur leagues at CastelnuovoSandrà, managed that Under-17 team. He remembers the moment differently: 'Salvioni hadn't been there long. He'd taken over from Marco Rossi, who had been sacked after the home defeat to Sambenedettese. He came to talk to me after he had seen what Mario could do in the practice game against the first team. We had a corner. The first team were zonal marking; Salvioni had given specific tasks to each of his defenders but no one expected Mario to try an incredible bicycle kick from the edge of the area. The ball hit the crossbar and bounced onto the line.

'In or out? I was refereeing and I gave the goal. It was too good a shot not to reward him. After the session, Salvioni came to me and said he was going to take Mario in a couple of Sundays' time. I told him I would be nothing but happy if he took him, that I would be delighted for him to make his Serie C debut. Then he asked me if I thought the kid was ready. What could I say but yes, absolutely ready? I was convinced.'

But things were not as simple as they seemed. Despite these assurances, Sandro Salvioni was told by the club management that Mario Barwuah Balotelli could not play.

'"What do you mean he can't play?" They said he was only fifteen. I asked if they were joking. He's good. When he has the ball at his feet he's not afraid to try things. He's got personality, quality, technique and speed. He may be fifteen, but when he is on the pitch he looks 30 to me. I'm taking him with me. I insisted,' Salvioni remembers.

But the response was the same: 'You can't pick him. He's fifteen and you have to be sixteen to play with the professionals. Talk to the chairman and the director of football and see what they have to say.'

'So I went. "Mr Chairman," I said. "This kid has to come with me. We're away at Padova on Sunday and I want him to play." He said I couldn't but I told him we needed Mario. We really did need him, as Lumezzane's two strikers, Carlo Taldo and Alessandro Matri, were both unavailable. We were going to have to bring someone up from the Under-20s or the Under-17s to put on the bench. Plus, we needed him because Lumezzane were second from bottom in the league and on the brink of relegation to Serie C2.'

Everyone at Lumezzane knew Mario was a good player, including Gian Bortolo Pozzi, the chairman, but to play with the professional footballers in Serie C1 you needed to be sixteen years old.

But Salvioni refused to give up. Eventually, the director of football told him: 'The only thing we can do is get authorisation from his family and try to ask for a special exemption for him from the league. We will send a letter explaining that we want the boy to play in the first team, with an attached certificate from our doctor attesting to his physical fitness. Then we will have to wait and see what they say.'

Salvioni asked how long it would take. The director of football replied that they would hear something either the following evening or on the Saturday. 'Send the letter and let me know.' Salvioni gets up from his sofa and continues his story.

'Mario trained with us the next day. But we didn't hear anything. Nothing. The chairman said they were still waiting for an answer. He asked if I was sure about taking him to Padova. My response was adamant; he was someone who could make a difference. "Come and train with the first team tomorrow," I told the boy. Mario said he had school but I told him he would have to skip classes for once: "I need you with me".'

'He turned up on Saturday before the game. We had a training session at 10 o'clock. I was on my way to the ground when I had a phone call from the director of football: "A fax has come through from the association. It's all OK, they have given us the exemption. Mario can play." I went into the dressing room and called Mario over. I told him everything was fine and that he was coming with us to Padova on Sunday.'

It was 2 April 2006, a sunny spring Sunday at the Euganeo stadium. Padova against Lumezzane, the 29th day of the championship, the return match in what was then Serie C1. Maurizio Pellegrino's Padova were fourth in the table and unbeaten at home. But after a brilliant start to the season, they were in danger of failing to reach the promotion play-offs. In short, they needed a win. On paper it should have been easy, given that Lumezzane were without half their first team players and had the unenviable distinction of having lost the greatest number of away matches with ten defeats so far. The Brescians looked as if they had been written off, were running out of time and in danger of automatic relegation. Yet, in the first half Lumezzane managed to dominate their opponents, who seemed listless and short on ideas. The only threats to Brignoli, the Lumezzane keeper's goal came about half an hour in: a header from the Argentine, Christian La Grotteria, was just off target and a rocket from Andrea Tarozzi went out to the side. As if this was not enough, Pellegrino, the home team manager, was forced to rethink his defence when, in the 23rd minute, Paolo Cotroneo, the central defender, was struck by tachycardia out of the blue and left-winger Andrea Suriano reported muscular difficulties in the 33rd minute. Unexpectedly, it was 0-0 at the end of the first half. The Lume boss suddenly realised he might be able to pull something off.

'There was not much more than half an hour left to go. I looked at Mario and told him to get ready to go on. 'I remember', Salvioni said, 'that I had another striker on the bench. I was playing 4-4-2 and had two forwards on the pitch and two on the bench. It was Giorgio Biancospino, an older boy, but I told him I was sorry but I was putting Mario on. I knew it wasn't fair, it should have been him, but at that point I preferred Mario because he had the qualities I needed on the pitch at that time. I took Luca Paghera off, another rookie, and put Mario on.'

In the 18th minute of the second half, Mario Barwuah Balotelli got up from the bench. He made his professional footballing debut aged fifteen years, seven months and

21 days. It was not an outright record (Catilina Aubameyang, who had played for Reggiana in Serie B, and Carta at Olbia in Serie C2 were both younger) but for Mario it was a huge debut for Lumezzane. He later claimed his initial surprise soon turned to fear. Looking out at the terraces in front of him, he saw the 3,643 spectators in the Euganeo stadium and his legs began to shake. But it did not show. Like it was nothing special, he skipped off and went through his warm up before going on in place of Paghera.

What were his first minutes of the game like? 'He started doing some of his tricks,' remembers Ezio Chinelli, the then manager of the Lume youth team, who was in the stadium on that fateful 2 April. What tricks? 'With his first touch, he conjured up a double stepover that left three defenders for dead, then a flip-flap feint, like Ronaldinho. Then he stopped the ball beneath the sole of his boot, challenging his opponent. Immediately, the Padova fans started booing.'

He had been called names because of the colour of his skin before when he was playing for the Lumezzane youth teams: against Lecco, when a parent got up and shouted 'that n*****'s a great player', as if it was a compliment; and in a derby against Brescia, when Mario was sent off for elbowing an opponent who had shouted 'filthy n*****' behind his back. It may have happened before, but at Padova he received the first racist boos of his career, something that would go on to torment him for years on the football pitch.

'The happiness and excitement of that debut', Mario would say years later, 'meant that I didn't hear those boos that were so full of hatred. They got stuck in my ears. As time went on, I heard every boo and insult very clearly, though.'

Ululating is a shameful and constant presence in Mario's life. Some of the touches made by that six foot one inch fifteen-year-old black kid, who no one had heard of yet, may well have deserved the tirade from the Padova fans. Marco Barbirati from Ferrara, the match director, referred to the incident in his report. The following day, Padova were concerned they were going to be landed with a fine from the federation, or worse still, disqualification of the ground due to the reputation of the Euganeo. It was not the first time Padova's fans had rained racist chants down on a black player, particularly the hard-core group known as the *Fronte Opposto*, who hoisted a flag with an eagle inside a shield on a black background and had links to the far right. It had even happened before against Lumezzane, just two years earlier. That time the supporters of the team from the Veneto had targeted Lassana Doumbya, a 23-year-old originally French midfielder playing for the Brescian team at the time. The federation had imposed the sanction of one match behind closed doors (a decision that was later revoked) and fined the club €3,000. But on 2 April 2006, as would happen many times on other pitches around Italy, the fact that a fringe element of fans was intent on ululating was not considered particularly important. No fine, no disqualification.

Let's get back to the match. Five minutes after Barwuah came on, exactly 23 minutes into the second half, Lumezzane took the lead.

'We scored from a corner won by Mario. I remember he set off down the left wing with his man in his sights. He tried to get away by the goal line and the defender kicked it out for a corner. It came in over the top from the left and Ferrara picked up the clearance from the Padova rearguard and sent it back into the middle. Mario was there waiting too, but suddenly this little guy came racing in – Emanuele Morini (five foot five and ten stone, a Roman who had played in England and Greece) – and scored. Mario played on until the end of the game. We won 1-0 and from then on he stayed with us in the first team,' Sandro Salvioni concluded.

The next morning's newspapers were over the moon. 'Lumezzane, a single shot worth double. Automatic relegation avoided and only four points from safety,' was the headline in *Bresciaoggi*, which went on to add: 'Salvioni praised the whole group: "They were an impeccable team".' At the start of the sports pages on page 30, there was even a column about Mario: 'Barwuah, record-breaking debut. On the pitch at only fifteen.' A handful of lines described 'the latest gem bred by the red and blues, born in 1990 to Ghanaian parents, takes his first steps in grown-up football. Showing no sign of nerves, Barwuah got straight into the flow of the game. Lumezzane, who, up to that point had taken few risks, suddenly found their weight going forwards and won the game.' His 'first night had gone well,' the paper stressed, adding: 'The young striker's debut was the cherry on top of a very successful cake.' In the player ratings, Barwuah came away with a six, the average mark in a team in which only Morini, the goal scorer, managed a seven. The verdict on Mario was positive: 'He shows athleticism and a running ability that should not be underestimated.' Three days after the praise heaped on him by the local press, the story of the jewel of Lumezzane reached the pages of the *Gazzetta dello Sport*. The headline was: 'The fairy tale of Barwuah, the fifteen-year-old playing in Serie C1.' Mario's fairy tale, of a boy born in Italy to Ghanaian parents, had well and truly begun. For better, football, and for worse, racism.

Chapter 2

The Son of Immigrants

He has never been to Africa, although it is where the Barwuah family come from. From the Dark Continent. From Ghana. A large coastal country on the Gulf of Guinea, Ghana shares borders with the Ivory Coast, Burkina Faso and Togo, demarcation lines that were imposed during the colonial period and do not respect the territorial limits of the region's many different communities. It has a surface area of 92,100 square miles and a population estimated at 27 million in 2014. Of more than 75 ethnic groups, the Akan is the largest, with 11.5 million people. English is the official language, but more than 80 other languages are recognised. Christianity is the most widespread religion, followed by Islam and animist cults.

Ghana was the first Sub-Saharan African destination for Europeans keen to trade in gold and the transportation of slaves to America. In 1957, it was the first black African nation to declare independence from the colonial British power. It was an example for other African liberation movements, as was Kwame Nkrumah, Ghana's first president and a leading exponent of Pan-Africanism and the Non-Aligned movement against neo-colonialism. In 1966, his presidency was overthrown by a *coup d'état*, which was followed by years of military rule and political instability. In 1981, another *coup d'état* at the hands of Jerry Rawlings, a flight lieutenant in the Ghana Air Force, gradually saw normality return to the country. In April 1992, democracy resumed with a constitution that authorised a multi-party system. By regional standards, modern Ghana is a model in terms of its democratic system, political stability and freedom of expression and the press. The country is well-administered with low rates of corruption. Thanks to the exploitation of oil fields, which began in 2010, cocoa (Ghana is the world's second largest producer behind the Ivory Coast), and mineral resources (gold, diamonds, manganese and bauxite), Ghana's economy now has the highest rate of growth in Africa. This economic boom has driven many migrants to return home. However, this was not the situation in the late 1980s, when Thomas Barwuah decided to emigrate in search of a better life. He and Rose, his wife, were born in Accra, the capital, but came from Konongo. A city of 40,000 inhabitants in the Ashanti region, it is characterised by red earth, brightly-coloured taxis, low-rise housing, tin roofs, markets on every street and now-exhausted gold mines. Konongo was home to Nana Kwadwo Barwuah, Thomas's father, and Enock and Comfort, Rose's parents. Enock was a former landowner who grew coconut trees for the confectionery and food industries; Comfort ran a small stall near the market. For the area, they were well-off. When their daughter and son-in-law left for Europe, it was they who looked after Abigail, Rose and Thomas's daughter, born on 9 February 1988.

Thomas was the first to leave. He followed the route taken by his fellow countrymen, who had begun landing in Italy, the gateway to Europe. The final goal, the dream, was England, Germany or the United States, but getting a visa was not an easy prospect. It was much simpler to obtain an entry permit for Italy, a long-standing country of emigration that was starting to become a country of immigration, so much so that the number of foreign residents was estimated at 500,000 in 1989. There was work to be found in the *Bel paese*. Many Ghanaian women were employed in Emilia Romagna as caregivers or maids in private homes; others ran small market bazaars or hairdressers. The men found work in the construction or agricultural industries in Sicily and Campania, or in the factories of the north, in Lombardy and the Veneto.

Thomas arrived in Palermo in August 1988. The first few months in Sicily's capital were tough. Barwuah got by with various odd jobs as a caretaker, cleaner and builder. Rose joined him in February 1989, earning small amounts as a cleaning lady. The couple lived at number 18, Via dei Candelai: two rooms on the second floor of a crumbling, dilapidated eighteenth-century building punctuated by wrought iron balconies inevitably strewn with dangling sheets, blankets and clothes, hung out to dry. Via dei Candelai is a narrow street that crosses Via Maqueda in the city's historic centre. At that time, its old buildings saw the opening of craftsmen's workshops and the arrival of new immigrants in search of accommodation. It is now a very busy street full of young people visiting its pubs, clubs, terrace bars and karaoke joints. Today, the Albergheria area, near the Ballarò market, is home to the heart of the Ghanaian community, Palermo's largest immigrant group.

12 August 1990. Sun, blue skies, temperatures in the high 20s: a peaceful summer's day. Little more than a month has passed since the magical nights of the Italia 90 World Cup, when Totò Schillaci, born and bred in Palermo's San Giovanni Apostolo neighbourhood, became an Italian hero thanks to his six goals. Too bad that the long-haired Claudio Caniggia and Diego Maradona, *El Pibe de Oro*, knocked Italy out on penalties in the semi-final. Third place and a bronze medal that is still being discussed on the country's beaches

a month later. Many are talking about it as if it is still going on. It is almost time for the mid-August Assumption Day break and Italy is on holiday. At the Ospedale Giovanni di Cristina, better known as Palermo's Ospedale dei Bambini [baby hospital], in Via dei Bendettini in Albergheria, Rose gives birth to a healthy, bouncing baby boy. Or so it seems.

He is to be called Mario, a name that his father Thomas has chosen as a sign of gratitude to Maria Pace, a Palermitan woman with five children who helped him when he first arrived in the city. Her daughter, Maria Brai, a physics professor at the University of Palermo remembers: 'I think my mother got to know him through a friend Thomas did housework for. She took him in, helped him and gave him money. He was very grateful and would often drive her to our country house, just outside the city. Thomas wanted to go to Canada and he asked me if I could do anything to help, but unfortunately, I didn't know anyone in Canada. I remember recommending him to a colleague, a professor at the hospital in Brescia, to help him find accommodation for his family when he decided to move to the north shortly afterwards. He found a job in a factory through a friend, a fellow Ghanaian who lived in Vicenza. I tried to help him find somewhere to live.'

13 September 1990. The sky is clear. Twenty-five degrees with a light, cooling breeze. Thirty-one days have passed since Mario Barwuah was born and he is back at the Ospedale dei Bambini. This time he was rushed here in an emergency. Screaming relentlessly, his stomach has swollen up like a football; he is not eating and has been vomiting. Rose and Thomas are terrified. They are afraid of losing their little boy, just as they had lost their first daughter Berenice years earlier. She was only four years old when she died in hospital in Accra. She had an infection, peritonitis, but no one was

able to explain why the little girl left this world in a matter of a few brief hours.

In the department of paediatric surgery at the Ospedale dei Bambini, the head physician, Manlio Lo Cascio looks at Mario's test results: X-rays of the abdomen with a barium enema. He diagnoses megacolon, a congenital disease that can lead to partial or complete obstruction of the bowel, as well as perforations. It is a serious intestinal malformation that could lead to the child's death. He needs an urgent operation. Now, 75-years-old and retired, Lo Cascio explains: 'It is a complex procedure but one that is carried out regularly. Devoid of the nerve cells that allow for normal movement, the diseased section of the colon is surgically removed, while the healthy section is lowered down to the anus. Unless complications arise, the operation lasts for between an hour and an hour and a half. Post-operative recovery is quick and favourable in the majority of cases'. Although 25 years have passed and Lo Cascio is not really a football fan, he clearly remembers the operation he performed on the baby that would go on to become a footballer. He also remembers that Mario Barwuah 'stayed in hospital longer than usual, for a few months. He needed constant medical care and his parents could not guarantee the best possible conditions, but I know very little about that. The nurses in our department looked after him'. The little boy's convalescence continued until June 1991 due to health and family problems. During those nine months, he was doted on by the nurses in the paediatric unit. In December 1990, they organised Mario Barwuah's christening in the chapel at the Ospedale dei Bambini. They gave him his bottle, changed him and bathed him every day. Rose and Thomas went to see him whenever they could; Rose slept beside her baby whenever circumstances would allow. They hoped he would recover and stabilise so he could return home with them. Finally, baby Barwuah was discharged at the beginning of June. He was cured. His mum and dad could finally hold him in their arms and take him for a walk in the Palermitan sunshine. Legend has it that one Sunday morning, at the entrance to the church of San Giuseppe dei Teatini near the city's Quattro Canti crossroads, an elegantly dressed woman in red came up to the Barwuah family, who were about to attend mass in the Baroque church. She looked at the little boy, thought for a moment and told them she was a clairvoyant, a fortune teller. She had a gift; she was not a charlatan and did not try to make money by duping fools. She spoke to the parents of the infant. Before leaving, she said: 'This child will do great things. He will be loved and hated. He will become a great champion.'

Chapter 3

Mum and Dad

Franco Balotelli was retired. Silvia Nostro had qualified as a nurse and operating theatre technician at the Gaslini hospital in Genoa and the Niguarda hospital in Milan but then chosen to devote herself to raising a family and to volunteer work. She had brought up three children of her own – Cristina, Corrado and Giovanni – and for seven years had provided a home for Loredana, Sonia and Simona, the daughters of her widowed brother. She had also fostered three children from troubled families who could only look after their offspring for a few hours a day. It was a wonderful human experience but a tough one, so tiring that Silvia and Franco had decided to put an end to fostering. They were now getting on in years; their children and nieces had grown up and they were starting to think about enjoying some rest. However, when a social worker called the Balotelli home in 1992 insisting that Silvia and Franco meet a family of immigrants and their child, neither of them was able to say no.

That child was Mario Barwuah.

Thomas Barwuah arrived in the north of Italy in late 1991. He left Rose and Mario in Palermo in the two-room apartment on Via dei Candelai and set off to take a risk on a new venture somewhere else, somewhere where there was plenty of industry. A friend had told him the foundries in the province of Brescia were looking for labourers. Italian manual labour was scarce and non-EU immigrants were considered fine for the toughest jobs. Thomas found work in a foundry in Poncarale and in time would also start his own small business, acquiring used tyres and sending them back to Ghana.

Once he had set himself up properly, he returned to Sicily to bring his wife and son back to the north with him. The Barwuah family struck it lucky with their first housing, an immigrant reception centre. The family of three then went to live with another African family in Bagnolo Mella, surrounded by orchards and vineyards, animal feed factories and foundries, 3 km from Poncarale and 12 km from Brescia. They lived in a single room, 18 feet by 15 feet, which was damp and covered in mould. It was not a situation suitable for a baby that had spent several months in hospital. Rose went to speak to the social workers to find a solution more suited to the needs of her son and the family as a whole. She asked for an apartment and financial assistance, insisting on the fact that Mario was still ill. But, according to her version, they refused to listen, telling her that there were no houses for them but also that they could not live in sub-standard housing with a two-year-old child that still had health issues. The solution proposed by social services was to have Mario fostered in accordance with law 184/1983. Article 2, paragraph 1 states: 'temporarily deprived of a suitable family environment, the child is fostered by a family able to provide him or her with the education and loving relationships he or she needs'. Little Mario was to be fostered by a local family until the Barwuahs' living and employment situation improved.

'We were not convinced about having him fostered but then we decided it might be in Mario's best interests. When we arrived in Bagnolo Mella, we had nothing, not even the money to pay for his medical care or to feed him,' Thomas would explain, years later. It was the social workers who suggested the Balotellis as a potential foster family for the boy; they knew they had already had similar experiences that had been successful. They were known locally as straightforward, reserved and very religious people with big hearts, committed to volunteer work. A meeting between the two families was set up, a meeting that no one present has forgotten.

'We went into a room with twenty Africans standing around a little black boy who could not keep still,' Silvia Nostro told the *Gazzetta dello Sport*. 'My husband had brought him a toy car and the child took his hand and said "Let's go, friend". We decided to take him on trial and loaded him into our Fiat Uno and went home.' Home was in Sant'Andrea, a hamlet near Concesio, a small town with 15,000 inhabitants in the province of Brescia, 27 km from Bagnolo Mella. Houses, terraces, factories and shopping centres are strung out along the road that leads up into the Trompia Valley. At the entrance to the town, a road sign reminds visitors that Concesio was the home town of Pope Paul VI: Giovanni Battista Enrico Antonio Maria Montini was elected to the papacy on 21 June 1963 and beatified by Pope Francis on 19 October 2014. His birthplace, in the heart of Concesio, is a destination for pilgrims from all over Italy.

Mario Barwuah spent his first night in the Balotelli's duplex apartment on a mat. They needed to get an extra bed for him so for the time being he slept on the floor in Silvia and Franco's three sons' bedroom. Mario's first memory was of the long hallway, where for years he would play never-ending matches with a foam ball against imaginary opponents. It was too bad for Silvia's vases and ornaments, which would often get caught in the crossfire and end up in a thousand pieces. There were also plenty of items of furniture and sideboards to be scaled and the tree in the garden became Mario's second home. He would climb up and refuse to come down. And then there was Max, the next-door neighbour's German shepherd who ran back and forth from morning till night and must have helped the toddler improve his motor skills somehow. In short, the peace and quiet of Casa Balotelli was shattered by the arrival of the mini-earthquake, who in just three months learnt to speak Italian with a Brescian accent he still has to this day. The child gradually overcame his physical issues, a legacy of the long months spent in hospital, and was able to run and play in the park near his home. He was like a whirlwind that could not keep still even for a second. His nursery school teacher remembers that even when it was cold during the winter months, they still had to take him outside to run around. Years later his parents would fill his days with sport to help run down his batteries: football, swimming, judo, karate and athletics, and from aged eight, scout excursions on Saturdays. Mario was a loveable rascal who got up to all sorts and was regularly on the receiving end of a scolding from Silvia. She was a strict mother who raised her voice, sent him to the corner and punished him when he had gone too far, but also consoled him when he cried and tried to protect him from the world and from those who teased him about the colour of his skin. Franco, his foster father, was more patient, willing to overlook his pranks and mediate between the boy and his wife; he was always happy to take Mario anywhere he needed to go, to scouts, the park or the parish sports centre. In the evening, it was Silvia who put him to bed. She held his hand, cuddled him and read him stories until he fell asleep, ready to return to his bedside if he woke up or had a nightmare. That was the nightly ritual until he was six. It was Silvia who took him to church and the parish sports centre, explaining that there was someone up there looking down on him and protecting him. One day, she told him about the contents of a box she jealously guarded under her bed: letters covered in blue crossings out sent from the Nazi death camps. Silvia's mother was a German Jew, born in Wroclaw, the capital of Silesia, a region that would become part of Poland at the end of the Second World War. The love of a pilot brought her to Italy and she managed to escape racial persecution, but her sister and parents died in the death camps. This was a lesson about hatred and the Holocaust that Mario the adult would not forget when he and the rest of the Italy team visited the camps of Auschwitz and Birkenau in 2012. But we are getting ahead of ourselves. For the time being, Mario Barwuah is still a just a little boy torn between two families, his biological family and the one that offered him a home. For the first year, the consensual custody arrangement progressed smoothly. At weekends, Silvia and Franco would accompany Mario to Bagnolo Mella to spend time with Rose and Thomas, before collecting him on the Sunday. Then, little by little, something went wrong and consensual custody became legal custody by provision of the Juvenile Court in Brescia. Sometime later, Silvia would remember that 'the support of his natural family was lacking. The only meeting we had with Mario's parents in court was when he was four. We did not hear anything more from them'. This is a version that Mario's birth family contests.

'No, I spoke to him often and I would take him back to our house. Then things changed. The relationship became colder. Every time we tried to take him back', Thomas Barwuah stated, 'the Balotellis extended the foster agreement. We could not afford to pay for a lawyer to defend our case so Mario grew ever more distant. He did not have the time to come to visit us or his brothers and sisters. We tried for more than ten years to get him back, but the court blocked our application every time.'

This is not how Mario Barwuah Balotelli sees it. He is adamant, and said as much when he was eighteen in an interview with *Sportweek*, the weekly magazine with the *Gazzetta dello Sport*, on 4 October 1998: 'Rose didn't want to keep me ... they gave me away. When I was with them, I spent more time in hospital than at home. Then I got better almost immediately after an operation. They say that abandonment is a wound that never heals: I say only that an abandoned child does not forget.' He adds: 'I have never had a good relationship with my natural parents. Now I see them two or three times a year, only because I want to see my brothers and sisters (Abigail, Enock and Angel). Whenever I see them, they are like strangers to me. I behave politely – How are you? How's it going? Even when I was little, they didn't do much for me, so I leave immediately and go out with my brothers and sisters. When I arrive, I say "*Ciao Thomas, Ciao Rose*". When I get home and see Franco and Silvia, I say "*Ciao Papà, Ciao Mamma*". It is true that my biological parents asked me to go back to them. But I really don't think that will happen. Did they ask because I was famous? Yes, I think so. I think they wouldn't care about me at all if I hadn't grown up to become Mario Balotelli.'

Rose and Thomas responded in an interview with the *Corriere della Sera* on 12 October 2008: 'We are not interested in the fact that he is famous now and we don't want his money. We are lucky enough to have what we need and if Mario came to our door without a penny to his name, we would take him back. We only want him to remember that we are his parents too. We have always loved Mario and we are extremely grateful to the Balotelli family for bringing him up. But we would also like to have an affectionate relationship with him. And above all, we did not "give him away".'

Mario Balotelli broke ties with his birth family in a harsh and cutting letter posted on his website on 5 October 2008. He wrote: 'Following the statements made to the press by Mr & Mrs Thomas and Rose Barwuah, my biological parents, I would like to publicly clarify a couple of things. They have been described as two people who were forced to "give up their child for adoption" because they were poor and unemployed. This is not true because I was never given up for adoption (although I am now waiting to be adopted by those I consider my REAL parents) and, above all, no one forced them to abandon me in hospital when I was a newborn and to disappear during the years following my foster placement. This foster placement was requested by them and, as everyone knows, has continued until today. It was not simply down to a social worker (another stupid thing I read in the newspapers) but due to a ruling by the Juvenile Court in Brescia, which issued a decree that was also signed by my biological parents (although they now claim to have been misled). I was fostered by the Balotelli family when I was two years old and the foster placement was renewed by court decree every two years. Has anyone stopped to wonder why? Why has no one asked Mr & Mrs Barwuah – who have recently had themselves photographed for the papers looking sad, carrying a photo of me in an Inter shirt – why they never applied to the court to take me back once my health problems had been resolved? Or why for sixteen years – apart from the odd visit at the beginning thanks to the patience of my mum and dad, who would take me to see them (even though on several occasions they were not at home) – they decided to disappear until they found out I had become a Serie A footballer? Has anyone wondered what the real reason was behind why my relationship with them has "cooled", as has been written, without even knowing what happened? For sixteen years, I didn't even get a phone call on my birthday. After I was two, I never lived with them again. Yet now they want everyone to know that they are my "real" parents and they want my affection, as if it were a right resulting from the fact that we share the same blood. What affection? What blood ties? There are no ties, except those that bind me to the people who loved me like a son. Anyone else is a stranger to me.

'It pains me that, despite my request to stop, they continue to give interviews, hoping to gain some kind of advantage, throwing false accusations at Mamma Silvia and Papà Franco. They were certainly not rich when they took me in; nor are they today. Papà was retired and Mamma was a housewife; they were normal people with other children. They never spoke ill of my biological parents in front of me (as has been falsely written) and still choose to remain silent and not to appear in public, for my benefit and my benefit alone. As I am expecting Mr & Mrs Barwuah to shortly begin making appeals in front of the TV cameras, I would like to state here and now that these opportunistic and belated appeals will not get a response. I repeat that I don't think Mr & Mrs Barwuah would care about me at all if I had not become Mario Balotelli.'

What is certain, as Mamma Silvia says, is that Mario 'like anyone else who has had a similar experience, has a hole in his heart'.

Chapter 4
Pink and Black

It was then that the fox appeared.

'Hello,' said the fox.

'Hello,' the little prince answered politely, although he could not see anything when he turned around.

'I'm here', said the voice, 'under the apple tree.'

'Who are you?' said the little prince. 'You are very pretty …'

'I'm a fox,' said the fox.

'Come and play with me,' the little prince offered. 'I am so sad.'

'I cannot play with you,' said the fox. 'I am not tame.'

'Oh! I'm sorry,' said the little prince.

But after thinking about it for a moment, he added:

'What does "tame" mean?'

'You are not from around here, are you?' said the fox. 'What are you looking for?'

'I'm looking for men,' said the little prince. 'What does "tame" mean?'

'Men', said the fox, 'have rifles and they hunt. It's a real nuisance! They also breed chickens. It is the only thing they are interested in. Are you looking for chickens?'

'No,' said the little prince. 'I'm looking for friends. What does "tame" mean?'

'It is something that is all too often forgotten,' said the fox. 'It means "to form bonds" …'

'To form bonds?'

'Of course,' said the fox. 'For me, you are still nothing more than a little boy just like a hundred thousand other little boys. I don't need you. And you don't need me either. For you, I am just a fox like a hundred thousand other foxes. But if you tame me, we will need each other. You will be the only one in the world for me. And I will be the only one in the world for you.'

This conversation is taken from the opening of the 21st chapter of *The Little Prince* by Antoine de Saint-Exupéry. It is a passage and a book of which Mario Barwuah Balotelli is very fond. He loved it and has read and reread it many times. In Year Six at junior school, he gave his teacher a wooden plaque inscribed with the words 'What does tame mean? It means to form bonds. Thank you for taming us, Miss Tiziana. Mario, Torricella. 1996–2001'. Next to it is a drawing of the little prince with his scarf, and the fox.

Tiziana Gatti now shows off the picture proudly, but as she puts it back on the bookshelf in her Brescian home, she says: 'I never managed to tame Mario, though.' Sixty-eight years old, she retired three years ago after a lifetime teaching Italian, history, geography and French. Signora Gatti was Mario's teacher throughout the time he spent at the Torricella junior school in Urago Mella, a neighbourhood in the west of Brescia.

'I saw him on his first day at school. He was small, a little whirlwind, with those big eyes that made an impression on you. I said to my colleagues: "This kid is going to give us a hard time". In fact, he made us suffer for five years. He was not a bad kid but he liked to play pranks and the others couldn't bear it. He would flick up the girls' skirts in the canteen; if I was in a meeting with a parent in another room, he would keep opening and closing the door. He would play a prank every single day.'

The worst was when they were having a kickabout in the playground. Mario brought down one of his classmates who was a very fast runner. His face hit the ground and he broke two front teeth. Can you imagine what the parents said? But that was not all: 'Towards the end of primary school, we were on a trip to Cervia. There was mayhem one night,' the teacher remembers. 'Mario was jumping on the beds, running from one room to the next, and even asked the barman if he would make them cocktails. My colleague, Paola, was at her wits' end. Whenever Mario was told to do something, it never went down well. It was always the same. He was a constant challenge to his classmates and teachers. He was the only black child among so many white children. He felt inferior, that he was not accepted and he tried to assert himself by saying stupid things and doing things they were not supposed to do. He wanted to be funny, to be the centre of attention and to make friends. Instead he was always getting into trouble.'

Is it true that he was not accepted? 'When he first came to us, for two or three years, he always drew himself with pink skin all over. Then he began to understand and drew himself with black skin,' Signora Gatti explains. 'Perhaps it was thanks to the work we did in class. I remember he was struck by Léopold Sédar Senghor's *Poem to my white brother*.'

The teacher quickly flicks through her French books and shows us the poem written by Senegal's first president, an ideologist of Négritude. It is worth reading.

> Dear white brother,
> When I was born, I was black,
> When I grew up, I was black,

When I am in the sun, I am black,
When I am sick, I am black,
When I die, I will be black.

While you, white man,
When you were born, you were pink,
When you grew up, you were white,
When you are in the sun, you are red,
When you are cold, you are blue,
When you are afraid, you are green,
When you are sick, you are yellow,
When you die, you will be grey.

So, between you and me,
Which of us is the man of colour?

Signora Gatti closes her anthology and adds: 'We read it in Year Four and we worked on *The Little Prince* to learn about how the words could help us, how they could influence our everyday behaviour. We even put on a school play about the theme of being tamed. Mario was enthusiastic about it.'

Signora Gatti, do you remember any incidents of racism against that little black boy? 'No, absolutely not. But some of his classmates' parents got upset with him when he played one prank too many. Even if it wasn't his fault, he always ended up being the scapegoat. The worst was the Syrian doctor, Alissa's father. Mario was not the only one, but he teased the boy because he stuttered. One day the doctor came into school. He had his son point out the boy who was teasing him and slapped him. Mario ran away, bawling his eyes out. It ended up with the headmaster, who wanted to report the matter to the police. Eventually, it was up to us teachers to put the pieces back together.'

The phone rings. It is Signora Gatti's sister. 'I'll call you back afterwards,' the teacher says. She comes back to the living room table and continues to tell us about how much that little black boy suffered: 'He never wanted to go and see his biological parents on Sunday. When he came back into class on Monday, he would always ask me if I thought they would take him to Africa. He was terrified by the idea that they would send him to Ghana to live with his grandparents. Silvia, his foster mother, was also terrified by the prospect, but in the end they managed to find the right solution so the boy could stay with them. The Balotelli family was a stroke of luck for Mario.' The teacher's Yorkshire terrier begins to bark excitedly; it has heard a noise on the first floor landing. Her husband has to pick it up and take it into another room so we can continue talking. What about grades at school? 'He was not great. He did well in French, English and maths, but in Italian his essays were this long,' she holds up her hand, showing a palm's width. 'You could not get anything else out of him, but he had good ideas.' Bad grades? 'Yes some, but that didn't make him cry. Mario cried if they wouldn't let him play or if someone was being mean to him. And it didn't take much for him to cry over a banana.' What do you mean? 'He never wanted to eat the bananas they were given at breaktime. He would pull a face and run away. I would go after him but couldn't do anything. For him, bananas were about Africa, and monkeys.'

You must have seen him grow up during the five years he spent with you? 'I watched Mario grow up with a football at his feet. As soon as the bell rang, he would run outside to play football in the garden. There were plenty of arguments because he always wanted to be the one to pick the teams, but sometimes his classmates wanted to as well. He was a good player, a very good player. I remember one day, we were going to the theatre and I said to him: "Mario, you are going to be a champion." "Do you really think so, Miss?" he asked excitedly. "Yes, I do. You're going to be a champion." I was convinced of it because he was such as fast runner and because of the way he played. But, unfortunately it is not because of his character that Mario has become a champion. I'm not a big football fan, but for me the true champions are the ones who give their all for the team. Mario, on the other hand, is an individualist; he thinks everything revolves around him. Perhaps I'm wrong, but I can see the same rage inside him that he had when he was at school; perhaps it comes from how he was treated by his biological family. Mario hasn't grown up, he hasn't matured. He is still screwing up in the same way he did at the Torricella school.'

Marco Martina Rini and Sergio Viotti, Mario's inseparable childhood friends, have a different view: 'Mario is calm compared to how he was when he was little. Back then, he would jump on the desks. He was a real live-wire. But he was clever, intelligent,' says Martina, a 25-year-old midfielder for Brescia. 'He would come over to my house with his football under his arm and we would go down to the parish sports centre.'

'Our life was all about football, the youth club and our bikes. We would play anywhere and everywhere: on the volleyball court, once we had taken down the net, or on the basketball court, with mini goals. It was the three of us against whoever else was there, even if they were older than us. And we always ended up winning. We liked to ride around the village on our bikes. We had fun ringing the neighbours' doorbells and then scarpering. Kids' stuff,' adds Sergio Viotti, born in 1990, now a goalkeeper for Monza in the Pro League. A boy from the Brescian district of Villaggio Badia, in 2012 he had a trial at Manchester City when his friend Mario Balotelli was playing there. 'When we were a bit older, we became passionate about PlayStation. We spent hours and hours playing, FIFA in particular,' Martina continues. 'Sometimes we could win at that, but on the pitch we couldn't do anything. Mario was always the best. It was him against everyone else. He always wanted the ball. He would even steal the ball from me, his teammate, so that he could score.'

'It was incredible to watch. He would go past the other kids as if they were bowling pins. Then he would score impossible rockets. As a keeper, all I can say is that if you find him in front of you, cross yourself and hope he hits it at you. I've seen a lot of great strikers. I was lucky enough to play for the national Under-15 and Under-21 teams, with people like Mattia Destro, Riccardo Saponara and Alberto Paloschi; they were all very good but nothing like Mario. He's in a class of his own. He always used to say that he would be the first black man to play for the national team and that he would win the *Ballon d'Or*. I'm convinced that if he takes control of himself, he could be the best in the world with the qualities he has. Yes, he's an exuberant guy with an unusual character, but difficulties are what make us stronger.'

Chapter 5

The Parish Sports Centre

'Do you like Balotelli?'

The question immediately elicits a chorus of voices.

'Put your hands up, children'. One by one, their coach had to order them to be quiet.

'OK, you next.'

'Although he left AC Milan, my favourite team, I still like him. He is a good player and he's Italian. I liked having him in the national team.' David, the first to have his say, is nine and a half and plays in goal.

'I like him because he has a yellow mohican,' shouts Marco, without waiting to be asked.

'I like him because he is a good player,' says Soel, a defender, born in Italy to Moroccan parents. 'He's great. He scores some incredible goals,' adds Stefano, a budding striker who wants to play for Barcelona when he grows up.

They all want to have their say on what they think of Mario and no one holds back, even for a second.

Let's try a different angle: 'Who doesn't like Balotelli?'

No one holds back this time either.

'I don't like him because he messes about sometimes,' says Pietro, a little boy with blonde hair.

'I don't like him because he never passes the ball,' complains Mario. 'Our coach always tells us to pass the ball to an unmarked teammate. He's always saying you mustn't try to do everything yourself.'

'Against Costa Rica at the World Cup, he played badly and missed a very easy goal,' remembers Mattia, who wants to play for Juventus when he is older.

'He isn't as committed as he should be.'

'He doesn't make the most of his ability.'

'He doesn't go back to defend.'

'He doesn't help out his teammates,' the chorus of voices insists.

'He thinks he's something special,' says Giammarco, judgmentally.

It is a late winter's afternoon. It is cold and the floodlights have been on for a while. About twenty children, nine years old at the most, are sitting in a circle around their coach on the seven-a-side artificial pitch at 26/A, Via delle Fontane in Brescia. Dressed in red tracksuits, they listen attentively to his advice. But when Lino Fasani, the chairman of the association that runs the Mompiano parish sports centre introduces a guest who wants to have a chat with them, from the shyest to the most talkative they are all happy to forget about their lesson on technique for a while. In no time at all, they line up for and against Balotelli, heaping both criticism and praise on the player. They all know that when he was their age he played at Mompiano, something that makes them happy and proud. Without exception; even the one who said Mario messes about sometimes. What they do not know is that the artificial grass on which they are sitting and on which they play twice a week was paid for in part by Mr Balotelli, turning a dirt pitch shimmering green.

We do not disturb them further and retreat into the youth club's offices to take refuge from the bone-penetrating damp. The large room is divided by a glass wall, containing the symbol of the club for all to see: a red and yellow cockerel playing football alongside shelves full of trophies. They have run out of room for all the cups. They are on the furniture, in the corridor, in cupboards and even in the dressing rooms. Mauro Tonolini, with years behind him working as a data processor and chairman of the youth club from 1988 to 2000, shows them off proudly. He provides a potted history of the club, founded in 1966 to offer sports facilities to the young people of the parish of San Gaudenzio. The church is lovely; just around the corner from the Rigamonti stadium, it stands on the main road of a village that has been swallowed up by the city. The former chairman takes us on a guided tour of the sports facilities and tells us about the early days when they were yet to have their own full-size pitch and had to play on other people's. Land was donated by the civic hospital in 1973, creating an almost regulation-size pitch, right across from where the Under-11s were just having their say. It boasts a wooden stand and artificial grass. Countless red shirts are running around. 'Our strip is red and white,' Tonolini explains. 'Although for a while, we changed the colours to black and white. Our sponsor was a Juventus fan and we had to keep him happy'. One final glance over to the kids kicking balls around and we go back into the warm, into the building overlooking a concrete courtyard. Two articles are displayed on the back wall: one is from *L'Équipe*, entitled '*La Différence*' and the other from the local daily *Bresciaoggi*, 'Balotelli Won't Make Mompiano Rich'. Needless to say, they tell the story of Super Mario and the time he spent at the youth club. The former chairman has more to show us. He takes out a blue folder where he keeps press clippings and pages from books about that black kid who used to play football here.

Lino Fasani is also sitting at the conference table: 'In the football section of the youth club, we have 265 players divided into ten teams. The youngest is five; the oldest is 32.

We also have 26 volleyball girls,' he explains. 'It's a family atmosphere, with an emphasis on religion. The aim of our association, as our statute says, is to encourage the growth of young people through sport, teaching them self-discipline, sacrifice and how to behave and relate to others. We educate and train. The technical football work is carried out by other clubs, like Brescia or Lumezzane. We don't pay our coaches or our players anything. They don't even get their expenses refunded. Our annual budget for all activities is between €70,000 and €80,000, not a penny more. This is part of the reason why our first team plays in the eighth division. It was our main objective. We haven't managed to get any further because, from the ninth division and up – and I think this is what is ruining football – so many players get paid. A market for players has started to exist. It is a world that is a long, long way from ours.'

We move on to Balotelli. Tonolini opens his folder, shrugs and throws his arms wide as if to ask what more can he add to the story of a champion about whom so much has already been said. Yet, they both begin to tell the story. 'He came here in 1997, if my memory serves me correctly. With Silvia and Franco, his foster parents. They brought him to our club because it was near Concesio. He had been playing at San Bartolomeo, another youth club in the area, for a few months.'

It was at the San Bartolomeo parish sports centre, on its dirt pitch at 25, Via delle Scuole, between Via Monte Lungo and Via Triumplina that Mario first kicked a football as part of a real team. There are plenty of rumours about that experience, which only lasted for one season. 'He didn't like it there,' Tonolini says, diplomatically. 'No, he didn't leave because he didn't like it at San Bartolomeo. There were other reasons,' says Giuseppe Magnani, a 63-year-old pensioner who retired from a life baking bread from 2 am until noon. Back in 1996, he was Mario's coach at San Bartolomeo.

Why did the boy leave then? Someone blurts out that he had to leave. He was asked to leave because of his unruly and excitable character, because he fought with his teammates, because he created a bad atmosphere and because the parents of the other kids threatened to remove their children if that nuisance did not leave.

'We never kicked anyone out! We never kicked Balotelli out! We did everything possible to make him fit in, even if it is true that, at one point, the kids complained about his behaviour in the dressing room and couldn't put up with his constant pranks,' explains Mario Sandrini, excitedly, a 66-year-old building contractor and chairman of the San Bartolomeo club at that time. To sum it up, he was a pain in the neck then?

'No, if he was a pain in the neck then so were many of the others. He spent a season with me when he was five and a half or six. He had just started school and lived next door to me. I knew him well. He was always cold and had a runny nose. He was a kid who liked to play and have fun. Of course, he was lively and liked to play pranks, but I never saw him do anything really stupid. I had no trouble putting up with him. Whenever I'd had enough of his stunts, I would say, "Look, Mario. Take your ball and go and do whatever it is you want to do so much over there in the corner." He already knew everything I could teach him.' Really?

'Yes, when it came to keepy-uppies and dribbling, he was the best and he had a powerful shot for a boy of his age. If the others could score from ten metres out, he could score from twenty. Technically, he was two years further on than the others. Physically, he was like a beanpole, but if you got a knock from him, it hurt. No, it wasn't muscle. It was nerves. Mario was all nerves. The first tournament he played in with us was at Lonato del Garda, a village in the province of Brescia. I put him on in the second half against Cellatica, a team from the town of the same name just outside Brescia. We were playing at another parish sports centre and, to be honest, in the first half there was hardly anyone watching. But when Mario came on, in his white shirt, people started flocking to the touchline. And to think that he was playing against kids two years older than he was.'

Did Balo score in that game? Magnani laughs, amused. 'Better than that, he scored two or three. That match at Lonato was one of the few he played in with me. They were early days. We didn't play in a league, just the odd friendly or local tournament. It was beautiful to watch him, though.'

'Yes, he was a very good player, but his head … it was the same as it is now. I remember that once, a team of older kids was short of a player and we put Balotelli on. At one point, he fouled an opponent in the midfield. The coach told him to shake hands and say sorry. He turned around and instead of shaking hands, started kicking him. I called the coach over and told him not to let him play on. It wasn't the only time I had to intervene. When his mum came to pick him up, he would throw his bag on the ground and start kicking and screaming. His mother and I would both tell him off, but he would listen for a split second before doing whatever he liked.'

He was a difficult character, yet despite the insistences of the chairman and coach, he was not banned. Why did he leave and go to Mompiano then? 'It was his family,' Magnani explains. 'They wanted to take him somewhere else. I told his foster father to leave him with us for a year and we would do something with him. His mother, Silvia, said that Mario was young and had to study to become a doctor and help his brothers and sisters. Football was just a way of letting him blow off steam. It was his brother Giovanni who chose Mompiano because he had played there.'

'Yes, Giovanni Balotelli played for us in the ninth division. He played with Valenti, who was Mario's coach here. The family knew us well,' Tonolini explains. 'His mother was also keen on the effort we put into education. It was easy to understand their choice. Mario was an exuberant boy and he fitted in here.'

So exuberant that no one has forgotten that youth club trip when Mario was just eight. 'We went to play near Bergamo. They put us up in a seminary because the tournament we had been invited to lasted three days.'

'That evening', Tonolini recalls 'we had real trouble getting them to bed. They were all over-excited. It was chaos during the night.' What did they get up to? 'They piled their mattresses up in a corner of the big hall where they were sleeping. They climbed up to a window and took turns at jumping off onto the makeshift mountain. It was pandemonium.' And it was Balotelli who was behind this acrobatic stunt? 'They all were, not just Mario,' Tonolini adds, brushing it off as childish high jinks. The fact was that Mario & Co got a good dressing down from the prior and the seminary refused to have them back the following year.

Exuberant, lively, full of energy: these same words are repeated by Don Giambattista in the sacristy of the church of Santa Maria dei Miracoli, as he removes his liturgical vestments after saying mass. Don Giambattista was at Mompiano from 1998 to 2002 before moving to a parish in the centre of Brescia. He remembers that Mario came to his first catechism lesson with his mother, who was much smaller than he was. He remembers that once, when Giovanni Valenti, his coach, was getting married, Mario was even an altar boy. He recalls that Silvia Balotelli was very religious and extremely concerned about her son's education. The priest smiles as he remembers the envy of his teammates and his parents: 'Why were they jealous? Because when Mario stepped onto the pitch, everyone noticed.'

'To start with he seemed like any other kid. It was only the colour of his skin that made him stand out. He was the only black child in Mompiano. Back then, there were very few black children. Not like today when every team has black players.' (*Author's note*: Brescia is Lombardy's second city after Milan in terms of immigrant numbers, 198,000 according to the most recent census.)

'For us', Tonolini explains, 'he was one of the many kids who came to the club. But when we saw him with a football … he was a prodigy. It didn't take much to see that Mario could be someone. It was obvious. Why? Because in those early training matches he would take the ball in defence, pass three, four or even five opponents and score. At that age it made the difference because he knew how to play. And he had such a powerful shot that lots of times I had to tell him to shoot a bit more slowly or he might hurt the other children. He also had a developed physique, like an athlete. It gave him a head start when it came to running and tackling. When we played away from home, we would often end up arguing with the parents of other teams. They thought we were playing a boy who was older than the others. But that was how old he was. He was one step ahead of the others. With the odd exception, he always played with children born in 1988 and 89, boys who were two years older than him. It was a bit of a waste for him to play with other kids born in 1990.'

The door opens with a blast of icy wind. In walks a guy wearing a windbreaker, football boots and tracksuit trousers.

Tonolini and Fasani introduce us to Andrea Ferrarese. They ask him to sit down and chat. Andrea, aged 24, plays for the Mompiano second team and coaches the kids at the youth club. Seventeen years ago, he was one of Mario's teammates. 'I was in the midfield; he was up front. When it came to football, he had something extra. His physical power was second to none. He had developed muscle mass and an incredible shot. Mario could easily score from the middle of the pitch. It was impossible to contain him. He would spend all day here playing football. I would often go with my father to Castelli Park, here, behind the Rigamonti stadium. He would be there, on his own or with his foster parents. He would mark out the goalposts with shirts or schoolbags and we would play one-on-one, which then became ten-on-ten. We were the youngest but we could stay there from three in the afternoon to seven in the evening.

'My brother, who played at the youth club on Sundays, would come for the game and Mario would always be here with his ball, playing on the grass where the car park is now. I remember a birthday party at his house. Mario's mum had organised games and activities for the kids but he wouldn't play. It was his birthday, but he wanted to play football around the house. He had an incredible passion. I think he took his football to bed with him. When he was a kid, he would always say to me "I'm going to play in the World Cup. I'm going to win the World Cup". He had this obsession. He always thought he was the best, better than me and better than all the other kids our age. Objectively speaking, he was right, otherwise he wouldn't have made his professional debut at fifteen or had the career he has had. At some levels, you play because you're good. You don't need recommendations or friends in high places. I played in the youth teams at Brescia and Lumezzane and now I'm back here. None of those I played with have made it as far as Mario. One in 10,000 makes it to Serie A and the national team.'

While Andrea Ferrarese is talking, Fasani goes in search of mementoes from back then: a yellow shirt with the name of the sponsor on the front and the number nine on the back. 'It was Mario's. We sent the other red and white one to Burundi', Fasani explains, 'to Sister Flaviana Gatelli, as a humanitarian donation. Perhaps it's still there, who knows.'

He also retrieves two group photos from a drawer. Ferrarese points out: 'That's me and that's Mario. He's easy to recognise.' It is the Mompiano Under-10 team. Someone has added the year on the edge in felt tip: 1998. Squatting on the artificial pitch at San Filippo, with a white football in front of him, Barwuah Balotelli looks serious. The other photo is from late 1999. It is a shot taken on a sunny winter's day on the pitch before a tournament for kids born in 1989. Mario is crouching again, still in the front row, still with his hand on the ball. He is wearing the red and white strip. One thing is odd: Mario is wearing gloves without thumbs, the kind mountaineers wear in the snow, and his legs are a strange whiteish colour. 'He was always cold. He played with mittens on for five months of the year. That white stuff was a coconut cream that his mother would smear on before matches to keep his muscles warm and stop his skin drying out,' Fasani explains. Three adults are standing behind the youth club boys lined up on the pitch for a souvenir photo: Mauro Tonolini, the chairman, Paolo Torre, the assistant coach and Giovanni Valenti, Mario's coach and lifelong friend.

Chapter 6

Circus Tricks

'Hey Mourinho!'

Giovanni Valenti laughs.

Moccia continues: 'Look, an ambulance has pulled up. Someone has just had a baby. See if you can get it to try out for you.'

'Under-1s?' Valenti replies.

Moccia leans in to explain: 'In England, kids play in the park on their own. They don't start playing in leagues until they are fourteen. You take them when they're three though!'

'We take them because if we don't they go to Atalanta, AC Milan or Inter. If truth be told, there are five Brescians born in 2004 playing for Atalanta. We're too slow ...'

The squabble comes to an end. Although not until Moccia advises a passing boy to try swimming: much, much better than football.

It is five o'clock in the afternoon at the San Filippo Sports Centre, a multi-purpose facility that is home to the Brescia club. Valenti has just arrived with a heavy bag on his shoulder. He has a training session today with the Under-11s. This evening's lesson involves a careful study of the construction phase of the game, plus the appearance of two special guests: the Filippini twins (Antonio and Emanuele), who played at Brescia alongside Pep Guardiola. Valenti is sitting at the table of a bar that happens to be closed that day. Before getting back to what we were talking about, he explains that Moccia was teasing him because at Brescia they try out children he thinks are too young. He winds him up by calling him Mourinho, something that is almost an insult for a manager who loves Barcelona, Guardiola and total football.

Valenti has not changed. He looks the same as he did in that photo with the Mompiano kids taken in 1999. He was nineteen then and played for the youth club first team. He was a mediocre player so decided coaching was a better idea. Now, aged 39, he is still teaching children how to play football. More than a coach, he is a teacher. That is exactly what he was to Mario Barwuah Balotelli for four seasons: 1998–99 and 1999–2000 at the Mompiano parish sports centre and then from 2001–2002 and 2002–2003 at Lumezzane. He was such a great teacher that his pupil wanted him in the stands for the biggest match of his career: 1 July 2012 in Kiev, the European Championship final, Italy against Spain. He only exchanged a handful of words with Mario that day. Wearing black-rimmed glasses, a yellow T-shirt with the words 'Super Mario Balotelli' and a barely outlined mohican, Valenti wished him good luck quickly before the game but chose not to disturb him further. It was not a happy day for the Italians but for Valenti it was one of the most exciting times of his life. He felt the classic lump in his throat when Mario's parents arrived to take their seats, meeting up with everyone who had supported their son since he was a child. He felt lucky to be there because Mario had grown up to become a great player, wearing the blue shirt of the Italian national team. Valenti felt lucky to have coached Super Mario when he was just an eight-year-old child, when he was just starting out as a coach.

What was Balotelli like back then? Valenti describes him as having been tall but not super fit. He says you could see he would be long-limbed, but his main gift was his incredible talent for football. It was pure fantasy. He was more interested in putting on a show, in circus tricks. He was more attracted by great play and by dribbling than by scoring goals. He would skin four kids but then shoot wide. They would shout from the stands for him to pass the ball, but he would carry on dribbling. He could do it any way he liked.

Nowadays the coach teaches his charges the Neymar, the Zidane, the Cruyff or the Ronaldo, feints that have been named after great players, but Mario did not need a catalogue or explanations, to him they came naturally. He learnt them from the great champions. He was an AC Milan supporter so their players were his favourites. He liked Marco van Basten but struggled to name the rest of the players in the team. Why? Because back then it was inconceivable that Mario would sit through an entire game, impossible for him to stay still in front of the TV for 90 minutes. Instead he watched videos that came with the *Gazzetta dello Sport*, which his dad, Franco, would buy for him regularly. Maradona, Pelé, Zidane and Ronaldinho; Mario would devour the clips with their fantastic displays of skill before trying them himself, over and over again. There was a time when he became obsessed with the bicycle kick and wanted to try it whenever and however. At least once per game. If he failed to find himself on the receiving end of the right kind of cross, he would take the ball, flick it in the air and create his own bicycle kick. Sometimes the ball would go out for a throw-in but Mario would be delighted because he had had the chance to try his precious bicycle kick. Valenti would tell him off for giving the ball away but Mario would answer right back that he had made his bicycle kick.

He was like that, an individualist but one who was also very altruistic. This was the case in the derby between Lumezzane and Montichiari, Brescia's two Pro League teams. Lumezzane were 3-0 up. Mario had scored all three goals but even when all he had to do was get round the keeper for his fourth, he waited for his teammate to arrive to grab the finish. Valenti remembers that match clearly. But apart from that case of generosity, did he get on with his teammates? Valenti is certain that he did on the whole, that everyone remembers Mario fondly, even if he could be moody and was constantly playing pranks. They were usually trivial things: if they were doing drills in groups of three and had to wait their turn for a minute, in that minute he would always have done something, even if it was just kicking the ball away. Nothing serious, never anything violent, according to Giovanni Valenti, who, like Magnani, the coach at San Bartolomeo, Tonolini and Don Giambattista insist that Mario was happy and likeable but extremely lively, almost hyperactive. The former Mompiano coach makes light of Mario's mischievousness as if it were on a par with letting the air out of his friends' bicycle tyres, describing Balotelli as an emotional softy, an all-round good guy. Confirmation comes when he talks about Niccolò, a small, frail and extremely shy little boy who was the butt of plenty of teasing until Mario took him under his wing and made sure no one gave him any more trouble. Speaking of past and present flaws, Valenti admits that Mario lacks self-control, a problem he also had as a child. But he adds that you have to know how to handle him the right way. Managers need to understand him, to press the right buttons. He explains that a manager dressing him down at half time in front of the entire team is not the right way to deal with Mario. He says that he can be touchy and that you need to try a different approach in order to get the best out of him. For example, he would go into the dressing room and tell him to stay calm in the second half because he needed him to win the game. He made him feel important and got him to understand that he was on his side. This is what Mario needs. But you can also be very hard on him, not that you have to let him get away with it. Being on his side doesn't mean turning a blind eye. You can also be tough with Mario and give him clear boundaries. But, according to Valenti, the problem lies in how to approach him. If you do not do that properly, you risk getting the exact opposite of what you want. Of course, when he was at Mompiano, things were easier because he was a child. His manager would tell him off and he would start to cry. He cried all the time when he was a child. He would end up on the bench or left out of the team. This was the case in a match they won against Milan. Mario had been left at home because he had done something stupid and Valenti did not pick him, with the agreement of Mario's family. Valenti says that a coach's role is to educate: not every child grows up to become a player but they all grow up to become men. And those who one day become players will become better players if they have received the right education. Giovanni Valenti proudly adds that Mario recognises him as having been one of the few coaches brave enough to have left him on the bench or to not have picked him when he needed to. Others, particularly in youth teams, were slaves to his talent and overlooked his mistakes.

The budding champion's coach at Mompiano, also his friend, offers up plenty of extenuating circumstances for Mario's behaviour. From ages eight to eighteen, things were difficult for Mario; foster care was precarious and it was only when he reached adulthood that he could be sure of being able to stay with the Balotelli family. When he was a child, having to go to court to renew his custody made him nervous and angry, instilling in him a rage against the world. Giovanni Valenti also takes some of the blame, saying that football clubs were undoubtedly less prepared than they are today when it came to welcoming immigrant children, black children in particular. The mauling received by Balotelli every other day on the front pages of the newspapers is another sore point. Valenti comments that all you have to do is sneeze and the whole world knows about it. This is something expressed more angrily by Andrea Ferrarese, Mario's former teammate at Mompiano: 'Why should we be interested in all the crap they tell us about Mario? Leave him alone.'

'In the face of all this media hype, he may well see it as a challenge and sometimes goes looking for trouble but the fault is ours and that of the journalists who focus on everything he does,' Fasani adds. 'A stupid mistake gets blown out of all proportion. They build you up one day and tear you down the next.'

It is all true, but Mario Barwuah Balotelli has been a media phenomenon since he was a child. When Mompiano played away against other teams, people in the stands would be talking about Mario and whether he was playing. Partly because he was black and partly because he was a very good player. In the province of Brescia, everyone knew his name. This was not the case for the other children. The mothers and fathers of the opposing teams knew him and he was closely followed by scouts from teams in Lombardy and the Veneto: Atalanta, Brescia, Chievo and Hellas Verona. It was Atalanta, from Bergamo, that were the first to come knocking on Mompiano's door. 'They had already taken Mattia Zagari from us (born in 1988, a midfielder who would go on to play in Serie C2, C1 and D). He came here when he was nine and played for two years. We were a good breeding ground for them,' Mauro Tonolini remembers. 'They wanted Mario but Signora Balotelli was concerned that letting him go to a professional club would mean taking him away from his home and his friends, removing him from an environment where he was happy, distracting him from his studies and going backwards and forwards to Bergamo three times a week. She was not convinced it was the best thing for a child and wanted him to stay here instead.'

'Atalanta did not give up and tried to take Balo on several occasions, as did Brescia and Chievo. They all came for him, they were desperate to get him. There was too much interest, too much attention on him. So much so that Silvia thought about sending him off to play basketball to stop all the stories about interest, scouts, trials, transfers and money.' No more football but basketball instead, a world that a certain level of business had yet to reach. Giovanni Valenti was the one who reminded Mamma Silvia that the Bible says God-given talents must be used, and that Mario had an incredible talent for football. Still today, Signora Balotelli teases him, telling him it is was his fault Mario became a footballer. Whatever the case, he continued kicking the ball and went to Lumezzane in 2000.

Tonolini remembers: 'A few years earlier we had signed an agreement with Lumezzane football club. At the end of every season they would come to take a look at our boys and choose two or three. If the trial went well and the parents gave their permission, they would go to the club in the Gobbia Valley, otherwise they would stay here. They would pay us in return or give us some sports equipment. It worked for us because we had trouble finding a sponsor to support our football academy. The agreement also stated that if the kids didn't like it there, they could come back to us. This is exactly what happened with Balotelli. They paid us in shirts, tracksuits, bags and balls to the value of less than a million lira (approximately €500). No lawyers or agents involved, just the word of two clubs.'

And, of course, the agreement of the Balotelli family. This time they said yes because Valenti was going to coach at Lumezzane and because they also knew others who worked at the club, such as Michele Cavalli. As a child, he had played at Mompiano as a striker; Carla, his grandmother, was a long-standing friend of Signora Silvia. He had also tutored Corrado Balotelli in maths after graduating from university. Now technical coordinator of AC Milan's Under-15 and -17 teams as he takes time out from his career as a maths teacher, Cavalli reminisces about meeting Mario as he enjoys a coffee and a glass of water in a Brescian square: 'I met him by chance in the square in front of the supermarket between San Bartolomeo and Casazza. I saw him dribbling and asked who he was. He told me his name was Mario and I guessed he was Corrado's brother. He was the kid Valenti had told me was very good. So, I decided to go to Mompiano to watch him train. I introduced myself to the kids and we eventually decided to bring Mario and one of his teammates for a trial at Lumezzane. The other boy was Andrea Ferrarese. We were curious to see what this boy we had heard so much about could do. But that late spring afternoon in 2000, Mario wouldn't train or play in the friendly against the Lumezzane players.

'He said he wasn't feeling well. He had hurt his knee so he went to sit near the goalpost and stayed there, watching. I asked him to go in goal just to involve him. He wouldn't hear of it. The other kid, Ferrarese, took part in everything we asked him to do and he did well, although his parents eventually decided he would go to Brescia. At first, I was perplexed by Mario's behaviour but later, once I had got to know him, I understood. He needs to observe the situations he finds himself in, to work out if they are suitable for his skills. He wanted to watch the kids that were there, to study the environment first to see if he liked it. It turned out that Lumezzane suited Mompiano's budding champion very well indeed. Dario Lazzarìn spoke with his parents to explain the club's training strategy and they were convinced.'

The decision was made. Or almost ... because the following year, 2000–2001, Mario was rested, or 'parked', at the Pavoniana Football Sports Club, a club linked to Brescia and now one of AC Milan's centres of excellence. How did this diversion come about? For the simple reason that Lumezzane were trying to broaden their consumer base to acquire young footballers. To do this, they moved their facility to the Club Azzurri in Brescia, a sports centre with four dirt and artificial pitches. It worked; enrolment at the football academy increased and the project took off. It was a shame that the youth scheme could not move forwards; the team Mario should have played in did not yet exist. Ezio Chinelli, manager of the Lume youth scheme for twenty years, recalls: 'Taking nine- and ten-year-old children up and down from Lumezzane was an ordeal, it was too complicated. So, with permission from his mother, we spoke to Pavoniana, with whom we had a good relationship, and asked Cervati, the president, if they would take him for a year so that he could play. We agreed with his mother that as soon as we had built the squad, which in fact happened the following year, he would come back to us.' This was how Mario ended up at the club where his brother Enock would play ten years later. It was a season that would occasionally see Barwuah Balotelli at the Rigamonti stadium, working as a ball boy for Carletto Mazzone's Brescia, a Serie A team that included Roberto Baggio and a young Andrea Pirlo. It is now the stuff of legend that one day, after a match, the 'Divine Ponytail' himself gave his shirt to that black kid everyone was talking about.

Chapter 7

Lume

A lush green bowl nestled between gorges and mountains in the foothills of the Alps. In front, Monte Palosso, a barren 1,157 metre-high peak; behind, the Colle San Bernardo and the Ladino, separating the Trompia and Sabbia valleys; further on, the Cavallo Pass leads down towards Lake Garda. Just 13 km along the Gobbia Valley from Concesio, the stands of the Nuovo Stadio Comunale in the town of Lumezzane offer breath-taking views. The athletics track that encircles the football pitch plays host to elderly joggers, while blaring music bores into your ears. They are testing the loudspeakers ahead of Saturday's match. Up in the glass-fronted cabin at the top of the stands, Giorgio Cavagna, team manager and son of the chairman of AC Lumezzane, is testing the microphones. He is tasked with the job of guide and pointing out the view: 'The stadium was built in 1988,' he explains. 'It seats 4,150 and two years ago the council christened it the Tullio Saleri Stadium in memory of the man who played in and coached the Lume team for twenty years. Before that, we played at Rossaghe, on the pitch that was built when AC Lumezzane was founded'. It was 1946, a year after the end of the Second World War, when the team in red and blue (the colours of Genoa, Italy's oldest football club) joined the second division, organised by the newly formed Brescia Provincial Commission.

The club's history stretches back 69 years, seeing them

gain promotion up through the divisions as far as Serie C2. It also includes a lull in the late 50s, when the team disappeared into thin air for five long years, as well as two potential promotions to Serie B, missed by a whisker. The trophy cabinet has a single occupant: the Coppa Italia Serie C Pro League cup, won in the 2009–2010 season. It is a small club with a handful of shareholders and a budget that barely reaches €2 million per year, yet it is has one of the largest academies in the Pro League with 280 youngsters.

Unfortunately, this provincial football club has been hit over the last few years, albeit indirectly, by the structural crisis and the shift that has brought an end to the 'phenomenon' of Lumezzane, once known as the 'workshop town' or the 'land of entrepreneurs'. With one company to every twelve inhabitants, including newborns, every firm was involved in the metal industry, from forging to turning, from chrome plating to printing, from pots and pans to cutlery, or from taps to accessories. Warehouses crowded every corner; factories and chimneys piled up, blending in with the houses, churches, plants and workshops that lined the road that climbs from the valley floor along the Gobbia River. Renzo Cavagna, manager of a fittings and machinery company for the brass industry for 35 years and chairman of Lumezzane since 6 July 2006, explains: 'The town isn't backed by so many companies any more. Of course, the large, well-established, healthy ones have stayed, but many have moved down to the plains, to the Brescia hinterland or villages elsewhere in the province for reasons of space, to build larger and more functional factories able to keep up with competition from new markets. With the factories, we've also seen the departure of their employees who filled up the stands. On Sundays, we have fewer than 200 spectators at the match, out of a population of almost 25,000. We've paid for the drop in attendance and the lack of sponsors ... yet we've been in Serie C for 23 years, a success for us when you look at the other larger teams alongside us with more resources, like Cremona, Venezia, Como and Alessandria. But to stay afloat, to survive in the Pro League, we have to use all the resources that come from outside: we get money from the league so the kids can play. We assess new talent and then sell it on to other teams.'

It is true that plenty of young players who have ended up at prestigious clubs have passed through here. Anna Bertolina, kit woman at Lume for seventeen years, remembers them all. In the bowels of the Nuovo Stadio Comunale, she is struggling with huge washing machines and baskets of shirts, shorts and socks waiting to be washed. She raises her head while she works and points to a wall, perhaps better described as a shrine, dedicated to the *Santini* (Little Saints) who have passed this way. There are photographs and newspaper cuttings about the little gems that have left Lume to go on to the million dollar world of top-flight football: Alessandro Matri, AC Milan and Genoa; Marco Cassetti, a defender for Roma, Watford and Como; Manuel Belleri of Empoli, Udinese and Bologna; Christian Brocchi, a midfielder for AC Milan, and Simone Inzaghi, who finished his career as a striker at Lazio. And Mario Balotelli, of course. There he is, smiling in his red and blue shirt before a game. 'The problem is that everyone has a go at him', the kit woman comments, 'but he's a good lad. When he came here, he was just a boy. I've never forgotten him. He's stayed in my heart.'

Just eleven, after a season spent at Pavoniana, Mario joined Lumezzane's Under-13 team. Dario Lazzarìn was his first coach. From the Veneto, near Rovigo, Lazzarìn joined Brescia at the age of eighteen, played one match in Serie B and scored one goal. He then moved on to C1 and spent a lifetime at Chievo as a player and now as the coach of the Under-17 B team. During a break from work, he recalls Balotelli's first few months: 'On the pitch, he was someone who could make a difference. He had unbelievable technique. He was acrobatic and had a good right and left foot. Despite being skinny and frail, he never fell over. He took knocks well. And there were plenty of them! He wasn't afraid of anything. For him, scoring a penalty at the parish sports centre or in the San Siro in front of 90,000 people was the same thing. The only thing he couldn't bear was to be the victim of injustice. Whether it was dished out by a friend or a stand full of 20,000 fans, he would snap.

'He was strong, quick and knew he was good. He knew, and from an early age he had decided he wanted to be number one. Even if sometimes he would switch off and there was nothing anyone could do about it. I remember once against Milan at Linate. It was a cold, foggy day and we lost 9-0. It was as if Mario wasn't on the pitch. I shouted at him to run and lose his marker but nothing. He wouldn't move, run, go back to defend, cover or attack. He was completely apathetic. Days like that happened, but they don't take away that football was his passion. He was always playing. His mother would tell us that whenever he wasn't with us, he was at the youth club playing with his friends. And if he wasn't playing outside, he'd be playing in the hallway at home. He never seemed to get tired. The difficulty for his mum was tiring him out so that he would go to bed at night.'

Lazzarìn pauses and then adds: 'We tried to give his mother a hand, to help her with Mario's education. We were in almost daily contact with her. She would tell us how he was doing at school and ask us how he was getting on with the other kids in the team. We worked with her. For example, if Mario didn't listen to his mother and father at home, he was told off. One of the punishments that hurt him most was stopping him going to training. But even if he hadn't trained with his teammates and his family asked us to let him play, we would send him on the pitch anyway. Or, on the other hand, if they called to tell us not to pick him on Sunday, we would leave him out even if it was an important game. The Balotelli family were fantastic, they were incredibly perceptive. They always protected Mario and brought him up with a lot of love, but they also knew when to be tough. Let's be honest, he wasn't an easy boy to handle. Every now and then he would pull some kind of stunt …' Lazzarìn smiles and adds that he liked to joke around but sometimes went too far: 'Like when he filled his teammates' bags with anything he could find and drenched them under the showers by ramming the taps on; or when he poured the shampoo his mother had given him all over the dressing room floor so everyone kept falling over.'

That black kid's countless pranks even reached the ears of Lumezzane's chairman. 'Mario got up to all sorts. He was only with me for two months, if he had stayed I would have had to ask the police to escort him to games and training sessions,' he laughs, remembering what Mario did in the nine-seater Mercedes that would pick him up twice a week for training and take him to away matches at Milan, Como, Piacenza, Cremona and Bergamo Varese on Sundays. 'He would go down to the back, pull down his trousers and moon out of the back window.'

Disma Bossini has ferried around Lumezzane's youth players for twenty years and remembers Mario as the naughtiest: 'I even slapped him once for being disrespectful: he would jump down from the minibus without closing the door and then come up behind me with the whites of his eyes rolled back to scare me. His father had given me permission to clout him if he didn't behave himself and warned me that he was lively and you had to be patient with him. He couldn't sit still for as much as a second without making some kind of joke and he would end up arguing with his teammates. Sometimes, I would have to stop the bus and bring them back into line. But he was bright, a good kid and I was fond of him. I'm still fond of him now. I'm a big fan,' Disma adds, interrupting his card game in a Lumezzane bar.

'As we say in these parts', Lazzarìn remarks, 'Mario's got a good heart. He was generous with his teammates. He was never rude or arrogant with me. He was respectful and knew how to say sorry if he did something wrong.' He remembers seeing him at the San Siro when he was with Chievo and Mario was playing for Mourinho at Inter. Mario did not hesitate for a second to go over and say '*Ciao*, Coach!' Lazzarìn has no doubt as to the lanky black kid's class: 'Still now, whenever I see Cavalli we bet on when Balo will win the FIFA *Ballon d'Or*. It's just a question of finding the right mental balance. Once he has done that his spark will come back.'

Midway through the 2001–2002 season, Dario Lazzarìn handed over to Giovanni Valenti before moving to another team. But he would be the one to accompany a thirteen-year-old Mario to a trial for Atalanta in Zingonia. 'Mino Favini was there that day. He had been in charge of Atalanta's youth development for 40 years and was the greatest talent spotter in Italy. I sat with him on the bench during the trial. He asked me if I knew how they could tell that someone was a champion: if you put him in one team and that team wins, then you put him in the opposing team and they win too. We put Mario in one team for the first half and then switched him to the other after half time. He won with both teams.'

As he would say years later, Favini spotted the boy's great

ease with the ball immediately. He knew he had great qualities and was clearly much better than other boys his age.
He tried to bring him to the Atalanta Bergamasca Football
Academy. 'They went to speak to the Balotelli family, and
I was there too as head of Lumezzane,' Lazzarìn explains.
'They talked for a long time and proposed favourable conditions, as well as offering to take the boy to and from Bergamo
in the club's minibus. But the family graciously thanked
them and ended the discussion by saying they would be happier if he stayed at Lumezzane.'

Chapter 8

Like the Champions League

He is smiling from ear to ear, the kind of smile only seen on the faces of those who are really happy, in seventh heaven. Mario Barwuah Balotelli was lucky enough to smile such a smile on 15 June 2002 in Padenghe sul Garda. The final whistle has just blown at the *Bresciaoggi* Trophy final and his teammates have lifted him up onto their shoulders. He is smiling, something he rarely does on a football pitch; his mouth is open and his eyes are full of joy. He is holding the cup that has just been won by the Lumezzane Under-13s. Years later, on 16 February 2014, three days before a Champions League game against Atlético Madrid, Mario would post this same photo on his Facebook page. It was his way of wishing himself good luck for the knockout phase of Europe's most important competition. Dragging up a distant childhood memory when you play for AC Milan may seem strange but far from it: for Balotelli, that victory was the greatest of his career, second only to his Champions League win with Inter. He has both said and written so.

Giovanni Valenti, his friend and former coach, confirms that this was an important moment in his life. Mario scored three goals. It was an unforgettable victory, a cup that was particularly dear to Balotelli. The *Bresciaoggi* Trophy was as big as the Champions League in the world of youth and amateur football in Lombardy and this time Mario's opponents were Pavoniana, the club with which he had spent a season.

Pavoniana were Lumezzane's long-standing rivals and there had been a pinch of extra spice since Barwuah had been welcomed back into the fold at Lumezzane. The bosses at Pavoniana Calcio took it badly: they wanted the boy to end up at Brescia.

On paper, the team from Pavoniana, in white and blue with Giulio Comai as their manager, were clear favourites. They were the strongest team in the province of Brescia and had been on a winning streak in recent weeks taking the league title and winning various tournaments around the country. They also had a thirteen-year-old called Adama Fofana, who had been born in Bouaké in the Ivory Coast but grown up, like Mario, in Brescia. He was a centre forward and reputed to be a very good player. This became apparent early on in that final in Padenghe: a cross came in from the right, Adama took it with his right foot, passed Bravìn, the Lume defender, with a rainbow kick and, on the fly, fired the ball past Gatta, in goal for the red and blues. The stands erupted into cheers; it was a goal that reminded older fans of the one scored by Pelé, the Black Pearl himself, in the final of the 1958 World Cup against Sweden. It had started ominously for Lumezzane but they refused to throw in the towel. Giovanni Valenti, their coach, started screaming and waving his arms; he told them to keep pressing up the field, fight for every ball and exploit their opponents' mistakes. In short, not to play as if they had already been beaten. It was time for Mario to get involved: from the edge of the area, he lifted a perfectly timed lob to surprise Bossini, Pavoniana's keeper. 1-1. A few minutes later, Barwuah helped his team take the lead. He won a penalty and scored with a powerful shot down the middle. It was 2-1. At the start of the second half, Fofana tried to draw Pavoniana level but failed. Mario took advantage of an error from Bossini as the keeper spilled the ball, possibly on the receiving end of a shove, and he scored easily. The final score was 3-2. Lumezzane's budding superstar, the youngest on the field (his teammates and opponents were all a year older), had proved that he was a fast, strong, decisive and opportunistic goal scorer. With a hat trick to his name, he had plenty to celebrate. But before he ran over to hug his teammates and coach, before they lifted him up, before the big smile even, Mario went over to Fofana, from the opposing team, another black kid just like him. It may sound as if it could not have been scripted better, but it really happened. Now 25, Adama Fofana, who has spent years travelling around Italy, Greece and Lithuania and now plays for Prato in the Pro League, remembers that moment well: 'The thing that struck me most about that final was that Mario came over to commiserate with me while the others were all celebrating. I was really upset. That trophy meant a lot to me and I had scored two goals. It did not seem fair to me that they had won, although looking back on it, they deserved it. That's how football is. Mario shook my hand, told me I had played a great match and that he was sorry we had lost. Only after I had told him everything was fine did he go over to his teammates. It is something that has stayed with me. I'll never forget it.'

Adama would have his revenge, however. He tells the story with a smile at the end of his afternoon training session: 'We went to the same comprehensive, the Lana Fermi in Brescia, near Via Oberdan. In the third year, we found ourselves against each other again in the final of the school tournament. My class against his and that time I won. I left everyone standing and scored the winning goal after they had taken the lead. Mario may have scored two goals, but that time it wasn't enough to beat me.'

Andrea Santìn was the captain of the Under-13s; the boy

lifting Mario onto his shoulders in the picture. He had come to Lumezzane from the Mompiano parish sports centre that same year, with Valenti. He played with Mario until he moved up to the first team. Thirteen years later, Santìn is still playing in the *Promozione* (sixth division) for Navicortina, a team from Nave, a town seven kilometres from Lumezzane. He plays for fun while studying Economics at Milan's Catholic University.

He remembers that famous match as one of the best moments of his teenage years. He remembers Mario as a 'good player, a very good player, although I never expected him to have the career he has had. He was undoubtedly talented and was in the right place at the right time. Above all, he was always convinced of his potential. When he was fifteen, I remember we were playing a friendly tournament at Mompiano. He was doing very well, he scored something like twenty goals and told everyone he was aiming to win the *Ballon d'Or*. Back then, we gave him a hard time about it ... but he was right. He hasn't won the *Ballon d'Or* but any kid would have signed up to get as far as he has. What is certain is his desire for football, something many now call into question, but it's something he's never been lacking.

'Last summer I met him in New York, where he was on tour with AC Milan. I asked him to come and play a practice match with the Japanese kids who were studying with me. He replied that he would have loved to but couldn't do anything to jeopardise the friendlies he was playing for the *Rossoneri*. He wants to play football, that's always been one of his strengths. Other kids develop different interests as they grow up: discos, cars, motorbikes, but Mario's never been interested in that kind of stuff.' Perhaps by now he has changed his mind about cars, discos and nightlife ... but Santìn is not convinced. He thinks many of the things written about Balotelli are not quite true, that they have been made up or are nothing more than gossip. He remembers when Mamma Silvia 'would not let him come out with us for pizza or when he went to a nightclub for the first time'. He was fifteen and ended up there with his team when they were celebrating winning the league.

Santìn is sure that Balo the celebrity has become more important than the footballer. He tells us after a lecture at the university: 'If he is going to rediscover the peace of mind he needs to play football, he has to be less of a target, less at the centre of a media circus.'

This is an opinion shared to some extent by Michele Cavalli. The maths teacher explains: 'Such interest in him has been sparked because he has become a celebrity and because he is talented. He has the kind of talent that is hard to tame. This is why they study him, follow him and put whatever he does under a microscope. It's also why they are slower to forgive him and look for the seedy side in everything he does. Mario is not someone who will hide. He has never done that. But now, he is so exposed to the media that he is expected, or rather it would be desirable if he behaved differently, but in some ways he still behaves like he did when he was a kid. Perhaps he needs a different kind of maturity to tackle what has been thrown at him. But let's not forget that he is only 24 and everyone screws up at that age. I defend him because I'm biased. I'm fond of him.'

Cavalli, the coach who watched Balotelli's trial at Lumezzane, does not find it hard to admit his weakness for the player he inherited from Valenti in the 2003–2004 season. He says that, unlike other black children, Mario could not be considered precocious: 'He was agile and rangy but he had yet to develop real muscle. He was still growing and didn't reach physical maturity until he was eighteen. But technically, he was already outstanding.' He also remembers the famous video tapes played on the minibus TV to entertain the group during long journeys to away matches. 'When they were talking about players the kids knew because they were still playing, like Roberto Baggio or Francesco Totti, they would all watch. But as soon as they went back further, where the colours faded, the images became black and white and they didn't recognise anyone, they would lose interest and go to the back of the bus. The only one who stayed, open-mouthed, was Mario. He would watch them all: Pelé, Maradona and Di Stefano. He watched everything that interested him and stored it away.'

It was the first year of the Regional Under-15s and Cavalli had a good group: 'In that league of eighteen teams, we finished fifth or sixth, behind AC Milan, Inter and Atalanta. We racked up 65 points, one of the best results in the history of Lumezzane's youth scheme. We even had T-shirts made up to celebrate those 65 points. As well as Balotelli, there were other valuable players, such as Marco Pedretti. He and Mario could both make things happen, they were both stars. But that chemistry, a relationship that would have helped the team a lot, was never sparked between them.'

So, let's get this right, they were like two cockerels in the hen coop, rivals on the pitch, budding champions that were constantly at each other's throats? 'Exactly. That's how it was,' Cavalli adds. 'So many times I tried to explain to them that if they would just work together a little, if they got to know each other a bit better, if they respected each other's skills and played together and not, as would sometimes happen, against each other, the team would benefit and be even more successful. But there was no way. I think Mario tried to win Marco over because he has always needed to have a relationship with people he thinks are good, particularly from a sporting point of view, but Marco was reluctant. I remember plenty of after-match sessions with me on the bench and the two of them sitting in front of me on the grass while the rest of the team was already in the showers. I would try to convince them to behave differently.'

Casalromano is a town of 1,600 inhabitants in the province of Mantua, in Lombardy. The village's amateur sports club is where Marco Pedretti now plays. He earns €500 a month to cover his expenses for the 60 km trip he does three times a week up and down to Brescia. Pedretti works as a postman, football for him is now almost a hobby: 'Ours was a love hate relationship. To be honest, whenever Mario called me and asked me to play in whatever tournament it was, I would go. I never turned him down. I never said I wouldn't go because he was going. In fact, I enjoyed it. On the pitch, I helped him score a lot of goals. Like now, he wouldn't do all that much. During training, he didn't like running or doing the drills the coach wanted, but when you passed him the ball, you knew he was going to score. The ball made him sing. The most exciting match I remember? That time against Brescia. All the kids knew each other and we wanted to make a good impression. We won 1-0; it was very satisfying. Mario scored with a rocket from outside the box past his lifelong friend, Sergio Viotti, who was the Brescia keeper.'

What was Mario like off the pitch?

'He liked to mess about like he does now, but he was a child back then. He wasn't bad. When it came down to it, he was a good guy. But he allowed himself to get dragged into things by others. He needed friends and didn't go out very much. He tried to get close to us, to become part of our small group whenever we went out in the evening or to eat pizza. Mario would have liked to have been part of our friendship group, but he went about it in the wrong way.'

What do you mean? 'He was constantly a real pain in the neck and would pull pranks all the time. Bad ones, sometimes. Instead of getting closer to us he ended up becoming more distant.'

What was the worst prank you remember? 'There were so many, it's not that I don't want to tell you.' Pedretti is reluctant to dwell on the matter but then admits: 'It's true that he would pee on our bags containing our clean clothes and he would pee on people too ...' The list of over-the-top pranks goes on and on and this by no means covers everything: hidden jackets, teammates' football boots thrown as far as he could, stunts that regularly provoked furious arguments with his friends.

Santìn admits: 'It's true that everyone remembers him as a turbulent child. Before he came to Lumezzane, there had been trouble with the odd kid, but they were things that happen in all the youth teams. They would argue with each other all the time. The only difference is that Mario is now famous and these episodes have become more important than they really were. He could be a pain in the neck, but nothing out of the ordinary'. Cavalli explains: 'Of course, there were times when we had to intervene to give him a dressing down or to tell him off, but I could name fifteen or twenty other kids who got up to all sorts.'

We leave it there.

What does Marco Pedretti, someone who played alongside him, think about how far Mario has come? 'I'm happy because I don't know what else he would have done with his life given that when I knew him, he always had his football with him. I ... I can say that I frittered away chances. Obviously, I dreamt about getting to that level and earning all that money, but in another way I feel lucky ... I don't know whether I have the right personality for the life of a top player. They can't enjoy their lives, they don't have any privacy, they get followed everywhere and their names are always on everyone's lips. Mario more so than others; trouble seems to follow him around like it did when he was a child. He doesn't do it to get noticed, it's just how he is.'

It's just how he is: 'A kid like any other, exuberant and boisterous,' Cavalli explains. 'With him you always had to find the right line between toughness and understanding. Between the stick and the carrot, if you like. He had plenty of character and knew how to show it. I'll give you a good example. We were playing at home against Mantova at the Rossaghe ground. Mario didn't start. I don't remember why, I think it might have been something to do with him having caused trouble during the week. It should have been an easy game for us but instead we were a goal down at the end of the first half. I decided Mario's punishment was over and put him on. He immediately picked the ball up in the midfield and went on a solo run, skinning four opponents and scoring. 1-1. Five minutes later he did it again, exactly the same thing. I remember he was on his own with just the keeper to beat and instead of scoring, he decided to kick the ball out. Did he do it on purpose? I don't know. After the match, which ended 1-1, I said to him in the dressing room: "Well done, Mario. That's what we expect from you." He smiled: "Of course", I added, "you could have scored the second goal as well." Mario looked at me, smiled and said: "Yes, I could have." I've always thought that because I decided not to put him on in the first half, he decided that a draw was enough. It was his response to my decision.'

Michele Cavalli stopped training Mario after a year and a half. He moved from the Under-15s to Massimo Boninsegna's Under-17s, because, as Ezio Chinelli recalls: 'When he was with us, he always ended up playing one category above his own, with kids who were older than he was.'

The professor and former pupil met again when Mario was already at Inter. 'That morning I had read in the *Gazzetta dello Sport* that he would be joining the first team training camp. In the evening, by chance', Cavalli recalls, 'I bumped into him at Brescia. It was summer and he was cycling around with a friend. "So, Mario. You're going to the camp. Are you happy?" I asked. "Yes, I'm very happy, coach." I've always been an *Interista* so for some reason I said: "Next time I see you, bring me Ibrahimovic's shirt." "Next time, I'll bring you my shirt, coach," he said. That sums Mario up. And he kept his promise. He came to the school and brought me the shirt he was wearing when he scored his first goal for the first team, against Reggina in the Coppa Italia. I thanked him and said: "You were right, Mario. I'm sorry."'

Chapter 9

An Army of Suitors

'I have no doubt he is going to make it to Serie A. And not just as an ordinary player, but as a great one.' This prophetic phrase was spoken by Massimo Boninsegna. He repeated it over and over when Giambortolo Pozzi, chairman of Lumezzane, asked him to tell him about the black kid. The coach of the *Allievi* Under-17 team was convinced, and he had good reason to be. In his first season, Barwuah Balotelli had scored fifteen goals in fourteen games; the team won the championship and made the national finals.

'Unfortunately, we could only get as far as the semi-final. We lost on penalties to Adria, the eventual winners.' Boninsegna now remembers: 'We were unlucky. We finished the match with nine men after a double sending off. We didn't have any defenders left and I was forced to take Mario off. It may well have been a mistake because someone like him could win the match for you at any moment. I had taken him with me, with the older boys born in 1988–89, midway through the season at the suggestion of Ezio Chinelli. He said I knew how to handle kids of that age. Balotelli was the youngest in the group. He was fourteen and I have to say that he fitted in easily and did very well. He was so much more talented than the others. He was physically strong and technically brilliant. I think he still hasn't shown us everything he can do, even now. He has much more to give.'

Really?

'Yes, we haven't seen the real Mario yet. Apart from Roberto Mancini, at Inter, he has never found a manager that gave him the right conditions to bring the best out of himself. You have to put Mario up front and let him do whatever he wants. You can't constrain him or force him to play in a position that limits him. You have to give him freedom. He has to be able to span the whole of the attack, to play as a traditional number nine or to vary it with being out on the wing. That's the only way he can make a difference and give the best of himself.' These are the words of someone who is passionate about football and who coached Balo until his debut for the Lume first team. Boninsegna adds: 'All sorts of things have been written about him. I can only say that we had a fantastic relationship that continued even after he had left Brescia. To my mind, he was just like all the other boys but had had a harder life than most of them. Outside his family, he was often discriminated against. It isn't talked about but I remember all the times I had to defend him, to line him up with his teammates and tell them off. If they did something stupid no one said anything; if Mario did something it ended up becoming a scandal.'

Boninsegna and those in charge at Lumezzane were regularly in touch with his mother and father about how best to handle the boy. 'Dealing with him was not easy. It was complicated; I think if he hadn't been at Lumezzane he may not have even become a footballer,' Chinelli assures us.

Why was it so difficult?

'Because to start with his name was Mario Barwuah and he was black. He hadn't been adopted, only fostered, so as far as the State was concerned, he was neither Italian nor Ghanaian. He didn't have an Italian ID card and he suffered because he could not be called up for the national Under-15 or Under-17 teams, although they tried on several occasions.

And on top of that, he was also a rebel. At one point, he didn't want to go to school anymore, so much so that his mother called me to ask if they could send him to a private school, to the Gianni Brera Sports School in Brescia. The fees were steep and the parents couldn't afford it', explains Ezio Chinelli, 'so we agreed to pay part of the fees and he studied there for a year or two.' The school, whose motto is 'Education and Sport', seemed a good solution for Mario who was no longer that keen on spending hours poring over his school books but was passionate about football.

Passion, character and desire are the qualities that everyone stresses, including Massimo Boninsegna. There are plenty of examples.

Character: the memory of that famous home game against Reggiana. The score was 0-0. It had been a lacklustre encounter until Mario managed to win a penalty with a solo effort. He put the ball down on the spot and fired it hard down the middle. The keeper stopped it. History repeated itself twenty minutes later: the referee blew his whistle for another penalty for Lumezzane. The number nine stepped back up to the mark. It was a terrible kick that ended up flying over the crossbar. It really did look as if the 90 minutes would come to an end with two glaring chances badly wasted and a meagre 0-0 draw. But with only five minutes remaining, Reggiana committed a nasty foul on a Lume player in the area. The referee had no doubt: penalty! Everyone was looking around puzzled. Who was going to take it this time? Of course, it wouldn't be Mario, who had already missed two and god forbid would miss a third. Yet, Barwuah Balotelli picked up the ball, went over to Boninsegna and said, 'I'll score, Boss. Don't worry.' His shot was hard and high, like the previous one, but this time it ended up in the back of the net. It takes guts to do something like that.

Passion: Boninsegna remembers: 'We did two-hour training sessions with the *Allievi* Under-17s, but that wasn't enough for Mario. He would stay on for another half an hour with me to practise scoring. We would bet on who could hit the crossbar from 30 or 40 metres out. He would hit it right in the middle six or seven times out of ten. The minibus drivers would complain because Mario was always the last. He wasn't finished once he had got home either. He would dump his kit bag and run outside to keep playing. Sometimes on Saturdays, the day before our matches, I would find him dribbling a ball around the town. The worst time was when I came across him at the San Filippo Sports Centre. It was June 2005 and we were playing Casale in a three-team play-off. The winner would go to San Benedetto to contest the national finals. I had gone to Brescia to watch the Under-15s. I was watching the match when the father of one of my boys came over and told me Mario was playing on the artificial pitch with his friends. I went over and, needless to say, there he was. "Mario, what are you doing?" I yelled from behind the fence. Calm as you like, he answered: "I'm playing five-a-side, Boss. Nothing's going to happen, don't worry." That made me angry so I laid down the law. "Go home now. We've got a match tomorrow." Like it was nothing, Mario insisted: "Come on, coach. It's just a friendly." I was furious and ordered him to get his stuff and go home or he wouldn't be coming with us the next day. Grumbling as usual, he eventually went home.'

There are plenty of stories about Mario's hunger for football and his desperation to play all the time. Here is another one:

'In those two months he was with me, he would leave immediately after training at the Club Azzurri in Brescia. He came on his bike, it must have been five or six kilometres.

He didn't want his brother to bring him in the car. One day, I took him to one side and said to him: "Mario, why don't you stay for a while after training and we'll try some shooting? A bit of practice and technique would do you good." "No, Coach. I've got to go home. I've got so much homework to do for school," he answered. I wasn't convinced. I let him go but I stopped him again the following day. "You told me yesterday that you had to go home to study, but I'm not convinced you're telling me the truth." "But Coach, if I tell you, you'll get angry." I promised I wouldn't and told him to tell me where he was going. I remember it well. He tried to sneak off down the steps and run away, so much so that I shouted after him: "Mario, I'm talking to you. Stop." "But Coach, you'll get angry." "I won't get angry, but now you really do have to tell me." "I'm going to play five-a-side with my friends from the parish sports centre," he told me. "Are you crazy?" I blurted out, before adding, "you can't waste this opportunity you've been given. What happens if you hurt yourself?" "But my friends don't go in hard, Coach. They know not to hurt me." "I know, but you can't risk it. You're fifteen years old and you're playing in C1 with no trouble at all. After all the work I make you do, you can't just go off and play again straight afterwards. Please stop doing it. You're old enough to be sensible." Mario turned around, he was angry. He went down the steps in two jumps and bolted. As soon as he had gone, I burst out laughing. I couldn't do it in front of him. How can you not laugh at something like that? You should have seen him when he told me, all worried and tense because he didn't know what I was going to say. The one thing that struck me was how he could keep playing when he should have been on his knees with tiredness.' This particular story comes from Valter Salvioni, the manager who gave Mario his C1 debut against Padova. He kept him in the Lumezzane first team until the end of the season.

The Sunday after his debut at the Stadio Euganeo, Barwuah Balotelli also started against Genoa. The match was played at home on 9 April 2006. 'My central defender was sent off twenty minutes in and I had to substitute him,' Salvioni remembers. 'He was on the bench for a couple of games. He would train with the *Allievi* Under-17s during the week and then join the first team on Thursdays. He even came with us to San Benedetto del Tronto when we went to contest the play-off final.'

It was 28 May 2006. Seven days earlier, Lume had won the first leg of the play-off at home against Sambenedettese thanks to two goals from Patrick Kalambay, the son of the Zairean boxer, Sumbu Kalambay. However, in the second leg in San Benedetto del Tronto, everything went wrong. Lume's red and blues went down 4-0 and were relegated to C2. It was a heavy blow after nine consecutive years in C1. All hell broke loose at Lume and the race to sign Mario Barwuah Balotelli, which had started a little while earlier, suddenly blew up.

There were plenty of clubs that wanted him: Atalanta, Brescia, Chievo, Milan, Inter, Cremonese, Udinese and Genoa. And there were plenty of people keen to recommend him. Salvioni was sacked by Lumezzane at the end of the season but admits: 'I called Federico Pastorello myself. He was the son of Giambattista, the former director of football at Parma and an agent I had got to know when I was working at Parma. I told him that the boy deserved all the attention he was getting and that it was worth taking him to Verona.'

In the meantime, the boy's foster brothers and sisters came forward to help decide his fate: Corrado and Giovanni were sales representatives, while Cristina was a journalist so began dealing with the press. The Lumezzane bosses were genuinely surprised. 'Until Mario made his debut at Padova, I didn't know his brothers and sisters. I didn't even know who they were. I had always spoken with his mum and dad,' Chinelli remembers. The two wannabe agents asked the club to let the boy go and Lumezzane did not take it well. However, they could not up their offer; their room for man-oeuvre was extremely limited and if the contract were to be extended, they could offer €22,000 gross that year, an amount only the most promising boys in the academy could aspire to. It was certainly not a large figure but it is worth remembering that at that time, the highest paid player in the first team earned no more than €60,000 per year. But it was also true that Mario's transfer had the potential to become a good deal for AC Lumezzane. The army of suitors was grow-ing ever larger. Among the throng, Genoa seemed to have the upper hand thanks to Bortolo Pozzi's good relationship with the Ligurian club. But they eventually gave up. Pantaleo Corvino, Director of Football at Fiorentina and someone who had cut his teeth in Serie C1 and B with Casarano and Lecce, had a reputation for being a talent scout (he had already discovered players such as Fabrizio Miccoli, Ernesto Chevanton, Mirko Vucinic and Cristian Ledesma) and had caught wind of the potential offered by the Lume number nine. Boninsegna remembers: 'Pozzi, the chairman, asked me to convince Mario but I told him I wouldn't convince any-one. I was only interested in the boy. I spoke to him, explain-ing that there could be an opportunity for him in Florence but that if he and his family were not convinced, there was no need to worry. Half the clubs in Italy wanted him.'

Whatever happened, Lumezzane gave the OK and a pre-agreement was signed. The family were invited to Florence to see the facilities, the school and the residence, where

Mario would be spending his future. It seemed as if the deal had been done. But something did not quite go as planned. Perhaps the finances did not add up for the wannabe agents, or Mamma Silvia may have become concerned about her son, who had not yet turned sixteen, living alone so far away from home. Whatever the case, time went by and the transfer that would have seen Lumezzane acquire a nice little nest egg (€500,000 or €800,000 according to the papers, although these figures were denied by Fiorentina, of course) went unfinalised.

Corrado and Giovanni Balotelli wanted to explore other avenues before giving the green light to the *Viola*. They thought that some time abroad at one of the great European football schools could have been positive, such as at Barcelona's La Másia. Without saying anything to anyone, without telling Lumezzane, they contacted Barcelona in mid-June and were invited for a trial. Chinelli still gets angry as he remembers the episode: 'I was in Spain, in Malaga for a weekend. They called me and told me Mario was going to Barcelona for a trial. But shit, even Barcelona … if we want to trial a boy, we send an official request to his club, however large or small it is, but they didn't do anything. So we immediately called the Catalan club to get them to send us the request and it eventually arrived by fax. As for what happened after that, we didn't hear anything more about it.'

'He did not spend long with us, three or four days,' remembers Fran Sánchez, coach at the academy at that time. 'He took part in some training sessions and one tournament. Three matches in all with *Cadete* B, where he played alongside Thiago and Marc Bartra.' Mario scored eight goals in those three matches. He got up to all sorts in the game against Hospitalet; after passing five opponents, he stopped cockily on the goal line and waited for the keeper to come back before kicking the ball into the back of the net. The Catalan coaches were impressed by the boy.

'Spectacular performance, good relationship with his teammates and the youth team coaches, and well-behaved at all times. He seemed like a good kid, shy and not very talkative,' Sánchez added. It looked as if Mario would go to La Másia but it was not to be. The versions, as in many footballers' stories, are conflicting. 'A financial agreement between the club and his representatives could not be reached. It was certainly not a footballing issue; we thought he had the qualities needed to stay here,' Sánchez stated sometime later.

'They never explained their reasons exactly. They only told us that they wanted to concentrate on training Spanish players,' the Balotelli family claimed. There are also those who call into question the complicated bureaucratic issues that would have needed to be resolved to bring Mario to Barcelona. Perhaps this explanation is less realistic given the number of kids from all over the world and from all backgrounds that the Catalan club has raised at La Másia. Mario's dream of playing for the same club as Ronaldinho, a player who he admired, went up in smoke. He often had his picture taken in Barcelona's bright yellow strip and would have loved to have joined the club. So much so that he sent Salvioni a postcard with the words: 'Coach, it's amazing here. I'd love to stay.' But it did not happen, he went back to square one, to Concesio. There was no need to worry, however. As Boninsegna said, half the clubs in Italy wanted him and some even say that English clubs such as Chelsea, Tottenham and, coincidentally, Liverpool were interested in that fifteen-year-old black kid.

Chapter 10

300,000 Euros

Thursday 21 August 2006: the football transfer window closed without causing a sensation. There had been plenty of interesting deals but no headline-grabbing transfers to win over the fans. The Ronaldo-Adriano swap that had been the topic of conversation for months in Spain and Italy had come to nothing. The Brazilian bomber and former Inter player stayed on in the Spanish capital. Those working for Massimo Moratti, the president of Inter, had failed to reach an agreement with Real Madrid to bring him back to Milan, something that had seemed like a done deal that morning. Fabio Capello held on to *El Gordo* and the Emperor Adriano stayed with Roberto Mancini. Despite this, the Milanese club concluded ten transactions on the last day of the transfer window, as detailed by an official statement issued at 11.51 pm that evening: 'In addition to acquiring Mariano Nicolás González on loan and lending out César, the Inter executives named eight other players as having come to or left the club from the Youth Scheme, as well as those who are still owned by Inter but have begun their careers elsewhere. Two boys born in 1990 will complete the *Allievi* Under-17 pool, coached by Daniele Bernazzani. The two players in question are the Ghanaian striker Mario Barwuah (already a Serie C1 player with Lumezzane) and the French midfielder, born in Cameroon, David Thukan (from the amateur San Paolo di Roma team).' This was followed by a list of sales and players on loan from the academy.

Mario Barwuah arrived at Inter on transfer deadline day when the fans were expecting the return of the *Fenomeno*.

How did this come about? It is a complicated story, one of torn-up pre-agreements, triangulations, bags of money, agents, missed appointments, meetings and confrontations. It is worth telling step by step, starting on 6 July 2006, when Renzo Cavagna took over the reins at AC Lumezzane from Giambortolo Pozzi. Among the many issues he had to deal with, such as the club's disastrous financial situation and the keenness of many of its members to wash their hands of football altogether, the new chairman also had to resolve the question of Balotelli.

'I absolutely wanted him to stay with us. I tried every possible way to hold onto him, even contributing financially out of my own pocket. I had taken a punt on him because, although I hadn't seen him in action much, I noticed immediately that he was phenomenal and a potential asset to our club,' Cavagna remembers in his office in Brescia. 'But despite my efforts, I didn't manage to keep him because his half-brothers and sister rightly saw fit to consider all the options to find the ideal place for him, somewhere bigger that could offer more than Lumezzane ever could.'

On that subject, do you know what happened with Fiorentina? 'When the boy and his brothers went to see Pantaleo Corvino to work out the final details of the contract – Pozzi had already established Lumezzane's fee – Corvino got irritated, probably by Corrado and Giovanni's requests. And do you know what he did?'

Why don't you tell me?

'He took the pre-agreement, ripped it into a thousand pieces right in front of the brothers and told them to get the hell out of there, that he didn't want to see them again.'

Once again, this is quite different from the Balotelli family's version of events, in which they maintain that they did not ask Corvino for more money but only for an apartment so they could be close to Mario. They claim the Fiorentina chairman refused, leaving Corrado and Giovanni to look elsewhere.

Let's move on. Chievo were also knocking on Lumezzane's door, but the Veneto club's spending power was limited so they only wanted the boy on loan. That was out of the question. In the meantime, Mario was training with the first team in Polpenazze del Garda. At that time, they were coached by Giancarlo D'Astoli, a former attacking defender who had already served a stint on the Lumezzane bench from 2000 to 2004. The assistant coach was Massimo Boninsegna, who time and time again found himself defending his protégé to senior members of the team, who were none too keen on the boy's messing about and laid-back dribbling; he would wind them up so much they would eventually go in hard with their tackles.

Boninsegna remembers: 'After about three weeks, the way things were going, I told him in no uncertain terms that if it was me, I would go and play for a big club's Under-20 team.' Mario seems to have accepted this piece of advice willingly: when D'Astoli tried to convince him to stay for another season to help the team now playing in C2, he told him he had made his decision and wanted to leave. On the corporate side, meetings between the chairman and Mario's brothers continued. Cavagna and his associates met with wannabe agents Giovanni and Corrado on several occasions. 'My opening offer was €10,000 but I went up to €20,000 and then €30,000,' Cavagna says. 'But then I got annoyed and realised this was potentially the most important deal of my life, an investment that would have taken the pressure off Lumezzane for two years. So, I took €100,000 from my savings and went to Polpenazze with a briefcase full of money, accompanied by two of my associates to witness that I was acting in the best interests of the club.'

Lumezzane were playing a friendly with Colognese, a Serie D team from Bergamo. Mario was playing and his two brothers were in attendance, keeping a close eye on him. 'I was supposed to meet with them for the umpteenth time. It should have been the most important meeting, the decisive negotiation but they didn't even turn up,' Cavagna claims. 'A little while later, I was at the clinic when I had a phone call from Lumezzane. I was told that the Swiss club Bellinzona were about to sign Mario but that Inter were interested. In the end we agreed on a respectable compensation sum with Inter: €300,000 plus three players. (Andrè Ballini, a defender born in 1987; Simone Bellini, a midfielder on loan, born in 1990; and Mario Rebecchi, a co-owned midfielder born in 1983). That's the story, in summary.'

Renzo Cavagna says that he has tried to forget the details of Mario Barwuah Balotelli's transfer to Inter because the triangulation upset him. This is understandable, but the story deserves to be told in detail. Corrado and Giovanni Balotelli, possibly under advice from Pietro Ausilio, head of Inter's Youth Scheme, and agent Patrick Bastianelli, hatched the winning plan. They used a trick, a football transfer market ploy used by many clubs but one that it is unlikely these first-time agents would have known. Ezio Chinelli explains: 'A triangulation works like this: you place the boy with a club in another, foreign association, exploiting a rule that allows young football players to be transferred freely within the European Union. The vendor then only receives the preparation premium calculated by UEFA. There is no negotiation between the parties, only compensation that, in Mario's case, would have been between €15,000 and €20,000. So, what happened at this point? Inter pretended to negotiate with Bellinzona, a club with which it was already on good terms, then they came to us with a paternal tone and said: "Go on, instead of sending him to Switzerland, we'll give you something for him and we can call it quits." It was the classic pat on the back. Where was the catch? Balotelli was no longer bound to Lumezzane. We could not sign him as if he were any old fourteen-year-old kid playing football for a club. We would normally place an option on him until he turned nineteen and then follow the classic procedure of a two-year pre-agreement before signing a proper contract. In the case of Mario, a foster kid without Italian nationality, the normal routes were not open to us. We had to re-sign him year on year, every 30 June. This was the problem … If he had been obligated to us, he might never have gone to Inter, or at least he would have gone under conditions that were very different as far as we were concerned. In co-ownership, for example, and then when he made his league debut we could have asked Inter to buy out our share. If they had tried to pull back, we could even have put half the player's price tag up for auction. In short, Lumezzane were extremely disappointed that Mario went to Inter on loan with the option for release. We were disappointed about how we had been treated by his brothers, not by his mother and father, for whom I have always had the greatest respect. And we were bitter about how we had been treated by Inter.'

What would it have meant for Lumezzane if Balotelli had stayed at the club?

'It's not every day a club like ours comes across a player like him. He could have meant a lot to us,' Chinelli remarks.

'One more year and we would have earned a minimum of €1 million instead of €300,000,' Cavagna cuts to the chase. He adds: 'Selfishly, I wanted to keep him with me but I couldn't and I don't regret it. Who knows, perhaps if he had stayed here he might not have had the career he has had. To have gone to Inter at such a young age must have helped him mature as a footballer. And when a kid is good, you have to let him go. I have let plenty go who are now in Serie B.'

Generosity aside, Lumezzane have made quite a sum out of Super Mario's various transfers. Every time he changes club, Lume receive a preparation premium, 1% of the value of the contract, compared with the 3% Inter receive. Balotelli's move from Milan to Liverpool earned them €200,000. When Inter sold him to Manchester City, Lume's coffers were swelled by the princely sum of €260,000, and when City sent him back to Italy, to AC Milan, they earned a further €240,000. Lume's bosses do not have too much to complain about. Those who do have a right to quibble, who have always ended up empty handed, are those at the Mompiano parish sports centre. Although they raised Mario as a footballer from aged seven to ten, they will never see so much as a penny. FIFA regulations on the status and transfers of players governing financial compensation paid to training clubs states flatly in chapter seven that it is to be paid to 'the club(s) with which the player has been registered since the season of his twelfth birthday'. A crying shame for the parish sports centre.

Chapter 11

Full Steam Ahead

'I'm determined, lively and sometimes I can make the difference to a team. As far as I'm concerned, football is just a game, fun that certainly isn't my job but I hope one day it might be. For the time being, I'm only thinking about smiling and scoring goals with my friends. As a player I don't like to be tied down by strategy, I prefer playing with freedom. I can be anarchic when it comes to tactics. I know I have to stay up front and score but that I need to improve the tactical part of my game as well. I also have to do better at school. I don't like going to school much but my family taught me that learning is important. I'm very close to my family; their affection and support is very important in football. I've started going to a secondary school that focuses on sport, so you could say that sport is my life now.

'What's my hobby? Football. When I'm not training at Interello, I go to the parish sports centre near my house for a kickabout with my friends. Sometimes we play on the PlayStation but I don't really like playing FIFA 2006, I almost always lose. Who are my idols? At the moment, I really like Robinho from Real Madrid because he always tries to show off his skills. Ibrahimovic doesn't mess about either. He's very tall and you wouldn't expect him to be able to do the things he can do with his feet. He has plenty of skill and really enjoys his football. Adriano is also very exciting because of his pace and power. And there's the phenomenon, Ronaldo, too. What's my dream? To win the *Ballon d'Or*. I know it's a big dream and that only a select few are lucky enough to win the coveted prize but if I work hard and get a little bit of luck along the way, who knows? Do I want to win the *Ballon d'Or* with Inter? Yes, of course. At the moment I'm on loan from Lumezzane and I hope to be able to stay at this important club. It's very well-organised and has great coaches. That's my goal, then Serie A and the *Ballon d'Or* ... it's free to dream!'

Only four months had passed since Mario moved to Inter, yet by 1 January 2007 he had already earned his first interview on the club's website. All the attention paid to him was understandable: he ended 2006 having scored fourteen goals in twelve games for the *Allievi* Under-17 team. He was top scorer in the league and his goals had helped Inter join Alberigo Evani's AC Milan at the top of Group B. Speaking of goals, the people behind Inter's website were perplexed by the fact that Mario did not celebrate when he scored a goal. Barwuah Balotelli responded to the question without hesitation: 'I've always scored lots of goals and I've always behaved like that. It's how I do things. Why should I celebrate or make a fuss? I'm a striker and my job is to score goals. The keeper's job is to make saves and a save is worth as much as a goal. If keepers don't celebrate, why should I?' Not a bad argument for a sixteen-year-old, who, in just a few months, had become the leading light of Daniele Bernazzani's team. To start with, Mario was not particularly happy to find himself in the *Allievi* Under-17 team, in fact he was downright disappointed. He told Valter Salvioni he had thought they would let him play for the Under-20s and Salvioni had to reassure him: 'You can't expect them to let you play for the Under-20 team if you're barely sixteen and they don't know you yet. They have put you in a team based on your age. When they see you have what it takes to play with the older kids, they will move you. You'll see. Listen to me and don't worry. Keep working hard and they will move you to the Under-20s.' The former Lumezzane coach was right: all Mario needed was some patience. Not much at all as it would turn out.

Barwuah Balotelli's Inter adventure began on 2 September 2006 when he joined the *Allievi* Under-17 training camp in Montecchio Maggiore in the province of Vicenza. They were playing in the summer 'Romeo and Juliet' tournament. Four other teams were taking part: Treviso, Atalanta, Cittadella and HamKam, a Norwegian team from the town of Hamar. Balo made his debut in the famous blue and black-striped shirt against Cittadella and scored. He scored another two goals against the Norwegians, helping Inter to an 8-1 win. The next month things began to get tough. The league championship began on 1 October. Ironically, Inter were drawn to play Lumezzane at home in the first game. It ended 1-1. Balotelli failed to score. He let his emotions get the better of him. A week later he scored the second goal against Montichiari to give Inter an outright lead. On 22 October, he managed his first hat-trick against Piacenza at the Interello Sports Centre.

In late 2006, Daniele Bernazzani, the Under-17 coach who would go on to become first team assistant coach to Mourinho, only had good things to say about his new purchase: 'He is physically strong and powerful and has a good head for scoring. That can be an important talent at this age. However, he can and must improve his individual technique and specific movements, but he is young and time is on his side'. He did not have any problems adapting to his new situation either: 'Thanks to his family upbringing, Mario fitted in immediately and established an understanding with his teammates straight away,' the manager told *Tuttosport*, undoubtedly supporting Mario's parents' decision to have him travel up and down from Concesio. The boy could have lived with his teammates in the Inter housing, but Papà Franco and Mamma Silvia preferred to take him back and forth so they could keep an eye on him. The journey from home to Interello took three quarters of an hour every day. Bernazzani maintained: 'They are right to keep him under control. At sixteen it is very easy to get distracted, especially when you are considered a great talent. Mario may not be all that enthusiastic about it, but in a few years' time, he will have nothing but thanks for his family'. He adds: 'He has started off on the right foot and is continuing to behave in the same way as the year goes on.'

This was a piece of advice, a warning that Mario seems to have followed to the letter. On 21 January 2007, after returning from the Christmas holidays, Barwuah Balotelli scored the winning goal, a penalty, to beat Lumezzane in the first of the return fixtures. He kept his emotions in check this time and made no mistake from the spot. But his days with the *Allievi* Under-17s were numbered. For a while, the three leading figures in the Inter Youth Scheme – Piero Ausilio, Beppe Baresi and Vincenzo Esposito, the Under-20 team coach – had been keeping an eye on the academy's new phenomenon. After an extraordinary first half of the season, they thought he was ready to move up a category but they were stalling: they were concerned about rocking the boat in the dressing room by throwing someone like Mario into the mix. The final decision was made in March. After the match between Inter and AC Milan on 25 February 2007 ended in a 0-0 draw, Barwuah Balotelli moved up to the Under-20s. He finally achieved what he had been hoping for since the start of the season. He had scored eighteen goals in eighteen games for the Under-17s, making him Inter's top scorer ahead of Mattia Destro, born in 1991, who had only scored nine.

On 3 March 2007, the sixth return fixture of the championship, Mario made his debut with the older boys in another Inter-AC Milan derby.

The sun was out and the terraces of the Interello Sports Centre were packed. There was a minute's silence before the match in memory of Benito Lorenzi, known as Veleno, a *nerazzurro* legend who had died that morning.

The Inter boys took the lead in the 28th minute through Pedrelli; Mario had already had two good chances but failed to convert them. His moment arrived in the 40th minute: Ribas shot on the Milan goal from inside the box; Facchin made the save but could not hold onto it. Balotelli pounced on the ball before the defender could get there and hammered it into the back of the net. It was his first goal for the Under-20 team, a goal in a derby that meant more than other matches, even in the lower age groups, a goal in a match that ended 4-2 in Inter's favour. To sum up, it was a fantastic debut.

'Mario was obviously one of the key players in that match, with a goal that wasn't difficult but important. He grappled with his opponent, made space in front of the goal and found the right moment to shoot,' Vincenzo Esposito now recalls. A former midfielder with Torino, Lazio, Atalanta and Prato, he coached the Inter Under-20 team from 2006 to 2009, before moving on to Ravenna and Prato, a team he still manages in the Pro League. From the small Tuscan town, he remembers Mario's arrival: 'He had come to me the week before that derby. I had already seen him on the pitch several times and I picked him because I needed a player with his characteristics. I immediately felt he was a natural showman and couldn't wait to get on the pitch to show what he could do. Otherwise, he was an extremely cheerful kid; straightforward, exuberant and generous, with a broad smile. But he was also instinctive, capable of moments of powerful individualism that could cause difficulties both for him and the group. When it came to football, he was phenomenal. He had so much talent, the like of which I had never seen before in such a young player. I called him up immediately.'

This indeed proved to be the case: in the seven matches Mario played for Esposito's Under-20 team he scored another three times against Chievo, Udinese and Triestina. Inter topped Group B in the championship, ahead of Milan, and qualified for the knockout stage. Super Mario (as he had been christened by the Inter TV channel after the plumber from the Mario Bros video game) scored two goals against Genoa in the knockout stage and one against Reggina in the quarter-finals. Inter beat Palermo in the semi-final. The final was to be played at 8.30 pm on Saturday 19 May 2007 on the municipal pitch in Bressanone. Inter's opponents were Sampdoria, managed by Alberto Bollini. They were a well-balanced and adaptable team that boasted three key players: the midfielder Danilo Soddimo and the strike force of Romeo and Ferrari, who had scored plenty of goals between them. Inter responded with strikers Sebastian Ribas, a Uruguayan born in 1988, and Mario Balotelli. It was a final and the tension was palpable. The first half could hardly be described as exciting. Samp and Inter were working each other out and holding back. There were few scoring opportunities. Sampdoria started better after half time and the match began to come to life. Short passes, long throw-ins to get around the back of the midfield, alert defenders, plenty of fouls and Balotelli making his presence felt. In the 27th minute, Fiorillo, the Sampdoria goalkeeper parried a free kick by the Inter number nine from twenty yards out, which was headed straight for the top corner. Seven minutes later, Mario was held back in the box but the referee let play continue. There was only one minute remaining when Jonathan Rossini, a Sampdoria defender, slid into Balotelli and brought him down. Cafari, the referee, blew his whistle for a penalty. The Samp players protested; they argued that the Inter striker knew exactly what he was doing and had intentionally tried to make contact with the defender's foot. It was no use, the referee's mind was made up. Balotelli put the ball down on the spot, looked at Fiorillo, took a run-up and shot. The ball went to the left and the keeper went to the right. Goal! Inter had won the league for that age group. It was the sixth victory for the Youth Scheme, the first since the Football League had decided to name the trophy after Giacinto Facchetti, the former Inter captain and chairman, who had died on 4 September 2006. As in the 1988–89 season, the Under-20s won their championship after the first team had won Serie A. Luca Facchetti, Giacinto's son, presented the boys with their medals. The party could begin, but before the celebrations, Mario needed to do something he had done before: he went over to shake the hand of Fiorillo, Sampdoria's goalkeeper, the vanquished opponent.

'When it was time to kick that penalty, Balotelli didn't flinch, he didn't bat an eyelid. For someone who was only seventeen, he was impressively cool and calm. In a team that could boast good players, he always made a difference and helped us lift two trophies that were very important to the club. Were there problems in the dressing room? Well ...' Esposito says with a smile, 'dealing with hierarchies was never his strong point. In football teams, as in everyday life, there are levels of hierarchy that need to be respected. You have to respect your teammates who are two or three years older than you are. And respect is shown through things that may seem trivial, like a seat on the bus or in the canteen. Mario didn't pay much attention to that kind of thing. He didn't recognise hierarchy; he couldn't stomach it. And this led to arguments.' With Dennis Esposito and Leonardo Bonucci, for example, the oldest in the group ...

'Dennis was a very fair and respectful boy. He was born in 1988, as was Leonardo, now a defender at Juventus and for the national team. They were a couple of years older and expected a certain precision from Mario that he was unable to give,' the manager explains.

Was it bullying? A kind of initiation?

'No, it was just that sometimes Mario made you lose your patience.'

How many times did you lose yours?

'He pissed me off in a playful, jokey way plenty of times. The worst was without a doubt when I received a call from the head of the Istituto Milano, his school. They told me Mario had got up from his desk, during class, while the teacher was explaining something, and walked out, saying he wasn't interested in what she had to say. He went home and ended up playing football with some friends in a square in Milan. He knew he had screwed up but couldn't sit there any longer. He definitely regretted it; I really punished him. I suspended him from an important match, against Empoli. I was reluctant because he was my best player, but I sent him to the stands. He needed to learn from such a punishment. You have to strike Mario with the thing he cares about most: being on the pitch in every game. I also had a duty to the group, who needed answers. They were intelligent kids and they understood that Mario wasn't doing it on purpose, that nothing with him was premeditated. He had his own difficulties'. Namely ... 'He had to get away from his ego, which was very strong at that time. He had to try to be less focused on Mario, or at least this was my opinion, and that of Giovanni Pasculli, who I worked with closely on the boys' psychology. Mario needed help to understand the value of the team, of generosity and solidarity, work and sacrifices for others.'

Despite what Esposito defines as Mario Barwuah Balotelli's personal difficulties, less than two months after the Under-20 championship final, he set off for the Riscone Sports Centre in Brunico, where, on 14 July 2007, the first team summer training camp had just got under way. Roberto Mancini had called him up alongside nine other boys from the Under-20 team. Mario, as always, was the youngest. He kept on leapfrogging milestones. In little more than a year he had made his Serie C1 debut, imposed himself on Inter's Under-17 and Under-20 teams and was now entering the orbit of the first team.

'In Appiano Gentile we all trained together and met to discuss things on a daily basis. I spent a lot of time talking to Mancini, as well as to Fausto Salsano (his assistant coach) and Siniša Mihajlović (his deputy); they all thought Mario was incredibly talented. Mancini, an intelligent and competent person, quickly realised just how talented the boy was and took him with him. Little by little, he joined the group and Mancini gave him his debut. In the five months Mario had spent with me, he had exploded.'

Chapter 12

Flat Out

A goal, a shot off the crossbar and another from twenty yards out. All in 40 minutes. Not bad for a boy playing only in his second ever match with the grown-ups. It was 21 July 2007 and Inter were playing a summer friendly against FC Sudtirol, a Serie C2 team, in Riscone di Brunico. Super Mario had already made an appearance against the Chinese Olympic team on 17 July, coming on at the start of the second half to replace David Suazo, the Honduran who had just been purchased from Cagliari. He had created the second goal for Santiago Solari before eventually being intimidated by Wang Dalei, the Chinese keeper, who had come off his line. Against the team from South Tyrol, Barwuah Balotelli, in front of 5,000 supporters, made no mistake. Five minutes into the second half he scored to give them a 2-0 lead: it was an easy tap-in on the end of a low cross delivered by Suazo. A few minutes later, he hit the crossbar with a fantastic header supplied by Solari and made his presence felt on two other occasions, in particular with a rocket from twenty yards out.

At the end of the match, an emotional young man spoke into the microphone: 'I'm delighted to have scored this afternoon. It was a great match. I've had the opportunity here at Inter to train with so many great players. They help me to learn new things and correct me when I make mistakes. They want me to improve because everyone here wants the best for me.' They tell him what Mancini said about him

('He's good … He is the future of Inter') and he smiles and replies: 'Coach hasn't said anything like that to me! Joking apart, I don't know if I will go on to become an important striker for Inter but I would like to thank him anyway and I will work as hard as I can to repay his trust.'

The manager was not the only one who was happy with the Brescian of Ghanaian parentage. After watching him at work in the Under-20s final in Bressanone, Massimo Moratti, president of Inter, suggested to Roberto Mancini that he select him for the last match in the league; he was enthusiastic about the boy. On his visit to Bressanone, he told reporters that Mario had promised him he would be the new Ronaldo in a few years, something Barwuah Balotelli himself confirmed. 'I'm inspired by Ronaldo and Cristiano Ronaldo.' One-liners aside, there was no doubt that Mario was the revelation of the training camp in the Alto Adige. Even his teammates said his future was certain. However, Julio Ricardo Cruz, *El Jardinero*, also had a warning for him: 'From what I've seen during the training camp, Balotelli has everything it takes to become a great player. But he's very young. He is just at the beginning of his career', the Argentine striker told the *Gazzetta dello Sport*. 'He needs to use his head and keep his feet on the ground, and not get over-excited about the first positive thing that happens. That's the only way you can deserve to play for Inter.'

Another Argentine, Santiago Solari, felt the same way, and still does. The former midfielder for Newell's Old Boys, River Plate, Atlético and Real Madrid came to Inter in the summer of 2005 and stayed until 2008. He witnessed the beginning of Super Mario's adventure in top-flight football: 'I remember his first training sessions with the first team. They consisted of a physical section, a tactical part off the ball and then we would finish with a friendly: eleven against eleven, four against four or eight against eight. You could see straight away that he was precociously talented. He had technical and physical qualities. Even at aged sixteen, Mario would use his body and there was no way to get the ball off him. He had so much pace and could score from any position. From the outset, you could see he would play in Serie A because he had a competitive nature. He was also a good kid, extrovert but shy at the same time and always on the defensive. He was well-received by the dressing room; the other players tried affectionately to advise him in the best way possible. At that age, if a dressing room is healthy, as it was back then at Inter, the other players are patient with you and try to involve and teach you. But if you're not sixteen but 25 and you mess about, your teammates will end up telling you where to go.'

How did Roberto Mancini help Balotelli, the new arrival? 'Although Roberto has many flaws, as does everyone, as well as a personality that is far from simple, I think he helped a lot. He is the type of manager who can argue furiously with a player, as I've seen him do many times, but if he recognises his quality, if he knows he can help him win a match, he picks him to play, whatever disagreements may have taken place.' When talking about Mancini's 2007–2008 season at Inter, Solari remembers a curious story: 'It must have been his first or second match with us. At the end of the first half, I went into the dressing room to wait for Mancini's tactical team talk and I see Mario with a PSP, a portable PlayStation. I told him to put it away immediately. He looked at me and replied incredulously, "Why?" "Mario, I'll tell you afterwards but now, please stop playing and put it away." In the end, he did as I told him.'

Solari laughs heartily as he remembers the episode and says: 'He was just a kid but he had this disconnect with responsibility for a match. Perhaps he got away with it because he was talented ... I am convinced that if Mario had combined his talent with the responsibility of a player like Raul, he would have won the *Ballon d'Or*. But, as I always say, everyone is who they are. I've always been the reliable and responsible type, but I never had Mario's talent. There is no doubt that he has grown up a lot; he has been able to overcome his problems, but at the end of the day, it is inconsistency that is most damaging to a footballer. To be capable of the best, to win a match on your own but then to disappear into thin air in the next one as if you weren't on the pitch. I know what a manager wants: he would rather have a player who always gives seven out of ten than one who gives ten out of ten in two matches and then two out of ten in all the rest. I think there always comes a time when quality and talent aren't enough to keep you in football's elite. You need perseverance, respect for your teammates, for your manager and the club, a calm private life and to take care of your body. Take Ronaldo, *El Fenomeno*. When he was scoring 30 goals a season, what did the manager care if he was fat and wasn't training, couldn't run or fetch the ball? But when he was down to ten goals a season, the manager began to wonder whether he really needed that player. When it comes down to it, it's simple mathematics.'

Solari now coaches the *Cadete* A, Real Madrid's sixteen-year-olds; he adds in conclusion: 'Do you know what I would give for someone like Balotelli in my team? My God ... I would give one of the fingers on my right hand for a sixteen-year-old Balotelli.'

Back then, there were plenty of people ready to lose their heads over Inter's new gem. At Palazzo Durini, Inter's head-quarters, the offers came flooding in, but the club's executives had no intention of letting the boy go. They added him to the 25 players on their UEFA list even though months would pass until he made his debut. The wannabe striker started with the first team at the Emirates Stadium against Arsenal on 30 July 2007, one of many summer fixtures. Compliments came from Moratti, who had withdrawn from the purchase of Alexandre Pato, the Brazilian seventeen-year-old with a €22 million price tag, convinced he already had a great alternative of his own. In fact, when the *Gazzetta dello Sport* asked him about the episode, he cut them off: 'Pato would have taken chances away from a product of our own academy who is maturing in a wonderful way. I'm talking about Balotelli.' What the president does not go on to say is that Pato would earn €2 million at Milan while Balotelli only cost the Inter coffers €60,000 a year.

After the emotion of the Emirates Stadium and the first team, Mario returned to Esposito's Under-20 team. He found himself back in England, in Sheffield on 8 November for a friendly organised to celebrate the 150th anniversary of the English club. He scored two goals, waiting for his time to come. And come it did at Sant'Elia on 16 December 2007, the sixteenth fixture of the first half of the Serie A season. It was the final minute of a quiet game between Cagliari and Inter. The *Nerazzurri* were winning 2-0. Mancini turned to the bench and said 'Mario, warm up'. The boy only had time for a quick run up and down the touchline before the third official held up the light board with his number, 45. Balotelli was going on as a substitute for David Suazo. He made his Serie A debut at age seventeen, in a white shirt with the red cross and Inter shield on his chest. His first appearance lasted for just three minutes.

The journalists at the post-match press conference asked him if he was happy and he responded with a laconic yes. Mario wanted more, he wanted to play and to play a key part. Training with the grown-ups wasn't enough for him, that little taster of football's top flight wasn't enough for him. He vented himself to the Under-20s coach, telling him in no uncertain terms: 'Coach, if they don't pick me for the first team on Sunday, I'm coming with you. I want to play.' Vincenzo Esposito calmed him down, told him to be patient and that his time would come. He was right. His opportunity came three days later in the Coppa Italia, on 19 December 2007. It was the first leg of the round of sixteen, against Reggina in Reggio Calabria. Mario Balotelli Barwuah started the game in a team that had been reshuffled to rest certain players. It included: Orlandoni, Ribas, Materazzi, Samuel, Fatic, Solari, Pelè, Burdisso, Cesar, Crespo and Balotelli. In three years in charge at Inter, Mancini had never faltered in the Cup, and he wanted to win this one too.

On a heavy pitch in a real downpour, it finished 4-1 to Inter with Mario as the star of the night. He scored two goals. In the 30th minute, he fired a right-footed shot into the back of the net from a short clearance by Nenad Novakovic following a header from Samuel. In the 85th minute, he intercepted a woefully short back-pass from Cascione, went around the goalkeeper and scored. He smiled with happiness while the other young players ran over to congratulate him. In the dressing room, Mancini reprimanded Mario for missing a third scoring opportunity. The manager tried to keep his feet on the ground but the following day's newspapers were triumphant about Mario, without exception. For example, *Tuttosport* ran with the headline 'Inter flying with Super Mario'. Another? *La Gazzetta dello Sport* gave him a seven out of ten in the player ratings and wrote: 'Balotelli (the Best) has arrived. He tormented Novakovic and stunned Cherubin. A champion in the making. Is he better than Pato?'

Super Mario was off to a flying start and in early January 2008 Inter flew to Dubai for the four-team Dubai Cup. Mancini took the boy with him to give him the opportunity to experience the atmosphere of the first team and international competitions, even if it was a minor event.

On 30 January 2008, Inter played Juventus in the quarterfinal of the Coppa Italia in Turin's Stadio Olimpico. The first leg in the San Siro had ended 2-2. Inter had to score if they wanted to advance to the semi-final. Because Suazo was out of form, Mancini picked Balotelli to partner Cruz up front. He was in the starting eleven and certainly made it count. In the ninth minute, a long ball from Maniche met the pace of the number 45, who took advantage of a mistake by Alessandro Birindelli; he got behind the Juventus defender, who had 200 matches in Serie A to his name. Birindelli fell flat on his face trying to stop him, while Mario controlled the ball with his shoulder on the half volley and calmly got past Belardi, the keeper. Four minutes later, the Juve captain Alessandro Del Piero equalised with a free kick deflected off the wall and Iaquinta later capitalised on a Stendardo header that came back off the post. 2-1 to the home team. Juve were ahead and Mario managed to get himself a yellow card. He lifted his elbow while in the air, giving Nicola Legrottaglie a black eye. Thankfully, Julio Cruz brought Inter level from the penalty spot, but a draw would not be enough, they needed to score again. Pavel Nedved, supplied by Del Piero, missed a sensational opportunity, firing the ball over Toldo's long arms. The young phenomenon made no such mistakes. A cross from Stankovic found Balotelli in the box with his back to goal. Marked by Legrottaglie, he turned, anticipated the move from Stendardo and let rip with a slingshot. It was unstoppable. 3-2 to Inter. Mancini celebrated at the bench and Mario smiled from ear to ear as his teammates hugged him. He talked about his two goals after the match: 'I think the best thing about the first one was my control. I would have been an idiot if I'd missed that shot. The second one? I thought I was going to pass the ball as I heard someone calling. Instead, I controlled it and managed to hit it properly. It was instinctive. A lot of my game is instinctive.' Two goals away at Juventus is not something that happens every day, only to great players. Everyone realised this and Balotelli-mania exploded. Italy was desperate to know more about Mario Balotelli, the boy with an imposing physique (6 feet 2 and almost 14 stone), who had just taken Juventus apart. His life story came out, followed by claims to his Brescian origins and an endless dissection of his strengths. He was even interviewed by *Le Iene*, a satirical TV programme on the Italia 1 channel. They had him dribbling the ball while reciting multiplication tables and tackling Pythagoras' theorem.

Meanwhile, the *enfant terrible* of Italian football, as he was labelled by those at *Le Iene*, went back to play for the Under-20s in Viareggio. The world's most prestigious youth football tournament was in its 60th year. It began on 28 January and ended on 13 February. By the time Mario arrived, things were well under way; he scored seven goals in six games to become top scorer, but more importantly he helped Inter lift a trophy that meant a lot to the club. His two goals in the final replay at Viareggio's Stadio dei Pini were decisive. Inter went behind twice against Empoli, but Super Mario took care of getting them back on equal terms. Firstly, from the penalty spot, complete with a *paradinha* dummy, and then a rocket of a free kick into the top corner. In the tenth minute of the second half, he even narrowly missed scoring with a bicycle kick: the ball clattered against the crossbar but just failed to cross the line. It was a good job that Mario had already bagged a winning bicycle kick, the trick he had loved so much as a kid back in Mompiano, on 6 February in the last sixteen against Cisco Roma: 'The ball suddenly flew up in the air and he pulled off such an incredible move that everyone in the stadium stood up to applaud,' remembers Esposito, who has not forgotten that hard-fought and vitally important final. After extra time, the match finished 2-2. The title would be decided on penalties. Balotelli scored the last of the required five by wrong-footing the keeper. Then Alberto Pelagotti, the Inter keeper, saved the fifth shot from Hemmy. It was mayhem! Turbo Mario, who had turned up to play with a mohican, ran around the pitch with a can of shaving foam, spraying his teammates, photographers and the cameramen white. It was over-the-top, or at least that was what the defeated Empoli team thought. 'He came right over to our bench. You should have more respect for your opponents,' the Tuscan right-back, Giuseppe Arvia, complained. 'It's not true and I don't do things like that,' Mario responded. Then he spoke to Italian state television about the victory, dedicating his success to his family, friends and his girlfriend Giulia. He spoke with real heart about the team, just as Esposito had done a few minutes earlier.

Now at Prato, Esposito recalls an unusual episode from that tournament in Viareggio: a prank the other kids played on Mario. 'Because at dinnertime he would always ask for something different compared to his teammates – he always wanted Coca-Cola instead of water or meat sauce with his pasta instead of tomato – they decided it would be fun to get him back,' Esposito remembers. 'While he was in the common room watching TV, they got a dead fish from the hotel kitchens, ran up to his room and put it in his pillow case. When Mario went to bed that night there was an unbelievable stench and he found the fish. He was furious and was awake all night, but he still played a decisive role on the pitch the following day.'

For Mario, the time for fun and games was coming to an end now that he was firmly in the orbit of the first team at an Inter that was in the race for its third consecutive Serie A title. On 6 April 2008, he scored his first goal in Serie A against Atalanta, away in Bergamo. Before scoring, Mario provided Patrick Vieira with an assist. In the absence of Chivu, Mancini had instructed Mario to take care of dead ball situations. He had spent a long time practising after training sessions with Sinisa Mihajlovic, Mancini's deputy and a dead ball specialist, trying to find the correct power and trajectory. It went well and he was able to put the lessons he had learnt to good use. He dished up a perfect trajectory from the corner flag and the French player gave Inter a 1-0 lead. There was more to come: another assist for Cruz that he squandered, followed by an absolute gem. Stankovic, Cambiasso and then a pass to Mario: he brought it down on his chest, sprang forward, sent Atalanta's keeper, Coppola, the wrong way and delicately nudged it towards the open goal. He would say later in the dressing room: 'My teammates asked me why it took me so long to shoot. And perhaps I was a bit slow.'

This may well have been true but moments such as those are to be enjoyed. It was pure happiness. Mancini took him off in the 38th minute to bring on Luis Figo and let him walk past the home fans keen to give him what for. Mario didn't notice and repeated that he was very happy. That it was great to have responsibilities and be able to do important things. Although he had played on the left wing and not in his favourite position, he had won over his manager and become one of Inter's youngest ever goal scorers. Only Mariolino Corso, the midfielder in Helenio Herrera's so-called *Grande*

Inter of the 1960s, had done better, scoring his first goal aged sixteen years and 322 days.

One goal led to another. A week later, on 13 April, another was to follow at the San Siro against Fiorentina. A Cruz throw-in found Mario on his own in front of the keeper and he scored the second goal. Five matches from the end of the league season, Inter had a four-point lead over Roma and Balotelli was receiving praise from all quarters. 'Super Mario helps the *Nerazzurri* overcome their problems' was the headline in the *Corriere della Sera*. Mario Sconcerti wrote: 'The boy who plays football with the maturity of a hundred-year-old has brought flexibility and freshness to the team.' The fact was that the number 45 was now one of the first on the team sheet. He had stolen Suazo's place. He scored himself and made scoring opportunities for others, such as against Siena on 11 May. To start with, a Beckham-style angled corner gave Vieira an assist before Mario scored with a header at the end of the first half to see Inter take a 2-1 lead. When Mancini brought him off in the eighteenth minute of the second half, the 83,000 fans in the San Siro stood up to applaud. In the dressing room, Mario burst into tears with happiness, believing his goal had been the winner and convinced he would soon be able to celebrate Inter's league title. He would celebrate with Mamma Silvia, who had come to the stadium to watch for the first time. But a goal from Houssine Kharja saw Siena equalise, ruining everything. It was a great disappointment for the boy who nevertheless went to meet his family in the stadium's car park with a smile on his face. He said: 'We'll win the title in the next match.'

The newspapers and TV pundits began to say that Inter were becoming dependent on Mario. It was certainly strange that a seventeen-year-old could have more of an

impact than so many great champions. But things would
soon be settled. 'From the match in Bergamo onwards,
Inter have always won when Balotelli is on the pitch. When
he wasn't playing (in the derby against AC Milan and the
second half against Siena), Inter managed a defeat and a
draw,' the *Corriere dello Sport* wrote, beneath the headline
'Balotelli Half of Inter's Value'. And that was not counting
the last sixteen of the Champions League, when Inter had
been taken apart by Liverpool, a defeat that would herald
the end of the Mancini era. Before that, the final match of
the league against Parma was still to be played, on 18 May
2008. Inter went to Parma after squandering four match
points and were now only one point ahead of Roma, with
82 points against 81. Roma were playing away from home,
against Catania; it was their last chance to move ahead.
Inter had to see it through on the swampy pitch in the
Tardini Stadium, against a team on the brink of relegation
that had to make certain of conceding nothing to Italy's
defending champions. Roberto Mancini picked Julio Cesar
in goal; a four-man defence with Maicon, Rivas, Materazzi
and Maxwell; Zanetti, Vieira, Stankovic and Cesar in midfield; and Cruz partnering Balotelli up front. It was a classic 4-4-2 with Balotelli moved to the right wing. He was far
from thrilled, but sacrificed himself and took some knocks
on the right before providing Cruz with the perfect cross
that was anticipated by Pavarini and only missed the goal by
a whisper. He received the ball in the box and guessed right
with a low shot to which the Parma keeper managed to
get a fingertip. In the 31st minute of the second half, with
Inter 1-0 up thanks to a goal from substitute Ibrahimovic,
Mario was taken off in place of Pelé. Two minutes later
he ran from the bench onto the pitch like a madman to
hug his teammate Zlatan. The Swedish player had given

the *Nerazzurri* the title with another goal. 'It was such an exciting moment, the best in a season that has been flat out. I will remember it as the one in which I made my debut for the first team, for the goals I've scored and for winning the title,' he confessed shortly afterwards to the *Corriere dello Sport*. Indeed ... he had played a key role in winning the league title (fifteen appearances and seven goals between the Coppa Italia and Serie A) yet he had not yet even turned eighteen. It was an honour that few great players in the history of football had experienced, names like Lionel Messi, Marco van Basten, Raul and Karim Benzema.

After a year like that, the boy was keen to get away on holiday, perhaps back to Brazil, where he had been at New Year with his brother to visit a social project, but before that he still had several commitments to fulfil: the final of the Coppa Italia against Roma in the Stadio Olimpico on 24 May for one. Balotelli started and finished the game but failed to score. Roma got their revenge for the league championship and bagged the trophy with a resounding 2-1 win. At seventeen years old, it was not all about football for Mario; there was also school to think about. At the Istituto Milano, Mario was preparing to take the exams that would allow him to advance to the final year, when he would be able to get his diploma. He had more time until he was to join Mancini's squad on a full-time basis. 'I would take public transport to school', he explained. 'I liked going especially because I got to spend time with my friends.' What about classes? Apart from maths, everything else bored him to death. He could not stay seated at his desk for more than half an hour or concentrate on a book. But he passed his exams. It was a shame that the final 'examination' of the season, the Under-20 final in Chieti on 8 June, went badly. He equalised to bring

Inter back to 2-2 but Mustacchio scored the winning goal for Sampdoria in the 82nd minute.

'He was the one who asked if he could come for the end of the tournament but he was tired after a long season with the first team,' Esposito said. 'If Mario had been at his usual level, we would have won that one too.'

Chapter 13

A Foreigner No More

13 August, 2008. 11 am, Piazza Paolo VI, Concesio. A crowd of people is waiting outside the town hall, decorated with flags. Boys and girls wearing Inter Milan shirts, brandishing notebooks and pens, whole families, curious onlookers, cameramen, photographers and journalists. They are jostling to find a scrap of shade beneath the arches of the town hall, some respite from the stifling mid-August heat. They are all waiting for Mario Balotelli. The young Inter phenomenon arrives by car, accompanied by his entire family. Silvia and Franco are very smartly dressed for the ceremony: she is wearing a white short-sleeved jacket and a dark skirt; he is dressed in a blue suit, white shirt and spotted tie. Mario, however, has opted for a casual look: a baseball cap on backwards with a white and navy polo shirt and washed-out jeans, all with the number 45 clearly visible and the logo of his clothing brand. Not to mention the two sparklers in his ears.

The previous day, 12 August 2008, Super Mario turned eighteen so is now officially an adult. He can finally become an Italian citizen. Diego Peli, the Mayor of Concesio, goes over to him. They shake hands for the photographers and TV cameras before the local police, dressed in blue, clear a path. They make one more stop to immortalise the moment before going inside where the ceremony in the council chamber can finally begin. Mario reads the oath; the mayor, with a tricolour ribbon around his shoulders, declares that:

'Mario Balotelli, born in Palermo on 12 August 1990, has acquired Italian citizenship on 13.08.08 in accordance with article, etc. etc. ...' The audience breaks out into applause and shouts of 'Bravo!' Even Super Mario timidly applauds then signs the documents with his left hand. Before handing it to its rightful owner, Diego Peli shows the public an identity card displaying photographs, stamps and the words '*REPUBBLICA ITALIANA*' written in large letters. The time for speeches has arrived. 'I would like to thank all those who have come here for this moment that is important to me, very important, the most important of all, I think,' Balotelli says softly. 'I would like to thank all my family as well as everyone else', and in a whisper he adds: 'I am proud to be Italian.'

Franco declines the invitation to speak into the microphone, shaking his head and making way for his wife, who does not hold back: 'Today, Mario has achieved something great, his right to be an Italian citizen. It is an absurd law that forces children born in our country to wait until they are eighteen before obtaining the right to citizenship,' Silvia explains, while twisting her ring around her finger. 'Mario was born in Italy. He has grown up here, was educated here, went to school here and learnt to play football here. He has assimilated all our customs and traditions and yet the limitations that have been placed on him, the sacrifices and humiliations have been many, only because by law he is considered a foreigner. It is now all behind him and we want to forget it,' she looks at Mario, 'yet, while we will forget it, we, my husband and I', she looks at Franco, 'hope very much that all the children and young people in our country in Mario's situation will be able to obtain this right to citizenship.'

The 'absurd law' described by Silvia Balotelli is law number 91, approved on 5 February 1992, governing new citizenship regulations. Article 4, paragraph 2 states that: 'Foreigners born in Italy who have resided here continuously until reaching the age of eighteen, will become Italian citizens if they declare a desire to acquire Italian citizenship within one year of that date.' It is a modification to law 555 dating from 13 June 1912 and is one of the most restrictive in Europe. Under Italian law, it is the *ius sanguinis* (an Italian citizen can only be born to an Italian citizen) that counts, rather than the *ius soli* (an Italian citizen is anyone born within national borders). In short, until 13 August 2008, Mario was a Ghanaian citizen, a foreigner in his own country. 'In Italy, life is much harder for a foreigner than it is for an Italian,' Balotelli tells the press. 'I could give you plenty of examples, such as when you have to stand in endless queues at the police station to renew your residency permit. I only did it once, with my mother, and that was enough. She had to do it for me dozens of times. Knowing that I was born in Italy and had never lived anywhere else, it was not great. And this was undoubtedly one of the most minor inconveniences.'

There were plenty of other 'inconveniences' that are difficult to talk about, starting with school trips abroad that Mario could not go on because he only had a birth certificate that did not permit overseas travel; he was Ghanaian so needed a passport and visas. Or when he was called to play for the Under-15 national team: his teammates could go but he was not an Italian citizen. Even if he spoke with a Brescian accent and had lived in Concesio for sixteen years, he was a foreigner, an interloper. He suffered and felt the situation was a great injustice. After the mayor had presented him with the medal of the town as a symbol of belonging to the community, a gift that was exchanged for one of Super Mario's Inter shirts, Mario told the TV cameras and microphones that he had been waiting for that moment for a long time.

He was more emotional than he had been when he made his Serie A debut, understandably so because his nightmare had finally come to an end. He was Italian and, as an adult, could begin the adoption process. Silvia and Franco had tried to adopt him under article 44 of law 184/83, governing something known as 'adoption under special circumstances', but it needed the backing of his biological parents, who were not prepared to give their consent. This problem had now been overcome and Mario would become a Balotelli in December 2008.

But there was more. With the ID card given to him by the mayor of Concesio, he also became a symbol for what would go on to be known as *Generazione* 2, or G2. The term is used to denote children of immigrants just like him, who were born in Italy or moved there when they were children; boys and girls who speak Brescian, Roman and Sicilian, who have grown up and lived in the *Bel paese*, who feel Italian in every way but are not legally so and are facing the same problems Mario experienced. Discrimination. Some 500,000 people, perhaps as many as 800,000, live in this limbo. These young people are on the receiving end of questions such as: 'You speak really good Italian, where did you learn it?' and 'How long have you been here?' just because they are not white, have Oriental or South American features in a country that, despite everything, struggles to recognise that it is now multi-ethnic. A country that has yet to change this absurd law.

In November 2011, Mario was received by Giorgio Napoletano at the Quirinal Palace alongside the other members of the Italian national team. He was struck by the words spoken by the President of the Republic, who asked the political classes for greater understanding of the rights of children born in Italy to foreign parents. In April 2013, Cécile Kyenge, the first black minister in Italian history, drew attention to the *ius soli* and announced a legal decree to reform citizenship law. Mario supported the Minister for Integration's proposal and agreed to represent the right to citizenship. A few months later, in the August of the same year in an interview with *Sports Illustrated*, Super Mario described the law that denies citizenship to minors born in Italy to foreign parents as 'stupid', explaining: 'I spent eighteen years in Italy but I still wasn't Italian. This is why I hope that kids like me will become Italian more quickly than I did.' For now, nothing has been done. Matteo Renzi, President of the Council of Ministers since February 2014, described citizenship for the children of foreigners as a question of civilisation. The plan has been set out: the *ius soli* would become a *ius soli temperato*, granting citizenship to children born in Italy to foreign parents on completing a course of study. Provided the Right agrees, it may become law in 2015.

For the time being, let's go back to Concesio on 13 August 2008. As well as talking about his life as a foreigner, Mario also mentioned disappointments and dreams. One missed opportunity was the Beijing Olympics. Because of his lack of an ID card, he could not be called up by the Under-21 Olympic team. It would have been a fantastic way to end such a great year. Another dream, or rather a goal, was to be called up by the senior national team, 'but even the Under-21s would be just fine,' commented Mario. Was the national team more important than the Champions League with Inter? He answered the question, striking while the iron was hot: 'Making those kind of comparisons is pointless. The national team is something you feel inside and is more important than anything else. I am Italian, I feel Italian and I will always play for the Italian national team.' Mario was adamant. So adamant that he did not even consider the possibility of playing for Ghana when, in the summer of 2007, they asked him to play in a friendly against Senegal planned for 21 August in London, with the prospect of a regular place in the team during the Africa Cup of Nations. The Ghanaians were so sure the boy would accept their offer that they shouted the news from the rooftops before being forced to change their minds. The Italian national team, the story of what had happened with Ghana and any expectations Mario may have had of being called up by Marcello Lippi for a friendly against Austria were all well and good, but there was no doubt that the journalists were most interested in finding out about his relationship with his new manager, José Mourinho. On 12 August, now officially an adult, Mario Balotelli had signed a new contract with Inter to run until 30 June 2011. The annual salary was €1.2 million.

Chapter 14

Mourinho, the Affectionate One

'I could write a 200 page-book about my two years at Inter with Mario but it would be a comedy, not a drama.' These words were spoken by José Mourinho in an interview with CNN in October 2012. Whether he is in London or Madrid, as a manager or a commentator, every time the Special One comes back to the question of Balotelli, he lets out a giggle and rattles off an anecdote. Like that time in Kazan ... or that other time when Mario snubbed him for the Formula 1 Grand Prix at Monza. And he usually ends in the same way as he did for Yahoo's microphones just before the 2014 World Cup: 'I always thought it was great fun and I have fond memories of that time. When he was a kid, you have your ups and downs ... but at the end of the day I enjoyed it. We won together and I think he enjoyed it too because some things he learnt and others he didn't, but the important thing was that, in the end, he was a Champions League winner.'

We all know we sometimes have a tendency to look at the past through rose-tinted glasses. On closer inspection it does seem as if Mourinho's two years with Mario at Inter may not have been a drama after all, but they were undoubtedly a constant battle. Let's start at the beginning.

On 3 June 2008, the Portuguese coach was officially unveiled as Inter's new manager at their Appiano Gentile training ground. Mourinho hammed it up in an interminable press conference, winning over his audience with jokes, silences and an '*Io non sono un pirla*' [I'm not an idiot] in response to an English journalist who asked him whether Lampard and Essien, Chelsea players, would be able to adapt to Italian football. It was a sneaky way of trying to find out whether Inter were interested in the two players. As well as triggering laughter and dishing out lessons from his lectern, Mourinho left this judgement on Balotelli for posterity: 'I started out at Barcelona with kids and I don't think a footballer's age matters: he is either good or bad, or fantastic. Balotelli? I don't know him but I'm looking forward to working with him. I want to get into his head and work out what's inside. In the meantime, I've watched him play and I can see he has absolutely fantastic potential. Balotelli has to aim to be the best at Under-20 level in two years and the best at Under-23 in five years' time.'

The manager would later repeat these ideas, word for word, on 15 July 2008 in Brunico, where the *Nerazzurri* were starting their pre-season training. After spending ten days on holiday in Sicily at the Zingaro Nature Reserve on a WWF adventure camp, Mario was happy to be getting back to work, even if Mourinho's words left him somewhat perplexed. He honestly thought his future had already arrived. Yet that was not the case, as was demonstrated on 24 August 2008 in the final of the Italian Super Cup at Milan's San Siro Stadium. Super Mario ended up on the bench against Roma. And it was not until the 67th minute, with the score at 1-1 that Mourinho decided to send him on as a substitute for the veteran, Luis Figo. Beppe Baresi, second in command on the bench, gave Mario his tactical instructions but they went in one ear and out the other. He wanted to prove his worth and he did so brilliantly. In the 84th minute, he caught a goal kick from Julio Cesar with a back-heel surprising the entire Roma defence, and beating Doni. Mario threw his arms wide with a stupid look on his face. It appeared to be all over, but Vucinic equalised from a David Pizarro corner in the 90th minute. Extra time: Mario received a yellow card for a foul on Okaka but then belted two free kicks that were miraculously saved by Doni. Penalties: Super Mario made certain he did not miss the second of the first five. However, Stankovic did miss for Inter, as did Totti and Juan for Roma. It came down to Javier Zanetti, the Inter captain, to score the final spot kick and give the club its first trophy of the Mourinho era.

There was nothing more to be said: the kid had done well, but as far as the Special One was concerned, his place was on the bench. As was the case on 30 August in the first league match of the season against Sampdoria, when he came on in the 65th minute. And on 16 September in Inter's first Champions League clash against Panathinaikos, when he failed to get off the bench at all. For Mario, satisfaction came with Pierluigi Casiraghi's Under-21 team. He made his debut for the Italian national Under-21s against Greece on 5 September at Castel di Sangro. He gave the Italians the lead with a right-footed volley and fell just short of securing victory with a scissor kick.

On 15 October in Tel Aviv, he went one better. He scored twice against Israel, earning the Italian team qualification for the European Under-21 Championships in Sweden. His first goal came from a free kick from more than 30 yards out, which Levita, the Israel goalkeeper, saw go past him in a flash; the second rolled in after grazing the post. Two goals, yet Mario did not seem happy: 'I missed a counterattack. Even my dog Jenny could have scored,' he confessed after the match. He explained that he had to be careful with the referees and opposing players as he had been yellow carded. He also said he needed to make sure he controlled himself more and did not lose his head. Mario almost seemed sad, perhaps because of the stories that had been doing the rounds in Milan: sports cars, evenings at the fashionable Tocqueville nightclub and showgirls. He answered stony-faced: 'Recently, while I was injured, the papers wrote that I was living it up and going out with showgirls. They got it all wrong. I have a girlfriend and her name is Sofia.'

The gossip in Milan seemed to die down but it did nothing to change his role as benchwarmer at Inter. He was not seen back on the pitch at the start of a game until 1 November against Reggina in Reggio Calabria. In the dying seconds of injury time, Cordoba converted from Mario's corner to give Inter a 3-2 win. Three days later in Cyprus on 4 November, Mario started against Anorthosis Famagusta in a Champions League Group B game. After thirteen minutes, he scored his first goal in European competition: a free kick from Ibrahimovic was parried by the keeper and Mario helped it over the line. The match ended in a resounding 3-3 draw: an embarrassment for the *Nerazzurri* but a great result for anyone who had bet on such an unlikely outcome. Balotelli would not score another goal in the blue and black-striped shirt until 21 February 2009, in the sixth Serie A return fix-ture of the season, Bologna-Inter. Why did it take so long? Because between sanctions, managerial decisions and disci-plinary action, he did not play much.

What had happened? Mourinho, the prophet, had dic-tated his commandments and Balotelli, the *enfant terrible*, did not appear to be one of the faithful. For this he was publicly admonished after Inter's match against Napoli, which saw them secure five consecutive league victories and first place in the table, six points ahead of Juventus. Mario was left out of the team alongside the Portuguese player, Quaresma 'for not training well during the week'. At the press conference in the belly of the San Siro, the Special One explained his vision of the world to the TV cameras and berated Balotelli. 'Sometimes in football, older players, those with more status and wins behind them, don't make great examples for others. They hide behind their status and don't set great examples for younger players. In this group, exactly the opposite is happening with Zanetti, Cordoba, Samuel, Figo and lots of the others. For guys like Mario, Quaresma and Santon, it's easy to look over and see how hard the others are working. If you're seventeen, eighteen or nineteen years old and you're working with 25 per cent of the intensity, concentration or desire the others have, how can you play? You only play if the coach wants to give you privileges and I don't give privileges to anyone. They have to change if they want to play with us. When it comes to Mario … I can only talk about Mario the player that I see at Appiano. I can't talk about his social, personal or family situation. Who am I to do that? What I can tell you, because I've told him, is that he has to work much harder. He has to work on his head, on his concentration, motivation, tactical thought and mental aggression. He's got to work on all these things.

'I refuse to accept a young man like him working less than players aged 34 or 35, like Figo, Cordoba and Zanetti. I can't accept that from someone who is nothing yet, other than hope, an investment in the future of Inter and Italian football. If he trained at 50 per cent, he would be one of the best in the world. I can't give a player a position on the pitch just because I chose him, like Quaresma, or because I want to protect myself from your criticism. I don't want to hide. I don't do it with Quaresma and I don't do it with Mario, because he's a great Italian talent and he's eighteen. I don't protect anyone and I don't protect myself. I make choices for the good of the team. But one thing that is good for the players is the fact that I forget. If the players that haven't been picked show me what I expect of them during the week, there will be no problem.'

There was no doubt about it, we had a Balotelli situation on our hands. Both Moratti and Zanetti had something to say on the subject and about the Special One's words.

The Inter president maintained: 'It was an affectionate thing that Mourinho said. I thought it was serious, affectionate and professional. And because Balotelli is intelligent, he will have understood it.' The captain's thinking was along the same lines: 'Mario has unusual technical and physical gifts and extraordinary potential. It would be a real shame to waste so much grace. He has to understand that Mourinho's words were full of affection and not intended to hurt him. The manager only has one goal: to get the most out of him and to take him to the highest possible level because this is also in the interests of the team and the club. And you can only make your mark as a footballer today by working hard. You can't allow yourself to have the same attitude at eighteen as a player that has already made it.'

That affection had little to do with the Special One's sermon may seem evident, but everyone worked hard to use the definition and even Mourinho sweetened his bitter Sunday pill a few days later: 'I'm happy when players like Zanetti and Crespo say that talent isn't enough to emerge as a player. For me, it's important because players are usually loyal to their teammates and have closer relationships between one another than they do with their manager, but they think the same way I do,' the Portuguese coach explained. 'They are fond of Mario, they want to educate him and help him become a great champion rather than an ordinary player.' In order to educate him, Mourinho assumed the stereotypical role of the cantankerous teacher, dishing out punishments. He did not pick Mario for the league match against Lazio and sent him back to the Under-20s 'to get him to understand the difference between youth teams and Serie A,' he explained. However, he announced that he was still open-minded and that the player, who some in the dressing room were already starting to call Mr Nobody, could make a return to the first team as early as the match against Werder Bremen. In fact, on 9 December in Germany, Super Mario came on in the 71st minute in a match that saw Inter's second Champions League defeat but also meant qualification to the knock-out stage after finishing second in the group. Before his reappearance, Balo had been on a carousel, playing for Vincenzo Esposito's Under-20s on 6 December in a home game against Treviso. It goes without saying that he scored two goals and hit the crossbar. But for Mourinho, the boy still needed to grow up and work hard in order to win his respect and to find his place up front for Inter.

By now it was December; January soon came and, truthfully, things between the pair worsened. The manager was losing patience with the constant rumours about Balotelli being up for sale. There was talk of a possible exchange with Antonio Cassano, then at Sampdoria. Or about Chievo, Bologna and even English temptresses such as Arsenal or Gianfranco Zola's West Ham. Mario's brothers and agents, who earlier in the summer were already getting concerned about whether there would be room for their charge in Mourinho's team, pushed for a six-month loan. It could be useful they said. Given the difficult time the boy was experiencing under the Portuguese manager, Corrado and Giovanni were keen to force a turning point. Mario asked for a meeting with the president, which was duly granted. On 12 January, Super Mario explained to Moratti that he wanted to leave to grow up in peace, to come back stronger. Massimo Moratti listened and then told the press: 'I've had a friendly meeting with the player. He seemed very happy to try to understand the needs of the club and is keen to comply with them. I'm sure he will do everything he can to get himself picked by his manager.'

Despite this, it seemed Mourinho had no intention of picking him. In fact, he did not even pick him for the Coppa Italia match against Genoa on 14 January 2009. This was how he explained his decision: 'Nothing has changed, neither in his way of working nor in his attitude. The only thing that has changed is that his brother has clearly stated that Mario wants to leave. I don't know whether it is him that doesn't want to stay or whether his brother is advising him. I really don't know what the situation is. I can only say that I like players who think for themselves. If someone is too dependent mentally on someone else, they are not able to take responsibility. Let's wait until 2 February when the transfer window closes and he'll understand he has to stay here. Who knows? Perhaps his attitude will change and he'll make himself available again. But, for the time being, he is not ready to play.' Mourinho was so convinced that Mario was getting bad advice and was distracted by the idea of changing clubs that he failed to pick him for the games against Atalanta, Roma and Sampdoria. After this latest blow, if rumours in the dressing room were to be believed, Mario went to his manager's office at Appiano Gentile to clarify his situation. He was told that he was not yet ready to climb the ranks of the Inter attack. When he replied that if that was the case they should let him go to England, he was told that things were not that simple.

The story did not end here ... far from it. His brothers asked for another meeting with the management and the following curt response came from the president: 'We have invested in you. We believe in you. You are not leaving.'

The sports pages, radio and TV channels were in their element, adding fuel to the fire. For example, on 28 January, Mario refused to join the team for an away match in Catania and received a huge fine from the furious club, who interpreted the gesture as an attempt to force the president's hand to let him leave. Mario was also said to have burst into tears. After a training session, the Inter number 45 apparently started crying after being told off by a teammate. The journalists had a simple explanation: the boy was unable to bear the tension of the previous weeks. It was all subsequently denied but Mourinho kept up his onslaught. On 30 January, he went back to his favourite subject: 'Mario is a good kid who some people want to see achieve a higher profile. If he's not prepared for it on the pitch, he is even less so off the pitch. If anyone thinks I enjoy keeping him out of the team, they're wrong. It upsets me. One day he'll understand who's looking out for him and who isn't, who's trying to help him and who isn't. I just hope he understands in time to become a great footballer'. Still not finished, the Special One predicted the near future in his crystal ball: 'I know it can be both easy and difficult working with me. Easy if you want to win and improve; difficult if you think you're the king of the world and don't like working. Difficult if you think everyone else is responsible for you but that you're not responsible for anyone. This is why it will be both very easy and very difficult for Mario to come back to work with us. It's up to him.' It proved to be very far from easy, but Mr Nobody would become Super Mario once more.

Chapter 15

Racism

'Balotelli is a filthy n*****'; 'There's no such thing as a black Italian'; 'Balotelli, your mother is a whore'; 'If you jump up and down, Balotelli will die'.

This is a catalogue of the racist chants Juventus supporters spat at the Inter number 45 on 18 April 2008 in Turin's Stadio Olimpico. In his report, Giampaolo Tosel, from the sporting authority, confirmed they had been heard 'on a number of occasions (with particular reference to minutes 4, 26, 35, 41 and 42 during the first half and 11, 19, 22, 25 and 30 of the second half) in various sections of the stadium'. Turin police opened an investigation into the incident, examining CCTV footage filmed inside the stadium and discovering that the chants had come from two of Juventus's most hardcore groups of fans, known as the *Drughi* and the *Bravi Ragazzi*, who were in the South stand. After the match, Giovanni Cobolli Gigli, president of Juventus, expressed fierce condemnation of the racist chants aimed at the Inter player: 'There are no excuses or justifications for such attitudes: football fans are passionate but episodes such as these are unacceptable. We must come together to try to foster a sporting culture that focuses on respect for your opponents and the fight against racism.' Massimo Moratti was scandalised: 'If I had been there, I would have pulled the team off the pitch.' The only dissenting voice was Mourinho's. For the manager, what happened at the Olimpico 'was not racism but simply an ignorant way of showing dissent to a hated opponent because he scores goals against you'. He was convinced that Italy was not a racist country and nor was its football: 'If I can say one thing in defence of Juve, it is that this wasn't the first time. It has happened in many stadiums, even in our own.'

On this, Mourinho was absolutely right: this was not the first time Balotelli had been the target of racist chanting. Padova's hooligans had done it on his Serie C1 debut with Lumezzane and it had continued at half the grounds across Italy, such as on 1 March at the San Siro in a league game against Roma, although on that occasion it was Balotelli who ended up on trial.

Ibrahimovic was out with a muscle problem so it was the turn of Mario, who was in the starting eleven for the first time in more than two months (the last time had been for the Siena-Inter match on 20 December 2008). Roma had a clear 2-0 lead at half time. At the start of the second half, the young player began his comeback, making the score 2-1. Brighi then appeared to give Roma the last word, scoring to make it 3-1. But seven minutes later all hell broke loose Super Mario produced his fifth goal of a tumultuous season. After dribbling the ball into the opponents' area, he ended up prostrate on the ground between Motta and De Rossi. The referee generously awarded a penalty. The Roma players' protests were prolonged; they claimed Mario had dived. It came to nothing. Right in front of the Roma fans, it was Balotelli who stepped up to the spot. With his usual calmness and a short break in his run-up, he side-footed the ball into the back of the net. 2-3. Immediately after converting the penalty, the boy wearing the number 45 put his index finger to his lips in an attempt to silence the fans from the capital. He then looked around him mockingly and stuck his tongue out. Christian Panucci, the Roma defender, saw what Mario was doing and came up to him shaking his head. Maicon then went over and what could almost be described as a brawl broke out. The match finished in the 93rd minute at 3-3 but the controversy continued for weeks. Balotelli was accused of being both faker and instigator.

After the match, Luciano Spaletti, Roma's manager, was the first to blame Balo the faker: 'From the bench, it looked to me as if Balotelli had dived. The TV pictures confirm it: it's clear that it wasn't a penalty. If the TV pundits want to take us for idiots … if you stay quiet you risk looking like an idiot. But we're not idiots.' But it was more than just that single thing that had set everybody off, there was also Mario's shushing the crowd. It was Francesco Totti who stepped up to denounce him: 'We can't tolerate a young player like Balotelli, who has great technical, physical and athletic skills behaving so badly towards his teammates, opponents and fans.' The Roma captain told the *Corriere dello Sport-Stadio*: 'I remember in the Super Cup final when he was getting ready to take a corner, I heard him say "Filthy Romans". It can happen in a moment of anger but insults like that shouldn't be repeated. Instead they were repeated over and over again on Sunday, in addition to him sticking his tongue out at my teammates, who resented it and took up the defence of the 2,500 fans who had been made fun of. I am not and I don't want to be in the Inter dressing room, but I believe Balotelli doesn't behave properly there either. Perhaps by coming into contact with great players like Materazzi and Gattuso, if he plays alongside them one day in the Italian team, he'll have the chance to learn these things, like how to behave properly. On the pitch we footballers have a code of behaviour. We can beat the living daylights out of one another but we always have to have respect for our opponents' fans.' The captain's rant was also tough on the issue of the argument with the Roma defender: 'It bothered me to see Balotelli behave so disrespectfully towards Panucci. Perhaps if Christian let him see all the trophies he's won in his career, he could take a souvenir photo ...'

From the Inter perspective, Massimo Moratti ruled out reproaching Mario for his behaviour, saying Roma and the TV channels had already taken care of it. He justified the behaviour with a simple 'that's the way he is'. The 'shush' gesture and sticking his tongue out earned Mario an investigation by the Italian Football Federation for a 'provocative attitude towards the Roma stand'.

Even Internet users were in no doubt that the boy had acted badly: 50,123 respondents answered a survey set up by *Gazzetta.it.* The question was as follows: 'A few days ago Balotelli told Cristiano Ronaldo to shut up (on 24 February during the second half of Inter-Manchester United, Mario had had no hesitation in telling the Portuguese *Ballon d'Or* winner to keep quiet) ... and now it's the turn of the Roma fans.' Readers of the website were asked to choose from four options: 40 per cent chose the first option: 'This behaviour cannot in any way be justified by someone who aspires to be a great player'; 35.2 per cent opted for the second answer: 'This behaviour is a sign of great immaturity'; 14.2 per cent decided that 'this behaviour is a sign of a strong personality'; while only 10 per cent chose the theory that 'such behaviour can only be justified if it has firstly been provoked'.

The latter was what Balotelli himself thought. He said that while he was preparing to take the penalty, he was on the receiving end of constant booing from the stands. He also said he was sticking his tongue out at his opponents because they had repeatedly shouted 'miss, miss'. He even said Panucci had begun insulting him before the kick off.

A teenage Mario playing for Inter against Juventus in January 2008.

Balotelli celebrates with the Serie A trophy in 2010
– his third league title in three years.

(*above*) With José Mourinho, who deemed him 'unmanageable'; and
(*below*) with Roberto Mancini, who brought him to England.

In action for Manchester City, November 2011.

Balotelli scores for Italy against Germany in the semi-final of Euro 2012 to set up a final clash with world champions Spain.

Stringer/Italy/Reuters/Corbis

(*above*) Mario celebrates with his new teammates after scoring against Udinese on his Milan debut.

Phil Noble/Reuters/Corbis

A rare high point in a difficult season with Liverpool: Balotelli celebrates scoring against Ludogorets in a Champions League group game.

The theory about the racist insults and provocation was one that few chose to believe, preferring instead to blame the boy. It was a shame; there were so many boos that the match official saw fit to write in his report: 'On two occasions during the second half of the match against Inter, the Roma supporters engaged in chanting consistent with expressions of racial discrimination towards a player from the opposing team.' It fined Roma €8,000 for racist insults against Balotelli.

Giampaolo Tosel would not be so lenient on 20 April 2009. Two days after the disgraceful scenes in Turin, he punished Juventus with the sanction of playing one match behind closed doors. It was a harsh sentence motivated by 'the gravity of the offence, the obstinate repetition of such behaviour, the absence of any attempt to disassociate themselves by other supporters or any intervention on the part of the club aimed at deterring fans from behaving in this way'.

Despite Giovanni Cobolli Giglio's fierce condemnation, Juventus appealed against the federation's decision. In the first instance, the Turin club succeeded. The Federal Court of Justice suspended the enforcement of the sentence pending a closer investigation of the case. The following week's match between Juventus and Lecce went ahead as normal. Meanwhile racist chanting became the topic of conversation across Italy and Europe as a whole. Michel Platini announced that UEFA was prepared to suspend matches for ten minutes in the event of serious incidents, while William Gaillard, a UEFA spokesman, called for zero tolerance on racism, explaining that 'these episodes are the responsibility of individual states and federations. It is up to the Italian federation to properly manage its own affairs and I am convinced that it will. Abete's thinking is in line with ours'. Giancarlo Abete, Chairman of the FIGC, moved from words to deeds.

On 5 May, he amended article 62 of the federation's regulations governing public order, inserting what would come to
be known as the Balotelli Rule. Football clubs would not only
be forced to remove racist banners but to prevent 'chanting,
shouting or any other manifestation of discrimination on the
grounds of race, colour, religion, language, sex, nationality,
country of origin or ethnic background that may interfere
with the playing of the match'. After the FIGC's decision, the
sentence of the Italian National Olympic Committee (CONI)
High Court of Justice for Sport upheld the ruling on 14 May
2009, rejecting the Turin club's appeal. Juventus-Atalanta,
due to take place on 17 May 2009, would be played behind
closed doors.

That same day, 17 May, Inter celebrated the seventeenth
league title in their history at the San Siro, the fourth in
succession and the first of the Mourinho era. AC Milan's
loss to Udine the previous evening had made Inter's win a
mathematical certainty. Inter fans held improvised parties in
the city's Piazza del Duomo and Largo Cairoli. Flags, banners, chanting and horns at full blast were seen and heard
throughout the city's streets. Against Mourinho's orders, the
players joined in the free-for-all. Instead of going to bed, they
boarded the coach in Appiano Gentile after their training
session and got off in the centre of Milan. Despite their wild
night of celebration, they finished things off beautifully the
following day against Siena at the San Siro with a 3-0 win.
'Champions again' sang the huge crowd in the stands. The
Special One bounced along to the rhythm provided by the
fans, who gave the whole team a standing ovation. Balotelli,
who had scored the second goal, was over the moon. With
his hair shaved into an intricate pattern, he smiled and celebrated in a way that for him was unusual. It was lucky that
Ibrahimovic scored in the 31st minute or the number 45

would have been on the receiving end of yet another sound telling off. Before the match, the manager had given precise instructions: pass the ball to the Swedish player, who was on course to be the season's top scorer. The boy failed to respect team orders but it did not matter because Ibrahimovic reached 25 goals for the season with a powerful diagonal shot and became top scorer.

All was well that ended well, although it should be said that Mario left the official Inter title celebration at Milan's Hotel Melia to go to Brescia to have fun with his friends. He needed a breather after a hard season and before the European Under-21 Championship in Sweden, which Italy were due to start as favourites with Balotelli as their undisputed leader. The adventure would come to an end on 26 June in Helsingborg in the semi-final against Germany: 0-1 and the third place bronze medal. Super Mario went home with a goal and a red card to his name, both in the match against Sweden.

At the training camp at La Borghesiana in Rome before flying to Scandinavia, the boy had summed up his season for the press. He said that his best goal of the season was the one he had scored against Juve, even if it had also been the worst night for him. They asked about his relationship with his manager: 'It's not true that if a manager is tough on you he doesn't care about you,' Mario explained. 'My mother is tough on me, but she cares about me. I feel very comfortable with this manager. I like him as a person and I also like his way of working. He's a one-off and I enjoy training. If I played badly and my manager didn't say anything to me, it would be a problem. If I play badly and my manager shouts at me, it's normal. There would be something to worry about if it was the other way around.' From Mourinho to racism: 'It exists in Italy. It's a minority but it exists. Italy is a multi-ethnic country but some people struggle to accept foreigners. In my case, it's not even because I'm black or have African roots, it's jealousy. They know this is the only way to make me angry. Racism exists but some people say so to make me angry and have no idea about what racism is. They are so ignorant that if you ask them, they don't even know what it is.' The Inter striker confessed: 'I made a mistake though, reacting like that. But my behaviour, sticking my tongue out or telling them to be quiet, was a response, not an attack. And it wasn't that serious compared with what they did. It's a normal thing; people have done worse. I live in a village called Sant'Andrea, Concesio, where there are loads of kids. I'm like an idol to them. Sometimes, I think it doesn't set a good example to these kids if they see a reaction like that when they're watching matches. On television, you can't hear what the fans are saying, you can only see what the players are doing on the pitch. It's normal for people to say "Look what Balotelli's doing", but they don't know that the fans have driven you to it. So, I understand now that reacting like that is wrong. It would be better for me to speak to the TV cameras after the match and apologise for the unnecessary things that happen on the pitch.'

This examination of his conscience led him to promise to change: he would no longer react to racist insults. Unfortunately, he would have to put these good intentions into practice just a few days later. It was Saturday, 6 June 2009. Pierluigi Casiraghi, coach of the Italian Under-21 team, had allowed his players to go out from 1 pm to midnight. Mario went with Criscito and Giovinco to have an early evening drink near Ponte Milvio. They sat at the tables outside the pub. A group of people went past and noticed Balotelli. They started chanting and insulting him. Worse was to come when they began throwing bananas. Balotelli and his teammates did not react. They went over to a police car and the racists vanished into thin air. Mario did not make a fuss about it, saying it was nothing, and did not press charges. He had changed his attitude and praise came from all quarters, starting with President Moratti, who, on the Inter website, paid him 'the most sincere compliment for having made light with great maturity of yet another ugly incident of intolerance of which he was the victim'.

John Foot, an English historian and author of the book *Calcio: A History of Italian Football*, commented on the affair a few days later in *Il Manifesto*. 'I remember this racist gesture when it happened a number of years ago to John Barnes, the England striker at Liverpool: some Everton fans threw bananas at him. Barnes picked them up and threw them away. Many Italians hate Balotelli, especially among football fans. This is partly because the boy plays for Inter, the team that has dominated the league for three years now. But the real reason goes much deeper. Balotelli reveals all the contradictions of foreign immigration in Italy, a country hit by a wave of racism (from north to south) that is unrivalled in the rest of Europe for its intensity. Many Italians cannot accept Balotelli as one of their own. He is different, black, African (in a negative sense) and inferior. He is a very good footballer and has also committed another crime: he knows no humility. They say he is arrogant and overconfident. He never lowers his head; he seems to enjoy the notoriety he receives. He is very good and he knows it. Wherever he goes to play, Balotelli is treated like a symbol of an Italy that many reject, a multi-cultural Italy not appreciated by those who want to defend the white essence of Italy against the arrival of outsiders. It is, of course, a situation we have already seen, in Italy and elsewhere. But things have changed in English stadiums since the days of John Barnes, although any fan of my generation grew up in the 70s and 80s hearing monkey noises ringing in their ears from the early days. But Italy is not the England of twenty years ago, things are getting worse here for one simple reason. Racism is preached from on high, encouraged by politicians and especially by those who hold the reins of power. Instead of opposing such behaviour, political parties such as the Northern League actively encourage it. Racism works in Italy. It wins votes. A worrying package of discriminatory measures was recently approved at both local and national levels. It included a ban on eating kebabs in public and playing cricket in the park, sending back boatloads of desperate immigrants, restricting immigrant marriages and – the most serious of all – attempting to isolate foreign children in schools and forcing doctors to report illegal immigrants who come to hospital seeking treatment. These measures have produced high-profile cases such as that of an immigrant woman persecuted while giving birth to her baby in hospital, later discovering that her residency permit had been delayed for bureaucratic reasons. Police violence against immigrants is so common that it has created a frenzy in the press, although, unbelievably, not in public opinion. The political authorities have blocked the construction of mosques across the country, and regional politicians, such as those in Trentino Alto Adige, have promised to keep their region free from Islamic places of worship. In this context, Mario Balotelli represents a high-profile target, constantly under attack from the world of Italian football, once a great sport but now in a depressing decline. What the Balotelli case reveals is a profound hatred towards a multi-cultural society. Italians – not all but many of them – find it simply impossible to accept that Mario Balotelli is really Italian. As far as they are concerned, there is no such thing as a black Italian. Immigrants are fine as long as they remain invisible, don't walk down the street, don't cause a nuisance and have no rights. They are good for nothing. They cannot be "one of us". Balotelli lifts the veil on these frightening contradictions. He is black, he is Italian and he is good at what he does. He rejects the role of being humble and inferior, of someone who averts their gaze through fear. This is why he inspires hatred and fear. It is the vision of a future that many Italians find profoundly disturbing.'

And they would continue to find it so.

Chapter 16

A Difficult Year

Kazan, the capital of the Republic of Tatarstan, Russia. 29 September 2009. Inter are playing FC Rubin, the local team, in the second match in the Champions League Group F. After a 0-0 draw at home to Barcelona, Mourinho is keen to get a result against the Russian champions. He opts for a 4-3-3 formation, a three-pronged attack consisting of Mancini, Eto'o and Balotelli. Mario is in the starting eleven for the first time. Not in the Italian Super Cup, which Inter had lost to Lazio in Beijing, nor in six league matches has he played from the very first minute. He has always started on the bench: five minutes here, twenty minutes there. But this time, the absence of Diego Milito and David Suazo forces the Portuguese manager to pick the number 45. In the 20th minute, Mario receives a yellow card for a foul on Salukvadze; in the 29th, he unleashes a right-footed shot that is stopped by Ryzhikov and the crossbar; and in the 60th minute he gets himself sent off after getting booked a second time for a late sliding tackle on Noboa. The Norwegian referee, Hauge, had it in for him since Balotelli answered him back. Inter are down to ten men. Years later, Mourinho would talk about the incident in an interview with CNN: 'Mario got a yellow card in the first half, so when I went to the dressing room at half time I spent fourteen of the fifteen minutes only speaking to Mario. I told him: "Mario, I cannot change you, I don't have a striker on the bench. Don't touch anyone. Only play

the ball. When we lose the ball, don't react. If someone pro-
vokes you, don't react. If the referee makes a mistake, don't
react. Mario, please." In the 46th minute [the Special One's
memory fails him here, but it makes the story funnier], red
card.' José and the reporter laugh heartily.

It goes without saying that he did not find it funny at the
time. After the match ended in a paltry 1-1 draw, the Special
One was furious. When they asked him about the episode,
he replied: 'I thought the sending off was right. I told him
what I thought after the game. I think it's right if you get
yourself sent off for a foul as the last man or for a handball
off the line, but only in those cases. Was it an error that can
be put down to a lack of experience? Don't make me answer.
Otherwise we'll be here in five years' time still talking about
Balotelli's lack of experience. Is he immature? Enough with
these questions!'

Mourinho unloaded on Balotelli and blamed him for
Inter's second consecutive draw in Europe's top competition.
But it was not just his manager who told him off; people like
Maicon and Zanetti continued to repeat the refrain: 'Mario
is still young and needs to grow up.' The following day,
Balotelli hung his head in shame and wrote on his website:
'Dear Inter fans, Please forgive me for the sending off in the
Champions League. Unfortunately, I paid a high price for
the stupid mistakes I made, which cancelled out the effort
put into the game. I hope to turn myself around positively
and will continue to give my best and be as professional as
possible.'

However, doing penance in cases such as these may not
have helped much with someone like Mourinho. Given the
build-up of the previous season, many thought things had
already deteriorated too significantly between the two. They
feared that after having been stigmatised, Mario would not

manage to get back on top. But the boy came back fighting. The 5-0 defeat Inter inflicted on Genoa at the Marassi on 18 October had his mark all over it. A through ball from Sneijder found Mario in front of Amelia. He guessed right with an angled shot just inside the far post. It was a great goal! José Mourinho recognised that Mario had played an exceptional match against Genoa but ... 'he had a terrible week in training'. This time the tongue lashing had become a sermon on young footballers. This is what the Portuguese manager said: 'I've spent a long time talking to the coach of the Under-20 team and I've decided there is a generational problem. Twenty years ago, players of that age were already men. Nowadays, young nineteen or twenty-year-old players who are satisfied with their small cars are the exception. Most of them they are thinking about a Ferrari or a Bentley and are worried about the car that their thirty-year-old teammate with a €5 million pay cheque is driving. Maybe young players are the victims in this situation rather than the guilty parties. Their families are also important, parents who don't worry about money, brothers and sisters who get on with their lives and leave them alone.' Any reference to Balotelli was, of course, purely coincidental ...

On 29 October, Balotelli had another fantastic game against Palermo. He scored two goals, provided the assist for the fourth goal from Eto'o and stirred up a touch of controversy. Super Mario won a penalty in the Palermo box. He placed the ball on the spot and stepped up to take it just as he had done when he was a child, but captain Zanetti took his hand and led him away. Orders had come from the bench that it was Eto'o's turn. The Cameroonian scored but Balotelli did not celebrate, apart from to make things up with his teammate with what seemed like a brotherly hug. But Super Mario's problems are never over. He often puts his foot in it himself, as he did when he confessed to the disabled children at the Don Gnocchi Institute: 'Didn't you know I'm an AC Milan supporter?' All hell broke loose. Mourinho joked about it: 'If Mario supports AC Milan, Pato supports Inter,' but he took the opportunity to make another clear dig at the boy's family: 'When someone close to him wants to be his press officer and control his social life [implying Cristina, his adoptive sister], and this person doesn't understand anything about the world of football, it causes problems for the player. I don't think Mario is responsible for the things I think are naive. He is surrounded by people who are not helping him. And when a naive boy is surrounded by people who don't help him [i.e. his brothers and agents, Corrado and Giovanni], he finds himself in a very difficult situation.' It would not be the only time the boy from Concesio's flirtation with AC Milan would get him in trouble. In February, he went to the San Siro to watch the match between AC Milan and Manchester United. A few days later, he was taunted by some Inter fans holding a banner that read: 'Mario, did you enjoy yourself on Tuesday? So did we,' a reference to the fact that the *Rossoneri* had lost 3-2. It happened again on March 2009, when the Italian satirical TV programme *Striscia la Notizia* ambushed him at Milan's Bar Silvan. The journalist gave him an AC Milan number 45 shirt with the name Balotelli printed on the back. He asked him several times to put it on. Mario refused but eventually, thinking the cameras had been switched off, did try in on for size, provoking the wrath of the Inter fans.

21 November, Bologna. An hour before the match, Balotelli was on the receiving end of whistles from the Bulgarelli stand, while others in the Stadio dell'Ara failed to spare him the usual boos. Mario responded with a thumbs down. Then, shortly after heading home his fourth goal of

the season, he shushed the audience again. But thugs are never silenced, instead they export racism and invent long-distance insults. For example, on 22 November 2009, Super Mario was minding his own business at a hotel in Barcelona; Inter had a Champions League clash against Barcelona on the coming Tuesday. What happened at Juventus-Udinese beggars belief. A hardcore group of Juventus fans started jumping up and down, singing about wanting him dead. Three days later, history repeated itself in Europe. Juventus were playing Bordeaux in their final Champions League Group A game in the Chaban-Delmas Stadium. Balotelli was in Italy, a thousand miles away, but before the match a group of Juve fans dedicated their chanting to him, singing '*Se saltelli muore Balotelli*' [If you jump up and down, Balotelli will die]. The loudspeakers reminded fans that UEFA had banned racism from its stadiums, but they shouted back their answers: 'There's no such thing as a black Italian' and 'A n***** can't be Italian'. Gianluigi Buffon, the captain, and Alessio Secco, Director of Football at the Turin club, went over to speak to the hardcore group and the chanting stopped. But the episode had been concerning, not least because Juventus were due to play Inter at home ten days later.

But before the big match came another episode in the Mourinho-Balotelli saga. The number 45, picked for the league match against Fiorentina, was sent to the stands. He was being punished for night-time partying and turning up late to training. Rumours were circulating that claimed Mario was a rebel, never listened to advice, failed to follow the rules, was out of line and always wanted to do his own thing. When Mourinho was asked on TV why Mario had been left out, he answered grumpily: 'Who is this Balotelli you're asking me so many questions about? Is he Maradona?

He's a player like all the others. I make my choices. I left him in the stands. My team won and for 90 minutes I forgot about him.'

Mario was on the bench on 29 November and then again at Turin's Olympic Stadium on 5 December. A few days earlier, Zanetti had said flatly: 'If I hear racist chanting aimed at Balotelli, I will ask the referee to suspend the match immediately.'

There was no chanting, but it made no difference because Mario's nightmare had begun two hours before kick-off. At the entrance to the stadium, the Inter coach was met by hundreds of hardcore *ultra* fans pouring out their hatred and singing 'If you jump up and down, Balotelli will die'. Jeers were aimed at Inter during the warm-up, accompanied by the same ditty, repeated every ten minutes with the addition of insults aimed at the young Inter player's mother. He was left on the bench for an hour. Perhaps because Mourinho wanted to punish him yet again or because the manager wanted to protect him. But Juventus took the lead in the 60th minute and Inter needed to take a risk. Balo came on amid a flood of boos. Every time he touched the ball there was a chorus of boos and insults. They called him every name under the sun. It mattered little that Alessandro Del Piero, the Juventus captain had reminded fans before the kick-off that 'football belongs only to one race, the human race'. There was no mercy for the number 45. In the end, a brawl broke out. Balotelli was on the receiving end of an elbow from Felipe Melo and threw himself to the ground, pretending to have caught it full in the face. The Juventus player was sent off. Buffon almost came to blows with Thiago Motta and Chivu head butted Sissoko.

The following day, the Turin newspaper *Tuttosport* reported: 'No racism, "only" sporting insults (so to speak) aimed at Balotelli, who did everything he could to prove those who have labelled him provocative and not simply a target for vulgar racism right. The worst fears were realised with the brawl that eventually broke out on the pitch following the umpteenth provocation from the young Inter player.'

The same refrain yet again, the same absurd theory: the blame lies with Balotelli who behaves in such a provocative way that he brings on the racist chanting and 'sporting' insults himself. This recurring theme was destined to be repeated on 6 January 2010. On the day of the Epiphany – when an old woman known as the *Befana* traditionally delivers gifts or pieces of coal to Italian children during the night – Inter were playing Chievo. Mario scored the winning goal, securing Inter's position at the top of the table at the midway point in the season. But it was an entirely different subject that hit the headlines: substituted in the 43rd minute of the second half, Balotelli had ironically applauded the fans. On the sidelines, he had then exclaimed to the Sky TV cameras: 'Every time I come to Verona, the fans disgust me more and more. They are unacceptable.' After all, he had said that next time he would tell the TV cameras what he thought instead of reacting on the pitch. He had done just that at the Bentegodi Stadium, although, in truth, there had been no sign of the racist free-for-all seen elsewhere. There had been plenty of whistling, but insults aimed Mario's way may not have come until he was being substituted. In fact, one newspaper printed a photo of a red-faced gentleman of a certain age wearing an Argyle sweater shouting something behind the departing player, while a child in a red anorak turned to look at him in astonishment. What is certain is that, for Mario, Verona was the classic straw that broke the camel's back. He could not take it anymore; he did not understand why they whistled at him even when he had done nothing wrong. He was the victim in a situation that got him down more and more, but yet again he was the guilty party as far as everyone was concerned.

He received criticism from all sides, starting with Stefano Sorrentino, the Chievo goal keeper: 'If he's so disgusted by Verona, he doesn't have to come back. I'm a father and I know that you have to teach your children. It doesn't matter whether they're four or twenty years old, children need to be educated. If no one says anything to him, he does whatever he likes and everyone lets him get away with it. He has *carte blanche*.' Franco Tosi, the Northern League Mayor of Verona, said: 'He is immature. Blaming the Chievo fans, who are among the most sporting in Italy, is paradoxical'. Luca Campedelli, president of Chievo, held forth: 'There were no racist attacks on the player, only whistling. It is not a question of colour but of Balotelli's attitude on the pitch.'

In the end, the boy was forced to put things right: He wrote on his website: 'I do not apologise to those who insulted me, but to the fans who had nothing to do with it and who I offended by expressing myself badly. I was exasperated with the boos I received during the match and when I was leaving the pitch. I should have made it clear that I was disgusted with the Verona fans that had booed, as they do in other stadiums in Italy.' He added: 'In Verona, I was ashamed of my own team's fans when I heard boos aimed at Chievo's Luciano. It is shameful and it has to come to an end.' His position could not be faulted but it was a pity Giampaolo Tosel, from the sport's governing body, also thought he was guilty: in addition to fining Inter €15,000 for the racist boos aimed at Luciano, Balotelli was saddled with a €7,000 fine because 'in the 43rd minute of the second half, he repeatedly provoked the crowd with applause as he left the pitch'.

This time the Special One sprang to his player's defence:

'I'm surprised by how the powers-that-be have reacted. I really don't understand why they saw fit to fine Balotelli. A player who feels a negative atmosphere around him but plays a good, sportsmanlike match gets a naive yellow card as he often does, without causing a fuss, then leaves the pitch, applauding for three seconds ... it doesn't seem fair that he should be fined. What I didn't like was how he generalised when talking about Verona, but he has apologised.' This *entente cordiale* between Mou and Balo was not destined to last, however. Sparks flew between the two again on 3 February. Mario played well against Fiorentina in the Coppa Italia, but at a certain point an argument was triggered. Mourinho was waving his arms around, calling Balotelli back to defend a Fiorentina corner, but Mario was on his knees. He later claimed he had lost a contact lens, belatedly running back and throwing his black gloves onto the pitch in a huff. Two minutes later, he was substituted by his manager and went straight to the dressing room, murmuring words about his coach that were presumably far from friendly. Three days later, a new purchase was unveiled at Appiano Gentile: the Kenyan midfielder McDonald Mariga. The Special One took it as an opportunity to talk about brain cells:

'You have no choice but to improve if you're training day in, day out with fantastic examples like Zanetti, Cordoba, Materazzi and Samuel. If someone works with these guys and doesn't learn anything, it's because they only have one neuron, one brain cell.' Was he talking about Balotelli? Many thought so, but Mourinho played it down a few days later. 'The joke about the neuron? Some parents have thanked me because their kids didn't know the word. I've helped popularise science!' In short, it was not about Balotelli. He clarified: 'I took him off against Fiorentina because at that point it seemed to me that he wasn't willing to suffer. He

has played well in the last few games. He is training as normal and in a positive way, even if it is in his own way.' Praise
indeed, echoed by Moratti, who declared at the Inter shareholders' meeting: 'Mario is a boy with exceptional footballing qualities; we are counting on him. He is an asset to the
club. There is absolutely no conflict of any kind between
the parties: Mourinho, Moratti and Balotelli are all working
towards the same goal.'

Little over a month later, this love-in disappeared into
thin air. Completely. The relationship broke down entirely.
Mourinho decided at the last minute that Balotelli would not
board the flight taking the team to London for their match
against Chelsea in the knockout stage of the Champions
League. It was a strange decision given that Inter had
reached this point thanks in part to Balotelli's involvement.
On 7 December 2009, it was his back-heel assist that had led
to Eto'o's goal, and his winning goal against Rubin Kazan
had allowed the *Nerazzurri* to qualify from the group phase.
Yet that was the decision Mourinho had made: Mario would
be watching the match on TV. There was talk of a violent
argument, of a confrontation between Mou and Balo on
the pitch at the Pineta Stadium after the manager had told
the player off and the nineteen-year-old had answered back
rudely. There was even mention of jeering. Whatever the
case, the horse had bolted. The Portuguese manager had
the full support of the club, who had not been happy with
Balotelli's recent exploits, such as when he played against
Genoa with a temperature of 100°F, and the knee injury
that had kept him out of the away fixture at Catania. That
was not all: the Inter management failed to understand why
Balotelli had chosen Mino Raiola, the man who had taken
Ibrahimovic to Barcelona, as his agent. After Mourinho's
decision, Raiola wasted no time jumping to his client's

defence. He explained: 'Mario is disheartened, sad and disappointed. He was looking forward to playing. No one has explained to us why he has been left out. It would be easy at this point to let everything go up in flames but we want to work on rebuilding a relationship with Mourinho.'

In the meantime, the stony-faced manager yelled at reporters before the game: 'I won't talk about him. I know you're waiting for us to lose so you can fill your pages with the fact that Balotelli has been left at home. But that's your job.' Marco Materazzi also stood firm: 'I give Balotelli advice in person and I give him plenty of it. But I have three children and I want to make sure I have some advice left to give them too.'

On 16 March, Inter beat the Blues 1-0 and stormed into the quarter-finals. It was Mourinho's revenge. Revenge also on Balotelli, the boy the press wanted on the pitch. Mario was seen in the stands at the San Siro for Inter-Livorno on 24 March. This time the gibes came not from his manager or teammates but from Inter's *ultras*. 'A dressing room that is united, strong and unassailable as never before: all we have to do now is keep out those who bring discord and trouble', proclaimed one very long banner. Another read: 'See you at the QI', a night spot frequented by Mario, if gossip was to be believed. The essay writing in the stands finished with a flurry: 'If someone still doesn't get it, he can wipe his ass with a Milan shirt'. Delicate words chosen to make the point clearly – Balo needed to stop flirting with AC Milan.

The truce, with his club and with Mourinho, was signed by Balotelli on 1 April. A statement of pure diplomacy read: 'I am sorry for the situation that has arisen recently. I am the first to be suffering because I love football and I want to play. I am now waiting in silence to be able to get back to being useful to my team. I would like not to have to think about the past any more but to look to the future to concentrate on my upcoming commitments and to be ready for them.' A face-to-face meeting between Mourinho and the number 45 was scheduled at Appiano Gentile before the match against Bologna on 3 April, after four weeks of not playing. In front of his home fans, the prodigal son scored to give Inter a 2-0 lead. But the point of no return was not far away.

20 April 2010. Inter were playing Barcelona in the first leg of the Champions League semi-final. They led the defending champions of Europe 3-1. Fifteen minutes before the final whistle, Mourinho sent Mario on in place of Diego Milito, the hero of the evening (he had scored the third goal and provided the assists for Sneijder and Maicon's goals). The Portuguese manager took his time giving the boy his tactical instructions, ending with an encouraging pat on the chest. The aim was to hold on to the ball and defend the result at all costs. Mario started well enough, chasing his opponents and intercepting, to the delight of the fans. But then he failed to control the ball, began playing around and gave the ball away, as if his heart was not in it. Mourinho shouted at him, reminding him of his orders. A roar came from the stands. Then came the act that enraged the San Siro. A pass from Eto'o bobbed up. Instead of controlling the ball, bringing it down and taking his time, Mario tried a shot from 40 yards out. It was a bullet that ended up some distance from Victor Valdes's goal. The Meazza howled in disappointment. Mario completely lost it, told everyone to f*** off and stuck his middle finger up at all of them, rotating it as if to say 'Yes, all of you'. Alone against the world.

That was not where it ended, though. The 'best' was yet to come: when the referee blew the final whistle, instead of celebrating with the others, the boy from Concesio walked towards the tunnel, took off his blue and black-striped shirt and threw it to the ground in anger. Lele Oriali, second-in-command, tried to calm him down as he muttered: 'You're all sons of bitches.' Insults could be forgotten, but throwing his shirt to the ground was sacrilegious. It was an intolerable insult to his teammates, manager, president and fans. According to Ibrahimovic, Marco Materazzi followed Mario into the tunnel, calling him every name under the sun and using his studs to teach him a lesson: 'He wanted to kill him. I'd never seen anything like it. If he had done it to me, I would have knocked him out in two seconds', the Swedish player explained. Lucio pinned the kid up against the wall of the dressing room to explain to him how to behave. Stankovic, who picked the shirt up off the ground and hid it in his shorts, was more understanding: 'Mario? He's just a kid. I understand, I have three boys myself.' This opinion was not shared by the fans, who, in the belly of the San Siro, fired insults at Balotelli, trying to attack him as he got in his car to go home. On live TV, José Mourinho shot back at all those who thought they knew better: 'I've been at Inter since June 2008 and if I think back to all the flak I've taken for trying to educate a very talented player, both personally and in footballing terms, I've been criticised so much by all of Italy's so-called football experts. And today, in a Champions League semi-final, the second most important match in European football at club level, something awful happened.'

The following day, Massimo Moratti said the following: 'What happened yesterday was public suicide by Mario. He is a boy with his own issues, which I don't want to go into.' The chairman explained that the club would take measures, but left the door ajar, hoping the player would 'reintegrate well into the team and with the group. We need him.'

Exactly the opposite of what the *Nerazzurri* fans thought. They wanted to kick him out, immediately, send him as far away as possible to any club prepared to take him. For example, the following appeared in an open letter posted on the website run by fans from the North stand on 23 April: 'Mario, we will remember you as the first (and hopefully the last) brat in history to have dared to take off his shirt at the San Siro and throw it on the ground in such a sign of contempt. You no longer exist to us, dear Mario, and with this we say goodbye.' This letter was posted just a few hours before Balotelli's umpteenth self-flagellation: 'I would like to apologise for my actions on Tuesday evening. When I came onto the pitch, I heard whistles from the crowd and my coach shouting,' Super Mario wrote on his website. 'I lost my head, I didn't know what was going on and I took my shirt off to vent my anger. I'm sorry for not being able to control the tension and frustration that has been building up in me for months now. I would like to clarify that I am not annoyed with the fans, least of all those in the North stand. They have always supported me even when others whistled at me. It is for them that I would like Inter to win everything. As long as I'm wearing an Inter shirt, I will do everything possible to honour it. I am going through one of the most difficult periods in my life. I am exasperated but I made a mistake by letting it show in that way.' Balotelli concluded: 'I hope now to be able to resolve the problems I have with some of my teammates and with the club with the help of the people who love me, as well as my agent.'

Problems are not so easily solved it seems, given that the same day, after a fifteen-minute interview with Mario, Moratti advised him to leave the Inter training camp immediately and go home in order to avoid any more tension. Excuses did not wash with the team and the manager. Once again, the young talented player was no longer part of the team. There was talk of an imminent parting of the ways, of the termination of his contract for just cause, of official inquiries and even of bullying in the workplace. In the meantime, Mario skipped the league game against Atalanta, the away match at Barcelona for the second leg of the Champions League semi-final and the game against Lazio on 2 May.

But then came the mending of fences, repairs made just in time for the end of the season. And behold, the lost sheep returned to the fold. On 5 May, he was on the bench at the Stadio Olimpico for the Coppa Italia final against Roma. Following a mid-air clash with Burdisso, Sneijder had to leave the field after five minutes. Balotelli came on. Thanks to a goal from Milito, Inter won their first trophy on the way to the Triple and Mario was on the receiving end of a kick from Francesco Totti. In the 87th minute, the Roma captain was chasing the Inter number 45 like a madman when, just inside the touchline in the Roma box, he finally caught up with his prey and brought him down. The red card came immediately; it was the act of someone not in their right mind. On 7 May, Totti explained his reasons to the *Corriere dello Sport-Stadio* – it is worth noting that he never names Balotelli: 'I made a mistake on Wednesday evening, that's undeniable, but everything goes back to the situation. During the match, "he" had a provocative attitude towards my teammates, something that has happened before. Do you remember when he stuck his tongue out at Panucci, what happened with Mexes, or when he celebrated in front of our fans? All this, all from the same footballer, has happened in almost every stadium in Italy, and in Europe, and it's probably one of the reasons he has never been properly accepted by his own team and is always seen by other clubs, and even by the national team, as a disruptive element. Those who know me know perfectly well that my reactions are always the result of provocation. Hearing a novice footballer, albeit one with great talent, repeatedly offending not just me personally but my fans, my city and my sense of belonging to Roma by telling me I'm finished, is unbearable. I'm not trying to justify it but it's simply the truth of what happened. We cannot tolerate the fact that "he" is always given the chance to be provocative towards anyone and everyone, including his own fans and those of his opponents, without taking his attitude into account beforehand. As I said, I was wrong and I will be punished, but there was one thing that felt strange … when I was sent off, none of the opposing team jumped to "his" defence.'

The theory of 'Balotelli the Provoker' was back. Mario gave his version in an interview with *Vanity Fair*. 'I only said something to him like, are you going to keep playing or do you want to be a baby? Then he called me a filthy n*****. I heard him tell Thiago Motta he was going to smash me. I smiled and walked away. Then he kicked me. I didn't know what had happened. It wasn't until I saw the clip on TV that I realised what he'd done. The insult hurt more than the kick. Totti was someone I admired.'

Meanwhile, the league title had yet to be decided. Mario started the game against Chievo at the San Siro on 9 May. He scored an impressive goal that was widely praised. It seemed the boy had been forgiven. On 16 May, the last day of the league, when Inter just scraped its eighteenth title, the fifth in a row, Balotelli was on the pitch and joined in the celebrations. Just six days later, the *Nerazzurri* won the title they had been waiting for since 1965 when Helenio Herrera's *Grande Inter* won their second Champions Cup beating Eusebio's Benfica at the San Siro. On 22 May at the Santiago Bernabéu, José Mourinho's Inter won the Champions League, beating Bayern Munich 2-0. Mario watched the victory from the bench but he was one of the most emotional and delighted about the Triple. He confessed to the Inter TV channel: 'It was incredible. I'm speechless. It was the first time I've cried with happiness because of a match'. A crowd of fans at Malpensa Airport welcomed the returning team home from Madrid but Mario felt light-headed. He leant against a car on his elbows as if he was struggling to breathe. But on hearing screams of 'Mario, stay, don't go', he straightened up. The party carried on without Mourinho. The Portuguese manager had stayed on in Madrid to hammer out the finer details of his contract with Real. On 28 May, he became the new coach of *Los Merengues*.

Wearing sunglasses, a thick necklace, white T-shirt, jeans and bright pink trainers, Mario Balotelli got out of his sports car on 29 June and went into Milan's Istituto Privato to sit the oral exam for his accountancy A-level, the exam he had been forced to postpone the previous year because of the European Under-21 final. He would answer questions on Italian, history, business administration, law and sports subjects. He would also defend his dissertation, entitled *Football: An International Story*. The exam lasted 45 minutes. When he came out, he told the waiting journalists that it had gone well (his final mark was 60 per cent). When they asked if he was going to stay at Inter, he replied: 'We'll see.'

Chapter 17

I'm Not a Bad Boy

Six English words spoken by Mario and topped off with a smile. Just like that: 'I'm not a bad boy.' They were the only words in the language of Shakespeare that Balotelli managed at his first press conference when he was unveiled as Manchester City's new striker on 17 August 2010. He explained: 'I know some English, but it's hard to understand when English people speak.' Everything else he said was in the language of Dante, making plenty of work for his interpreter. 'I'm not a bad boy, despite what they say in Italy. I'm an unusual boy. I'm neither bad nor particularly good. I'm full of energy, but normal.'

Roberto Mancini, his new, as well as old, manager and mentor, weighed in on the issue to lend his support: 'We were all bad boys when we were young. All of us here. It's normal to behave badly from time to time when you're young, then, little by little, you change. I think Mario's a good guy, a normal guy, and what's important is that he is a good player.'

Mancini did not skimp on praise for his new purchase: 'Mario has everything it takes to be a fantastic player. He's young, he has great technique, he's quick and he heads the ball well. In the future, he could be one of the best players in the world.'

The compliments between teacher and pupil went both ways: 'The fact that Mancini was the coach at City was fundamental. If it had not been for him, I would not have come. Many teams wanted me, including one in Italy, but I told my agent I wanted City because of Mancini. He gave me my start in Serie A and has always had faith in me. Now is the time to repay him.' His agent, Mino Raiola, confirmed: 'There were four or five other clubs that wanted him [rumour had it, Milan, Arsenal, Chelsea and Manchester United]. When City realised this, they decided to speed up the process.' The negotiation, which had been complex, was concluded on 13 August, when the Citizens' website officially announced their new signing. The deal earned Inter €28 million plus a bonus of €3 million linked to the player's performance over the coming seasons. Mario signed a five year contract with a starting salary of €3.5 million per season plus a bonus (between €350,000 and €600,000 depending on the number of goals scored and the achievements of the team), almost double what he would have earned at Inter (€1.9 million). The wealth of City owner Sheikh Mansour had no doubt played a part in Balotelli's choice, but the decision to leave had been made much earlier: on 20 April, by the shirt thrown to the ground and Materazzi's studs at the San Siro. Mario said as much at the press conference at the Carrington Training Centre: 'Pages and pages have been written about me in the newspapers. Living in Milan was difficult. I told my agent I wanted to leave.'

He wanted to leave Italy, the criticism and constant insults; to leave the war with his manager and the fans; to leave the boos, the racism and a type of football that was sick and becoming increasingly deranged; to leave and get far away from home to find peace. Super Mario explained his reasons in an open letter that appeared just before 7 pm on the evening of 13 August, after he had passed the medical and signed his City contract. His farewell was bitter: 'I am about to start a new adventure. I'm sorry to be leaving Inter and Italy. I would have preferred to continue to grow professionally in my own country. I am going somewhere where I hope to find the space to play because this is very important to me. I need to play, to make mistakes, to learn and to play some more. I also need a calmer atmosphere around me. I'm putting a difficult year behind me. I have recognised my mistakes but I believe I have often been at the centre of pressure and criticism that in some cases has left me exasperated. Now, I'm only thinking about helping my new team in the Premier League. I want to give it my all! I would like to thank my family, who, with so much patience and affection, have been with me in the good times and bad. I would like to thank President Moratti, the team with whom I shared so many victories, the fans who supported me, my entourage and my friends.'

No mention of Mourinho. When the journalists at the Carrington Centre asked him about the Special One, he said: 'He's not my manager any more and I don't want to talk about him. He said I was unmanageable? Forget it, I'm not interested.'

Mario thanked Massimo Moratti: 'He's a great president. When I see him, I'll buy him a drink,' he said. After a long meeting with Inter's new manager, the Spaniard, Rafa Benitez, Moratti made the decision, albeit with a knot in his stomach, to walk away from the boy he admired so much.

'Balotelli Sold' was the blue and black headline in *Corriere dello Sport-Stadio*. 'A senseless decision,' the editorial claimed. The entire Italian media was scandalised. 'This is no country for young men,' wrote *La Repubblica*, a play on the title of Cormac McCarthy's famous book. The paper added: 'Nor for young talented men or those whose skin colour is decidedly unfashionable in Italy.'

At the World Cup in South Africa, Italy, the defending champions, were knocked out by Slovakia, Paraguay and New Zealand. It was an unmitigated disaster. Experts such as Arrigo Sacchi, Roberto Baggio and Gianni Rivera were called to the sickbed of Italian football. Everyone pinpointed a need for renewal and to focus on young talented players like Balotelli, who had just made his debut for the national team at senior level but ended up in England. In short, it was a heavy defeat, the umpteenth for Italian football. It became extremely dramatic, blown out of all proportion. Meanwhile, Mario was showing off his light-blue shirt sporting the eagle and three star crest. The young talented Italian player smiled and posed for the usual photos at Mancini's side outside the City training centre: Raiola commented: 'It was great to see him so happy.' This happiness was short-lived, although things seemed to get off to a good start as far as City were concerned. On 19 August, Super Mario made his Europa League debut against the Romanian team, Timisoara, coming on for Barry in the 12th minute of the second half. A quarter of an hour later, he deflected a rocket from Adebayor into the back of the net. 1-0 to City. He then got a yellow card for a foul before staking his claim to goal of the season with a lob that grazed the post. The following day, the British papers were unanimously triumphant. 'Thanks Balo,' said the *Sun*; the *Guardian* claimed he had saved the club from £180 million-worth of shame; the *Daily Mail* had no doubts when it came to glorifying Super Mario, while the *Telegraph* wrote: 'Regardless of what José Mourinho might think, Mario Balotelli is clearly worth the trouble that seems to act as the Manchester City forward's shadow. The bad boy of Italian football he may be, but when a twenty-year-old, with a £22 million price-tag, marks his debut with the kind of bewitching performance that transformed City in the

Europa League against FC Timisoara in Romania, the bad angels that often outnumber the good can only be viewed as an occupational hazard that comes with working with the prodigious forward.'

It was a shame then that the twenty-year-old Brescian picked up an injury at the end of the game against the Romanians: he grimaced during a tackle, clutching his right knee. Roberto Mancini hoped it was nothing serious and that Mario would be on the pitch the following Monday for their Premiership clash with Liverpool. But he did not make it and the balance sheet of his first few months at City finished in the red. An injury, a car accident, a knee operation, a mistimed anthem, a house guest who would have been best avoided, a motorbike he would have been better off not getting onto, two flirtations and pages and pages of gossip in both the UK and Italy. On 28 August, Balotelli, who was not yet used to driving on the left, hit a black BMW with his Audi R8 on his way to the training ground. The breathalyser test was negative but legend has it the police officers found £5,000 in cash in his car. 'I'm rich,' was his simple explanation. Pictures of the car did the rounds on the internet. This was not to be Mario's only transport-related issue. According to the *Sun*, he was the recipient of an average of three fines per day during his time in England. His Maserati had been towed as many as 27 times and the fines paid amounted to the princely sum of £10,000.

On 9 September 2010, Mario underwent surgery on the cartilage of his right knee at the Policlinico San Matteo hospital in Pavia to repair the injury he suffered in the match against Timisoara. But before the operation, he stuck his head out of the hospital window sporting a green surgical cap. To the delight of the reporters camped out below, he shouted '*Forza Milan!*' and sang the club anthem. The operation was a success, but it would take six to eight weeks of recuperation before he could play again. In the meantime, the gossip merchants went all out on Balotelli. On 17 September, a video was shown on the *Mattino Cinque* morning TV programme on Italy's Canale 5 in which a certain Janine, a Milanese singer, was seen entering the home of the Manchester City striker at 4 am and did not leave until 2 pm the following day. Melissa Castagnoli, the girlfriend who had come to England with Mario, dumped him on live TV. But it did not end there ... the voyeuristic Italian TV channels also showed images of him getting onto a motorbike when he was still supposed to be on crutches. A few weeks later, on 1 October, Mario drove into the car park of the women's prison in Brescia in his convertible Mercedes. His car was intercepted by prison officers. They asked to see his documents and eventually recognised the footballer and his companion, his brother Enock. Both men were detained for half an hour until the affair could be resolved. Super Mario justified himself by saying he had seen the open gate and was intrigued by the fact that it was a women's prison. He claimed not to know he needed a special permit to enter. He apologised and left disappointed.

Luckily, for him and for City, Mario seemed to have recovered by the end of October and was ready to make his Premier League debut. City were due to play Arsenal at home on Sunday 24 October. The number 45 came on, again for Barry, in the 72nd minute with the Gunners 2-0 ahead. Bendtner scored in the 88th minute, giving Arsenal a commanding lead. In short, it had been a disastrous afternoon. Nevertheless, Balotelli's day did eventually come. For better or for worse. It was 7 November: Manchester City beat West Bromwich Albion 2-0. Super Mario scored twice, his first Premier League goals. He was described as both match winner and match sinner. He received a yellow card, followed by a red card for kicking Youssouf Mulumbu. Mancini disagreed with the refereeing decision but was angry with Balotelli: 'I told him to be careful of the referee. I wanted to substitute him so he wouldn't be sent off but I didn't do it quickly enough.' The FA came down heavily on him: the bad boy received a three-match ban. He missed the derby against Manchester United, vitally important as far as the fans and the club's league position were concerned, as well as the games against Birmingham City and Fulham. His teammates were starting to get fed up with him and put him on notice. In the *Manchester Evening News*, the Dutch player Nigel de Jong told him he needed to have more self-control and learn from his mistakes. In short, he said Mario needed to calm down. The boy seemed to have got the message and, on 1 December at the Etihad Stadium, he scored two goals in the snow against Red Bull Salzburg in the Europa League. It was a great job, marred by the fact that two days later he reacted angrily to a challenge from Jérôme Boateng in training. Chaos ensued. It took a few seconds before the peacemakers arrived to separate them, but the sequence of photos published by the English newspapers yet again made the case for Balotelli's temper and flawed temperament.

He was a boy capable of giving the best and worst of himself, even where fashion was concerned: the British tabloids went as far as dissecting the number 45's style. Fashion experts went wild over his so-called chicken hat, the woollen five-pointed hat Mario had found on a stall at a Christmas market and premiered before the match with Everton. Or his black 'skeleton' gloves, which looked like part of a Halloween costume in contrast to the plain black ones worn by his teammates.

Back on the pitch, he scored a hat-trick in the home game

against Aston Villa on 28 December. He performed in front of Mamma Silvia, who had come to visit him for Christmas to make him his favourite dish: lasagne. The journalists asked him if it was true that he wanted to go back to Italy, to Milan even. He answered: 'I'm happy at City, even if you're trying to tell me I want to leave.' Roberto Mancini explained that he was 'probably homesick. He's only twenty and he has left his family for the first time. It's normal for him to miss them. I don't think it's a long-term issue.' He reiterated: 'It is very important that we keep him. He is a very good player and he has plenty of room for improvement.' Mancini was understanding when it came to the endless questions that had already been asked in Italy about why Mario does not celebrate his goals, but he admitted frankly: 'When you score three goals in a Premier League game, you should celebrate. Every day I fight against Mario and sometimes I would like to give him a punch.'

However, the match against Aston Villa would be Mario's last before another prolonged break. The problem with his knee began to resurface. Kept off the pitch for almost two months, he was still the centre of attention as far as the British tabloids were concerned. In the first few weeks of the New Year, they linked him to Sophie Reade, a Playboy bunny and Big Brother winner. It was hardly a scoop, given that she was the one who told the *News of the World* the raunchy details of their relationship. In an interview with the *Gazzetta dello Sport*, Mario brushed off the episode: 'I met her once and she started bombarding me with messages. I had to delete her number. Once *Big Brother* wasn't popular any more, she went to the newspapers to find work.' Talking about the subject, he explained: 'If a girl says she's the girlfriend of a footballer, everyone thinks it's true. You can't defend yourself.' It was a good job that Balo was about to go on a trip. He went to the

United States, to the mountains of Vermont, where it was snowing and the temperature was minus twenty. He went to the Killington Medical Clinic, run by Bill Knowles, the physiotherapy guru who had treated sportsmen such as Tiger Woods and Jonny Wilkinson. It took two weeks of intense work to rehabilitate and strengthen his right knee, to solve the problems that had been tormenting him since August once and for all.

He returned to action on 21 February 2011 for the home FA Cup tie against Notts County. Controversy flared up immediately. In the 60th minute, Mancini called Mario back to the substitutes' bench following a clash of heads in the air with Krystian Pearce, the Notts County defender. Balotelli lost his temper and threw his snood on the ground, before storming off to the dressing room without acknowledging Mancini. The manager chose not to make an issue of it: 'We had agreed on the substitution as it was his first start after two months. I know he wasn't happy about coming off, but I need him fit for the next two months.' He explained that he had played well and had not felt any problems with his knee. It seemed as if Mario really had overcome his physical issues: he scored against Fulham on 27 February and against Aston Villa in the FA Cup quarter-final on 2 March.

But this streak of positivity came to an end on Thursday 17 March in the second leg of the Europa League knockout phase against Dynamo Kiev. In the first leg, the Light Blues had been on the receiving end of two goals from Andriy Shevchenko and Oleh Gusev, losing 2-0. At the end of the first half, Mario had a swollen face. They gave him two anti-histamine injections in the dressing room at half time but he had to come off after only twelve minutes of the second half. He was itchy and uncomfortable. It was an allergic reaction to certain types of grass. Apparently, it was an ongoing problem; the medical staff were already aware of it but this time the antihistamines were not strong enough.

On 17 March at the Etihad, Mario did not have any problems with the grass but it turned out to be his Black Thursday. It began during the warm-up when he was struggling with his bib. He just could not get it on properly. He had his head in the armhole and then started fighting with the elastic. One of Mancini's assistants came over to help him put it right but to no avail. Mario threw it to the ground angrily and tried with a blue one instead, with the same result. With the TV cameras trained on Mario throughout, a never-ending video came out, lasting almost a minute and a half. While the channel was rebroadcasting the match, the video had the Sky TV commentators in stitches. It went viral on YouTube and resulted in countless imitations, not least from his teammate Dzeko. Imagine how the *Sun* revelled in the episode: Their article was entitled: 'He can't even dress himself. What do you expect from someone like him?' If the story had ended there, it would have been a mere blip. At the beginning of the game, Mario missed a sitter from three yards out, firing a ball that should only ever have ended up in the back of the net high into the sky. He then unintentionally deflected a shot from David Silva, which could have given City the lead, out for a goal kick. The worst was yet to come. In the 36th minute, he made a blatant, chest-high kung-fu challenge on Goran Popov. The Turkish referee, Cuneyt Cakir, wasted no time in taking out his red card. Ten-men City were knocked out of the Europa League. It was a stupid mistake broadcast all over Europe that made Mancini furious: 'Am I angry? What do you think? If Mario used his head, he would be a fantastic player. But that's his problem. When he does stupid things, it becomes more difficult for him, for me and for the team.' Mancini explained in the post-match press conference: 'If we had kept eleven on the pitch, we would have scored two or three goals. Coming back from a 2-0 defeat is already very difficult, but when you have to play with ten men because of a stupid red card, it becomes even harder. There is a big difference.'

The manager kept a lid on his anger, unlike the British tabloids. The *Daily Mirror* opened with 'Euro Stupid'. The *Sun* was tougher, describing him as 'an idiot called Mario Balotelli', then went on to praise 'the brave ten men of Manchester City while a coward skulked in the dressing room'.

The number 45's excuses appeared right on time on the club's website as on so many previous occasions: 'It was not my intention to hurt anyone; I want to express my sincere apologies to Popov. I was trying my best for the team as I always do. The ball was in the air and I went for it with my foot high. I never tried to make contact with Popov and I certainly didn't want to hurt him. In retrospect, however, the tackle was poor and I'm very sorry to my teammates in particular that I got sent off so early in such an important game. I should have shown more consideration, but I was so involved in the match'. He continues with a thought for Mancini: 'It was not a good way to repay the manager who has shown so much faith in me or the owners and fans who have made me so welcome since I arrived from Italy. I hope they will forgive me.'

Forgiveness comes at a high price: it cost him two weeks' pay. But this was not why Mario decided to sort out his head. He narrowly escaped a street fight outside one of his favourite Italian restaurants, the San Carlo in Central Manchester. On 25 March, Jenny Thompson was sat at the table next to Mario. An escort girl, she had become famous following a fling with Wayne Rooney. What did the kid from Brescia do?

As soon as he saw her, he started singing 'Rooney, Rooney', before blowing a raspberry in the face of her companion, a property developer. Things became heated and insults flew until Super Mario told his adversary he would see him outside. The waiting staff intervened to make sure things did not deteriorate further, but it was clear the tabloids would have a field day. Two days later, the Italian would get up to something even worse. He took it upon himself to throw darts at Man City's youth team players from a first floor window at the Carrington Training Centre. No one was injured and there was no damage, according to the *Sunday People*, which added that, on being asked for an explanation, Mario responded: 'I was bored.' It may have the makings of a story invented out of thin air by a tabloid newspaper but to corroborate their story, the English papers dug up the account of a sultry Sunday afternoon in June 2010 when, in Milan's Piazza Repubblica, police patrol cars rushed to the scene of a supposed shoot out. Instead of an armed gang, they found Mario in his car with four friends. He was holding a toy pistol. He admitted: 'I fired five shots but I didn't expect all this fuss.' The incident was resolved with a dressing down. The darts stunt, if the press were to be believed, cost Mario Balotelli a £120,000 fine and an official warning from the club. All these episodes, some of which attracted more attention than others, saw criticism of Mario abound.

Harry Redknapp, the manager of Tottenham Hotspur, labelled him as both 'arrogant' and 'frightening'. The 64-year-old manager said: 'He looks like he hates every minute of what he's doing. I've never seen anybody with that sort of attitude. It's frightening. He doesn't know how to smile. He's doing a job he should love yet he looks as if the routine is getting him down.' The final blow came from Rodney Marsh, the talented former City player who never fulfilled his potential: 'I absolutely do not want my name to be associated with Balotelli's.'

Everyone at Man City and in English football began to wonder whether the boy was ill-suited to playing in the Premiership but the tabloids were rubbing their hands with glee: they had found a new protagonist for their media circus. The paparazzi followed him everywhere, unearthing a new story on a weekly basis. It was a real soap opera. He was thrown out of Liverpool's Rude Lap Dancing Club for violating the 'no touching' rule. He tried to pick a fight with five bouncers at the club. Yet there was still another side to him: Mario won £25,000 at the Manchester235 casino and promptly gave away £1,000 of his winnings to a tramp. When a kid who asked him for an autograph told him he was being bullied at school, Mario put him in his car and drove straight round to the school. Balotelli the hero took up his cause and told the headmaster to take steps against the bullies. He reportedly paid for a full tank of fuel for all the cars at the petrol station where he had taken his Maserati. In a pub in one of the most infamous parts of Manchester, he bought drinks for everyone and challenged them all to a darts match. He walked into a library and offered to pay off the overdue fines for students who had returned their books late. He parallel parked his luxury Bentley outside Xaverian College because he was desperate to go to the toilet. All these stories have been denied by Mario, apart from the one when he used the money his mother had given him to get groceries to buy himself a trampoline, or when he invited a magician he had met on the street back to his house to teach him magic tricks. Despite everything, anecdotes about Super Mario proliferate like the best urban legends. In the few months since the boy had arrived from Italy, he had turned himself into a popular hero, a terrible yet lovable Greek god, someone capable of good and evil, a jester and a king, one thing and its exact opposite. He was someone who was either loved or hated, someone who made people laugh. And sometimes he even made the City fans go wild with joy.

14 May 2011. London, Wembley Stadium. Manchester City against Stoke City in the FA Cup final, watched by 88,643 fans. In the 74th minute, Yaya Touré, the big Ivorian, scored just as he had in the semi-final to knock out Manchester United in the same stadium. This time the move started with Tévez supplying David Silva, who spun away from his marker to the left of the Stoke goal. He passed back to Super Mario, who let rip with a belter. Coming off a defender, the ball ended up at the feet of Touré, who fired a half volley from the penalty spot into the back of the net. It was a superb piece of skill. Tévez jumped out of the way but Thomas Sorensen, whose saves had kept Stoke in it up to that point, could do nothing but watch. It was the goal that secured the 130th FA Cup for City, their first title after a 35-year drought. It was Mancini's first victory with the club, or rather his second, having achieved their objective of qualifying for the Champions League in a Premiership that had been won a few hours earlier by Manchester United. Spurs had lost out this year, after pipping City to the coveted spot a year earlier. City would eventually finish the season in third place ahead of Arsenal.

Touré said: 'This win is fantastic for us.' Fantastic for the team and fantastic for the City fans, who had not seen one of their players lift a trophy since the League Cup win in 1976. And fantastic for Balotelli, especially after the controversy of the semi-final against United, when he had shown his light-blue shirt to the Red Devils' fans in provocation and almost started a fistfight with Anderson and Rio Ferdinand. After his Italian coach defended him ('It looks like it is always his fault.

What are we gonna do, send him to prison?'), he was Man of the Match. With his shirt off and his mohican cut high, Mario struck again when speaking to the Sky microphones as the Light Blues were celebrating: 'Was that the best game you've ever played for Manchester City?' the reporter asked, thrusting his microphone forwards. 'All my season was shit, can I say that? My season wasn't good. Today maybe I played more for the team. This is important.'

The interviewer countered: 'Mancini wants you to be like Cantona. Do you feel a bit like Cantona today? He was a winner here at Wembley.'

'Cantona is really a big player. I'm different. I'm Mario. He knows that every player has his quality. I have my quality and if I give it to the team I can be important.'

'You are the Man of the Match. Congratulations,' said the journalist, offering Mario a bottle of champagne. He smiled and hugged Mancini, while the presenter back in the studio commented: 'In answer to Mario's question, no. You can't use language like that. Our apologies if you were offended by that. I know there are a lot of kids watching but emotions are running very high straight after the final whistle as Man City win the Cup.' The *enfant terrible* had struck again.

Chapter 18

A Modern-Day Rock Star

Oh Balotelli he's a striker ...
He's good at darts.
He's allergic to grass,
but when he plays he's f****** class.
Drives round Moss Side
with a wallet full of cash,
Can't put on his vest
but when he does he is the best.
Goes into schools,
tells teachers all the rules.
Sets fire to his gaff
with rockets from his bath.
Doesn't give a f***,
'cause he did it for a laugh,
Runs back to his house
for a suitcase full of cash.

Manchester City's fans affectionately dedicated this chant to Mario Balotelli. To the tune of Leonard Cohen's *Hallelujah*, they sang it from the stands of the Etihad, on trains to away games, and in the pub both before and after matches. The song was constantly evolving: with every new Balotelli antic came a new anecdote about his life off the pitch, inspiring a new verse. The final lines were composed on the eve of the Manchester derby, except this time they were based on real events rather than hearsay. On the night between Friday 21 and Saturday 22 October 2011, fire fighters were called to extinguish a fire that had started in Balotelli's home in Mottram St Andrews, a residential area on the outskirts of Manchester.

'Four breathing apparatus and two hose-reel water jets were used to deal with a fire and a large fan was used to clear smoke from the property,' reported a statement from the fire service. 'Crews managed to put out the fire within half an hour of arriving, but remained at the scene until 2.45 am to prevent any possible flare-ups. The five occupiers were able to get out unharmed. The fire was caused by a firework.'

It seems that at around 1 am, Mario and his friends started setting off fireworks from the bathroom window. Towels and curtains caught fire and the situation got out of control. The flames spread and the air, thick with smoke, became unbreathable. Once the fire crews arrived, Mario reportedly took a big risk by going back into the house to recover a suitcase full of money. Or at least this was what the tabloids had written and was picked up on by the fans for their final verse.

Super Mario gave his version of the facts in an interview with the BBC in March 2012. 'It started like a joke. It was stupid. I was bored. I was with my friends and one of them was sleeping. So I got a bin, a metal one, and put the fireworks inside. Nothing was going to happen so I left the room and left the fireworks in the bin but didn't light them. I walked out and my friend went into the room and just started screaming. The fireworks were going off. They put out the fireworks in the toilet but the curtain caught fire. That's it. That's why the firemen came.'

The fact is that 24 hours before the fireworks incident, Balotelli had publicly declared he was a changed man and had grown up, in short that he had got his head together. He spoke to the press before the Manchester derby: 'It is the real Mario who is coming now and it isn't the same Mario as last year. This is partly because I am training well and feeling good and getting better all the time. I don't live in town any more ... so it's quieter. I try to stay at home more with my family. They weren't here last year. They came sometimes but they were not based here. That's definitely helped. Now I miss home a little bit less ... There is only one problem with life in England – the weather.' He joked about the climate before coming back to his manager: 'With Mancini I feel comfortable. I've known him a long time and he's a good manager. He believes in me. Even when no one in England believed in me, he did. And he kept on believing in me. I want to do something important here at City with him.'

It was undeniable that the City number 45 had been doing well since late September. On 15 October, he opened the scoring with a spectacular bicycle kick against Aston Villa in the eighth fixture of the season. He scored his third league goal in succession after those against Everton and Blackburn, the fourth if you count the League Cup. He helped City lift themselves up to the top of the table with a two-point lead over United. 'Who needs Tévez with Super Mario in top form?' the *Daily Mail* asked. On 27 September, Tévez, *El Apache*, had refused to take to the pitch in the Champions League game against Bayern Munich. Roberto Mancini said he would not play for City again. The Argentine went back to Buenos Aires and would not reclaim his position in the side until the following March. Many were sad to see him go, until Mario's star began to shine.

In the first few months of the season, Balotelli had suffered on the bench or in the stands. He was unhappy to be the Light Blues' fourth striker behind Sergio Agüero, City's most expensive signing (Sheikh Mansour had paid Atlético Madrid €45 million for the player), Dzeko and Tévez. But when his manager did decide to include him in his first eleven, he began to wreak havoc. The fireworks incident had been unfortunate but luckily they were repeated on the pitch on Sunday 23 October. On the Monday morning, Mario appeared on the front page of the *Financial Times* beneath the title 'Blue Fireworks. United hammered in Manchester derby'. Nothing could have been more appropriate: Super Mario, the derby's key player, scored two goals and caused the sending off of Jonny Evans. He began the systematic demolition of Sir Alex Ferguson's team. After threading the first goal into the right corner of De Gea's goal with millimetric precision, he lifted up his shirt to show the slogan 'Why Always Me?' These three words provoked plenty of discussion. Football's powers that be took it as yet more proof of the black Italian's arrogance when it was simply a lament, a request to be left in peace. He wanted people, the tabloids and the critics to stop speaking ill of him when they had never met him. He wanted the paparazzi to stop following him here there and everywhere and stop lurking outside his house. It was a way of asking people to leave him alone: Why Always Me? The rapper Tinchy Stryder turned the three words into a song and the fans would never forget it.

The Mario and City show went on and this time Manchester's so-called Noisy Neighbours were shouting for joy. United's fans, with so much pedigree and too many trophies to count, supporters of the world's richest club with 330 million fans worldwide were not used to losing 6-1 to City. For United it was their first home defeat since April 2010, when they had lost to Chelsea and their worst result since losing 5-0 in 1955, also to City. The Red Devils had not conceded six goals at Old Trafford since 1930, when they lost

6-0 to Huddersfield and 7-4 to Newcastle. Sir Alex Ferguson complained: 'It's the worst result in my history. I can't believe the scoreline. Even as a player I don't think I ever lost 6-1.' City took the lead in the Premiership, five points ahead of their local rivals. Mancini was as happy as Larry but poured cold water on the celebrations: 'This is important for our squad and I am happy for the three points, but in the end it is just three points.' He did not hold back when it came to Balotelli: 'I think Mario played very well. If we want to talk about Mario as a football player, I think we can put him in the top five players in the world. The problem is that he is young and can make mistakes.'

He had made a mistake during the club's US tour, infuriating his manager. The team were playing a friendly against LA Galaxy on 24 July. Balo had already scored from the penalty spot when David Silva gifted him another ball that almost became his second. All he had to do was help it on its way towards the goal or pass to Dzeko, who was free to his right. Mario thought both solutions were too ordinary and looked for the most difficult option, as he had done as a child: a Marseille turn with a back-heel. From two yards out, the ball ended up crashing into the advertising hoardings. Dzeko could not believe his eyes and threw his arms in the air in despair. On the touchline, Mancini jumped to his feet and told James Milner to warm up before putting him on in Balotelli's place. Super Mario was having none of it: he made a scene in front of the bench for the fans at the Home Depot Center, threw away a water bottle in anger and stormed off to the dressing room. After the match, the manager said: 'We need to be always professional, always serious, and in that moment I did not think Mario did this. That is why I took him off. In football you should always be serious and if you have a chance to score, you should score. I hope he has learnt his lesson. It is punishment enough for him to be substituted after 30 minutes.'

Water under the bridge, or at least it seemed that way after the thrashing dished out to United. Super Mario was in full flow: he scored in the Champions League against Villarreal and against Napoli at the Stadio San Paolo, but City failed to get out of the group stage. In the Premier League against Liverpool on 27 November, he received two yellow cards in eighteen minutes and was sent off. Back in the dressing room, he kicked and subsequently damaged a door. Mario seemed to have a permanent cloud hanging over his head: there was no end to the controversy. Every day brought something new, such as his shouldered goal against Norwich on 3 December. He received the ball from Adam Johnson and tried to jump over the Norwich keeper, who got a hand to it, sending the ball up into the air. As usual, Mario picked the unlikely solution and shouldered the ball into the back of the net. The delirious City fans almost blew off the roof while Norwich supporters were talking about deliberate provocation. When not focusing on the unpredictability of his football, the diatribes turned on his bedtime. Mario had dinner at 1 am at the Zouk Indian Restaurant in Central Manchester the night before the Chelsea game. His chicken curry resulted in newspaper headlines claiming City had introduced a curfew 48 hours before important games. Despite this, Super Mario scored against Chelsea on 12 December but the team suffered their first Premier League defeat of the season. The Blues imposed themselves for a 2-1 win. After fourteen positive results (twelve wins and two draws), the City machine was brought to a grinding halt.

Three days later, Balo was embroiled in yet another scandal. If it had been Jérôme Boateng who was on the receiving end of his anger last time, this time he ended up incurring the wrath of Micah Richards, the City defender, following a training session friendly. Fists were raised and their team-mates had to rush over to separate them. The pair made peace and Richards tweeted: 'Me and Mario are all good! Things happen in training & we shook hands. It shows passion!' But nothing could prevent the sequence of photos ending up in the newspapers. By this point, all City could do was erect new fences to keep out spies and the paparazzi.

22 January 2012 saw a home game against Tottenham. Super Mario secured the win by converting a penalty in the 95th minute. The 3-2 win was vital in the race for the title but a polemic broke out after the game. Harry Redknapp hit out. What happened? In the 84th minute, Balotelli, who had already been cautioned for a foul on Assou-Ekotto, collided with Scott Parker and appeared to deliberately stamp on his opponent's head.

The Tottenham coach said: 'Scott's got a lovely cut on his head. I'm surprised the linesman didn't see it. The first [stamp] could have been accidental, but the second one? He backheeled him straight in the head. I don't like talking about people kicking players in the head but when you see that, it's wrong.'

There was no doubt it was wrong, given that the FA gave Mario a four-match ban after reviewing the TV footage. He did not play again until 25 February when he scored at home against Blackburn and lifted up his shirt to reveal the words 'Raffaella ti amo' [Raffaella, I love you]. His love story with the Italian showgirl Raffaella Fico had begun in June 2011. Betrayals, reconciliations, angry scenes, a rumoured wedding and a pregnancy would provide months of material for the paparazzi and gossipmongers. Cynics claimed his message of love was Mario's way of asking forgiveness from Raffaella for a fling with the porn star Holly Anderson, who the tireless

British reporters had spotted at Mario's side. Flings were a constant feature in the life of the twenty-one-year-old footballer. He was caught yet again by the *Sun* coming out of the X strip club in Liverpool on the eve of the match against Bolton. The photo was published on the front page next to the time it was taken: 2.45 am. The following day, Balotelli scored City's second goal. Mancini commented: 'Mario played well. He had a lot of chances and maybe if he got more sleep he could have scored three or four goals'. The manager also chose to dish out some useful advice: 'I'm sure he understands he has made a mistake. Mario is like that, but there's nothing we can do if he does not eventually realise he cannot keep doing this. He is his own worst enemy. When you are a professional, you should know that you cannot stay out until after two o'clock in the morning so close to a game. Now he is young, but at 25 or 26 it will be different. If you do not have a good private life then you will not be able to play at the top level. Sometimes I feel a bit let down. These things will happen at his age but after a hundred times, I think he should understand what is going on around him.' He ended on a joke: 'It could be that marriage would help him.' For Mario, it was more than some advice about tying the knot and the usual lecture: his night out cost him a £250,000 fine for breaking the curfew imposed by the club.

Noel Gallagher, the former Oasis frontman and die-hard City fan, spent an hour interviewing Mario for the BBC in March. It was a chat between two naughty boys with complicated pasts and a present marked by both genius and recklessness. More than the questions and answers on a variety of issues, it was the following assertion from Gallagher that was most interesting: 'Balotelli is a modern-day rock star. He's a little bit crazy, a little bit unreliable and a little bit flamboyant.' In short, he described him as a pop icon in the best

Mancunian tradition, which has given rise to bands like The Fall, The Smiths, Joy Division, The Stone Roses, The Happy Mondays and Oasis. It mattered little that Mario did not know who they were. Gallagher described him as the perfect mix of talent and irreverence: 'Footballers in general in this country are quite boring and dull ... I love you because you make me smile.'

He certainly provided plenty of entertainment in the game against Sunderland on 31 March 2012. City lost 3-1 at home and Super Mario got into an argument with Aleksandar Kolarov about who should take a free kick. Vincent Kompany, the captain, had to drag him away amid boos from the crowd to stop the situation from worsening. Mario scored two goals and earned City a draw but Roberto Mancini was furious: 'Yes, in the end Mario scored two goals but he didn't play well. In a game like this the strikers should make the difference, but not in the last two minutes, in the minutes before.' The manager was tough on the spat with Kolarov: 'It can happen on days like this, but this is the last time.' It really did seem as if he was getting fed up with his pupil. The same could be said of the club, who informed Mario that he was at risk of being sold if a serious offer came in during the summer transfer window. A week later, it seemed as if the affair between Mario and City had come to an end once and for all. At the Emirates Stadium, he got up to yet more of his antics against Arsenal: he almost broke Alex Song's leg and then got sent off for a second bookable offence. City slid to eight points behind United in the table and the dream of winning the Premier League seemed to have vanished into thin air. The Italian manager's comments about his striker left no room for doubt: 'Balotelli has to change his attitude. I didn't see the Song tackle from the bench but now that I've seen it on TV, I can say that he should have been sent off. I am disappointed in him and I have no words for his behaviour. I love him as a guy, as a player. I know him. He's not a bad guy and is a fantastic player … I've seen players with huge talent finish in two or three years because they do not change. I hope, for him, he will. I am very disappointed in him. He continues to make a lot of mistakes. With Mario, it's always a big risk. Every time we risk one [man] being sent off. I'm finished. We have six games left and he will not play.'

The patience of the father figure, mentor and coach, who had twice placed his trust in Mario Balotelli, at Inter and at City, appeared to have run out. Mancini had tried to help the boy, who resembled him so much, to grow up, but he had not grown up and continued to do whatever he liked, with the excesses of a rock star and the madness of a cursed poet. It seemed as if the closing credits were about to roll, but this turned out not to be the case. Instead it was the umpteenth plot twist. Three days later, Mario's father figure changed his mind. 'I thought it would be a six- or seven-game ban for Mario, that's why I said he wouldn't play again this season,' Mancini said after the win against West Brom on 11 April. 'He only got three games so he will be back for the game against Manchester United.' On the eve of the most important game of the season, the Italian manager dismissed it: 'Despite some stupid things he has done, Mario has done some important things, like his double strike at Old Trafford this season. It's difficult to say if I will recall Balotelli but everyone is available and I will make my choice on Sunday. It's like a family when a child does stupid things. With him anything is possible.' It may well have been this fatherly affection, as well as the need to have one more striker to call upon in the last throes of the race for the title that caused him to cut short the punishment. The Bad Boy was back in the squad at the Etihad for the match against Manchester United on 30 April on Big Monday, the most important derby in history.

But he did not get off the bench. Thanks to a header from Vincent Kompany, City won 1-0 and went back to the top of the table, level on points with United.

Two days later, Mario was in trouble again. The British tabloids reported a violent argument between Mario and his girlfriend, Raffaella, so violent that the player was said to have called City executives, who in turn alerted the police. When the officers arrived at the house in Alderley Edge in Cheshire, they were told there had been an argument about money. They were greeted by a peaceful family scene and left. Obviously the reporters at the *Sun* were not satisfied by the official explanation and dug the knife in. Along with the other tabloids, they maintained that Mario's flings were the real reason behind the dispute. Raffaella was said to be unhappy about the revelations about Super Mario's lovers. One of these was Chloe Evans, the footballer's personal assistant, who told the *Sun* she had been with Mario for two years and peppered her story with salacious details such as the player's weakness for wearing make-up and women's clothes in their most intimate moments. The row between Raffaella and Mario had taken place on the evening of 29 April and apparently it was not the first time, although this time it was responsible for the breakdown of the couple's relationship. Already playing the role of the ex-girlfriend, Raffaella Fico was interviewed a few days later by *Chi*, an Italian weekly magazine. She offered her own version: 'I remember the police car, the cold, the confusion, the stomach cramps and an intense pain. Mario, why did you do it? Go away, go away, he kept saying. I didn't hear from him any more after that and I don't know the real reason behind his attitude. There is something serious that I can't explain.' The Neapolitan showgirl confessed that she had forgiven him for his flings and spoke about Mario's marriage proposal: 'We were supposed to get married in my home town next year.' This was not the end of the story, there was more to come …

Meanwhile, it was the penultimate day in the Premier League. City were playing away at Newcastle and, right on time, the *Sun* dug up another story about Mario with the headline: 'Mario & The Four Escorts'. This time Super Mario was said to have organised an X-rated party with four escort girls the night before the match. When the kid from Concesio claimed he was under attack from the tabloids, which wrote nothing but stupid things about him and told lies, adding that papers that put naked women on the front page were disgusting, it was hard not to understand.

13 May 2012. 3 pm and the final matches of the 2011–2012 season kicked off. Both Manchester City and Manchester United were on 86 points. City were ahead on goal difference by eight goals. United were playing away at Sunderland; City were at the Etihad against Queens Park Rangers, fourth from bottom of the table and risking relegation. It would all be decided in 90 minutes, or in 94 as it turned out.

Mario Balotelli was on the bench: he might turn out to be useful in what was 'a crazy finish to a crazy season'. Minute by minute, this is what happened on that unforgettable afternoon of football.

In the 20th minute, Man Utd took a 1-0 lead against Sunderland: Wayne Rooney headed the ball past Mignolet, giving the Red Devils the advantage in the title race.

In the 38th minute, Man City made it 1-0 over QPR: Paddy Kenny, the QPR keeper, deflected a shot from Pablo Zabaleta into his own goal. City were ahead again.

In the 45th minute, the injured Yaya Touré left the field; Nigel de Jong came on in his place.

In the 48th minute, QPR scored against City thanks to an equaliser from Djibril Cissé. The goal would have given United the Premier League title and seen QPR climb out of the relegation zone.

In the 55th minute, Joey Barton was sent off for a revenge foul on Carlos Tévez and a knee in Sergio Agüero's back. QPR were down to ten men.

In the 65th minute, QPR scored to take a 2-1 lead: Jamie Mackie headed a cross from Armand Traoré past Joe Hart. It appeared to be all over for City and QPR looked safe.

In the 69th minute, Dzeko came on for Barry.

In the 76th minute, Balotelli came on for Tévez.

In the 79th minute, Kenny parried a shot from Balotelli.

In the 84th minute, a free kick from Balotelli was blocked from Shaun Wright-Phillips and the ball was loose for a few seconds.

In the 90th minute, Mario got his head onto the end of a corner but Kenny pulled off a miraculous save.

In the 92nd minute, City equalised for 2-2 thanks to Edin Dzeko with a well-timed jump to convert the umpteenth corner. It was the second minute of injury time but it was still not enough for the title. City needed to score again.

It was the 94th minute at the Britannia Stadium and the match between Stoke and Bolton had ended 2-2. Bolton were relegated and QPR were safe.

In the 94th minute at the Stadium of Light, it was still Sunderland 0 Man Utd 1 when the final whistle blew. The Red Devils were virtual champions. Sir Alex Ferguson and the players awaited the latest news from the Etihad.

In the 94th minute, City took a 3-2 lead. Supported by Balotelli, Agüero made a run into the area. Flat out on the ground, Super Mario provided Agüero with an assist that met the Argentine in full flow: he found just the right amount of space to thread his shot through the forest of legs and beat Kenny. It was the goal that saw City take the title. United had been champions for all of thirteen seconds.

Mike Dean, the referee, eventually blew the final whistle in the 95th minute. City had won the Premier League for the first time in 44 years. Chaos ensued on the pitch and in the stands.

Mario Balotelli celebrated with a medal around his neck and the Italian flag wrapped around his shoulders.

On Monday 14 May 2012, the streets of Manchester celebrated with the biggest light-blue party the city had ever seen. The open-top bus carrying the City players crossed the city through a throng of overjoyed fans. Mario Balotelli was not part of the parade. He had flown home to the waiting Italian national team.

Chapter 19

The Hug

Once upon a time, there was a boy who didn't like dark chocolate but loved eating white chocolate. Papà Franco would buy him a bar and slip it into his bag when he went to play football. It was his magic potion, like Getafix's, brewed for Asterix, or spinach for Popeye. Whenever he felt tired or his legs began to give way, he would have a bite before running off to score lots of goals. Franco Balotelli had decided not to make the tiring journey to Warsaw to see Mario play for the national team against Germany for a place in the Euro 2012 final, but he remembered the bars of white chocolate his adoptive son loved so much. He bought a supply and entrusted them to his wife, Silvia, to take to Poland. They were a panacea, an amulet, a lucky charm and a message of love made from cocoa beans and milk.

Until 28 June 2012, Super Mario had been conspicuous by his absence. At the Euro 2012 tournament in Poland and the Ukraine, Mario had been disappointing in the first game against the World Champions, Spain, on 10 June. He had squandered a goal-scoring opportunity: in a one-on-one with Iker Casillas, he had too much time to think and ended up losing the ball to Sergio Ramos. He was cautioned before being substituted in the 57th minute for Antonio Di Natale.

In the second Group C match against Croatia in Poznań, Balotelli was once again in the starting eleven, but his mistakes in front of goal were decisive in the 1-1 draw that left

Italy in trouble. The *Azzurri* were at risk of going home. To make it to the knockout phase, they needed to beat Giovanni Trapattoni's Ireland and hope that other results in the group went their way. Balo started to feel the pressure. The paparazzi caught him out walking with a new flame. The papers accused him of failing to grow up, reporting rumours from inside a dressing room that allegedly preferred Di Natale, whether for personal or tactical reasons. Several days later, Balotelli explained the situation in a press conference: 'Even as a child, I was moved when I thought about wearing an Italy shirt. But it hasn't affected me here. I was nervous in the first few games because it was my first European Championships, but there wasn't anything wrong with me. I wasn't angry, I didn't have any problems with the team or in my private life.' Pointing to one of the journalists, he added: 'Unlike what your colleague said, I didn't have "my bum in the Nutella". I was fine. The only problem was that I wasn't scoring goals.'

Balotelli's goal would come in the decisive game against Ireland. This time, he failed to make the starting eleven; the manager picked Di Natale instead. He came on in the 29th minute of the second half amid an avalanche of boos. But in just fifteen minutes, he tore the entire Irish defence apart before his moment finally arrived in the 90th minute. Andrea Pirlo floated the ball into the box from a corner. With his back to goal, the Italian number 9, tightly marked by John O'Shea, conjured up an amazing half bicycle kick. He lent against his marker, who was trying hard to pull him over, but scored with a right-footed scissor kick. Shay Given, the Irish keeper, did not even see it. Angrily, the boy from Concesio went to give the finger and put his foot in it in the usual way, but luckily, Leonardo Bonucci came running to put his hand over Mario's mouth. Diplomatically, he told the press afterwards: 'Mario said whatever it was in English and I didn't understand.'

Mario was venting against the boos, what had been a difficult week and the pressure and accusations he had struggled to cope with. It was a goal that released the tension and began to win him credit. Commentators and the press started changing their minds, saying he was the player Cesare Prandelli's Italy team needed to move forward. To advance, they would need to beat Roy Hodgson's England in the quarter-final in Kiev on 24 June.

'It will be fun to play against my Manchester City teammates', Mario confessed to the microphones. 'I hope we win because I want to win and even though they're my teammates, I hope they lose. Milner, Hart and Barry are my friends but I'm not afraid of anyone. Hart says there are two Balotellis: one who can win a game and the other who could get sent off at any minute. He's lucky he knows two of me!' Mario relished the challenge. The Italian press listed the five factors that might help him play a great match: 1. He had broken his goal drought against Ireland; 2. He was playing against 'his England', the country in which he had just won the Premier League; 3. Defenders Terry and Lescott could cause him plenty of problems, but he knew them well; 4. He would be on the pitch with the inspirational Antonio Cassano; 5. Enock, his brother, would be watching in the stands. Even the English press were putting Mario on the front page; they could not wait to beat Italy and break the curse of the quarter-final, which had been their downfall on far too many other occasions. It was Steven Gerrard, Liverpool and England captain, who put everyone on notice: 'Balotelli is an excellent and dangerous player. We watch him week in, week out in the Premier League. We know all about him. We'll have to try to contain him.'

On 24 June 2012, Italy-England was decided on penalties. For 120 minutes, the Italian team proved superior, but thanks to an organised defence set up by Roy Hodgson, the Three Lions held firm. It finished 0-0 and came down to a penalty shoot-out. Mario, who had missed several good scoring opportunities, was the first to put the ball down on the spot, face to face with Joe Hart. After a short run-up, the ball sailed to the right of the City keeper. He had dived in the right direction, but the shot from the Italian number 9 had accuracy and power. There was nothing he could do. This was followed by mistakes from Montolivo, Young, whose shot clattered against the crossbar, and Cole, whose fourth penalty was saved by Gianluigi Buffon. Two mistakes from the English and only one from the Italians. It was up to Diamanti, who made no mistake. Italy were into the semi-final. After losing six out of seven penalty shoot-outs, England said goodbye to Euro 2012 and went home. Mario ran over like a lunatic to hug Diamanti. He had played well, but the hero of the night was Andrea Pirlo, who had the audacity to make the City keeper look slow with a leisurely chipped penalty.

The semi-final would see Italy take on Germany in a classic of European and world football. It was to be a match brimming with memories and emotions. From the famous 4-3 win in the Estadio Azteca in Mexico City in the 1970 World Cup, to the 3-1 win at Madrid's Santiago Bernabéu during the 1982 World Cup in Spain, not forgetting 4 July 2006 when Grosso and Del Piero ruined Germany's dream of playing in the World Cup final in Berlin.

It was time for a white chocolate bar. In the hours before the match, Mamma Silvia wanted to see Mario to give him a kiss and deliver the chocolate Franco had asked her to bring. But there was no way to get the gift from Concesio to him. All she could do was speak to her son by telephone. She would only see him for a brief moment in the stadium during the pre-match warm-up. But after the game, wearing his Italy tracksuit to match his mohican, Mario went over to the stands to his waiting friends and mother. Struggling to get through the crowd of people, Silvia leant over the railing: mother and son embraced for what seemed like an eternity, face to face, with kisses and tears of immense joy in a scene that moved all those watching their TVs back at home. Also moved, the bad boy with a heart of gold confessed to the TV cameras shortly afterwards: 'I told her "These goals are for you". My mother is not young any more so I had to make her happy when she came all the way here'. Signora Silvia would later explain: 'I knew how much Mario wanted to prove himself. He often tells me: "Mamma, I'm not arrogant but I feel I have something special within me." Before the Ireland game, we struggled to contact him and he wouldn't answer messages. When he feels in difficulty, under attack or betrayed, Mario reacts by clamming up. He isolates himself from others. Those two goals in such a wonderful and important match have liberated him, as his talent and the little genius inside came out. He managed to finally show what he can do. That's why I wept with joy.'

It was in the twentieth minute of the game against Germany that Mamma Silvia wept with joy. Antonio Cassano was on the receiving end of a pass from Chiellini to the left of the area. With his back to the goal, he turned like a magician and floated in a cross that pinpointed Mario. Balotelli scored! He leapt up, over a foot above Badstuber, the defender who was meant to be marking him, and, with a perfect header, the ball ended up in the top corner. Manuel Neuer, the German keeper, had been wrong-footed. Super Mario had given Italy the lead. In the 36th minute, a long, looping pass from Montolivo found Mario on-side. The Italian number 9 controlled the ball with his left foot and sprinted off. He ran into the penalty area with all the power and rage pent up in his body and unleashed a cannonball, a bolt of lightning. Neuer was on his knees. Mario scored again to make it 2-0. Super Mario took off his shirt and stood there showing off his impressive muscles before being submerged by his teammates. His mother did not approve: 'Players should always keep their shirts on out of respect,' she said later. She was also concerned about the yellow card and worried Mario would miss the final. Her son Giovanni, who had accompanied her to the stadium, explained that he would still be able to play under the new regulations. She was also worried when Mario was substituted in the 70th minute but he was not injured, Giovanni told her, they were just cramps because he had done so much running. This time he had conquered the world's front pages for the right reasons:

'Finally, a star is born. In the centre of the pitch, as arrogant as a Greek statue in a PlayStation game: the symbol of the new Italy. Super Mario Balotelli, the dream boy,' wrote the *Gazzetta dello Sport* in its editorial. There was no doubt that the bad boy had become a hero for millions of Italians. It had taken less than two years, in only his thirteenth match in the royal blue shirt. The story of Mario and the national team had got off to a late start. Balotelli was dreaming about the World Cup as far back as March 2010.

'I'll bet you a dinner that I'll go. If I'm called up, you have to buy me three dinners. If we win the World Cup, I'll buy you 40, however many you want, all year!' he joked with an interviewer on the *Iene* TV show on Italia 1. Imagine how he must have felt on 11 May 2010 when Marcello Lippi, the national team coach, released the list of the 30 players pre-selected for South Africa. Balotelli's name was nowhere to be seen; Lippi had placed his trust in the old guard, in those who had won the World Cup in Germany four years earlier. There were plenty who supported Mario's inclusion in the team: teammates, pundits, fans (not only Inter fans), the football press and authorities such as Arrigo Sacchi, who believed: 'Mario is a unique talent. In a positive context, if he is well-managed, he could bring added value. He is a good kid. He doesn't always behave with maturity but he isn't someone who would disturb the harmony of the dressing room or the game. It's a gamble but one without downsides. Think about it, Marcello.'

Marcello did not think about it at all. He did not call Mario up to play for Italy, nor for the pre-tournament friendlies. Three years later, he would justify his choice: 'I didn't think he deserved to be called up because he wasn't playing for his club team. They would often punish him or make him play for the Under-21s and he was a troublemaker. Why should he have been rewarded?'

For Lippi and the players, South Africa was a debacle. Marcello was forced to hand over to Cesare Prandelli. The former Parma, Roma and Fiorentina manager was a breath of fresh air. When he first took over on 6 August 2010, he brought eight new faces into the group. Mario Balotelli was one of them. Mario made his debut for the senior national team at the Upton Park Boleyn Ground in London on 10 August. It was only a friendly against the Ivory Coast and Italy lost 1-0 thanks to a goal from Kolo Touré, but he had made a good first impression. On a rainy night in London, Balotelli did not disappoint the thousands of Italian fans who had travelled to the West Ham stadium. In the 59 minutes he spent on the pitch, he showed both skill and personality that were convincing. Prandelli said: 'It was his first match. We wanted him with us and he showed things that were interesting in certain situations.' Test satisfactorily passed.

Mario's second outing in a royal blue shirt came on 17 November in Klagenfurt, another friendly against Romania. It was a rough night. The boos started as soon as he touched the ball. They came predominantly from the section of the stands occupied by Romanian fans, but also from elsewhere. A hundred or so Italian extremists from the Ultras Italia group did not give Mario as much as a minute's peace. While the Italian national anthem was being played, they performed the fascist salute and shouted: 'There's no such thing as a black Italian' and 'Italy for the Italians'. The message for Mario and Cristian Ledesma, the Lazio midfielder of Argentine extraction, who had received his first call-up from Prandelli, was clear. Still not content, half an hour into the second half, the fascists held up a sign, removed after only a few minutes, which read 'No to a multi-ethnic nation'. Oddly enough, the match was being played in the name of solidarity (the Romanian federation had unfurled a banner to raise awareness of the fight against racism and intolerance towards the Romani people), yet no one intervened to bring an end to the racist chanting. The Italian extremists were not identified by the police until after the match and only after three years of investigation were seventeen of them charged with 'the dissemination of ideas based on superiority, discrimination and racial or ethnic hatred'. Balotelli did not allow himself to be intimidated. He played on and did not react as he had done in exasperation on other occasions. At the end of the match, he commented: 'I don't know these people. I can only say that where I live in Brescia, a multi-ethnic Italy already exists. Perhaps those people haven't noticed, but now that I'm playing in England, I would like to see people talking about these issues in our country. People should face up to racism rather than discussing my girlfriends.' He added: 'This time I behaved well and no one can say that I provoked it. Judge for yourselves … the worst thing you can do to a person who insults you is to ignore them. Indifference. I have learnt with time, but I'm still angry and bitter.'

The following day, Gianni Mura wrote the following in *La Repubblica*: 'Bravo Balotelli, not so much for how he played (one of the least bad, anyway) but for how he endured such a hateful and unacceptable situation […] One may wonder whether such a situation is too heavy for such a young man […] We must also question whose words will protect Balotelli. The captain (a boy himself) or even Prandelli could have asked for silence […] It is now time for everyone, starting with Abete, to start worrying about the dignity of our national team. This does not mean winning matches but silencing supporters of which every civilised country would be ashamed.' Cesare Prandelli, who had hugged Mario when he substituted him, said: 'If something like this happens again, we will make a powerful symbolic gesture. We will all hug him.' The idea would never be put into practice but the boos and racist chants against Balotelli continued, whether he was playing for the national team or his club side.

Mario would not play for the national team again until the friendly against Spain on 10 August 2011. He was not called up for the matches against Slovenia and the Ukraine in March. Prandelli had applied his code of ethics to the letter, Balotelli having broken it with that savage challenge against Dynamo Kiev in the Europa League. In the match against Vicente del Bosque's Spain, he would not appear until the 59th minute. This pattern was repeated in the two subsequent Euro 2012 qualifying games. On 2 September against the Faroe Islands, he came on in the 83rd minute, and in the 76th minute against Slovenia. There were two points to be made. One was that during the match against the Faroe Islands, Prandelli had lost his patience because, according to dressing room rumours, Mario had turned up to the bench with his iPad. Secondly, Italy's 1-0 win against Slovenia had earned them qualification to Euro 2012. Mario's role had been far from decisive: he had only played in chunks of the matches and had not yet scored. He put this right on 11 November 2011 against Poland in Wroclaw. After the match, the *Gazzetta dello Sport* ran with the headline: 'Balotelli Number 1. Magical Applause and his First Goal for Italy.' In the 30th minute, Marchisio picked up the ball in the midfield and found Balotelli with a pass. Lifting his head, he saw the keeper off his line and unveiled a magical piece of skill. From thirty yards out, he found his target and sent up a right-footed lob that slipped under the crossbar, tricking Wojciech Szczesny, Arsenal's Polish goalkeeper. He then lifted up his royal blue shirt and kissed the shield two or three times before being overwhelmed by his teammates. It had been both a convincing goal and a convincing match. Everyone believed the bad boy, the hopeless and unmanageable footballer, had grown up. All that was needed now was to sit back and wait for the first black Italian to score in an Italy shirt to do even better at the European Championships.

And that was indeed what happened. Super Mario helped the Italians forget about the *Scommessopoli* football betting scandal that had even seen the Guardia di Finanza finance police turn up at the Coverciano training camp to investigate some of the players. Prandelli would later say: 'If you told us for the good of football we should not participate, it wouldn't be a problem for me.' The Italian Prime Minister, Mario Monti, suggested that professional football in Italy would benefit from a break of 'two to three years'.

This was all forgotten after Balotelli's two goals against

Germany. Completely forgotten. Italy was as moved as its number 9, who told the Rai microphones: 'This was the greatest night of my life and I hope Sunday will be even better. Papà Franco will be there for the final and I hope to score four goals this time, not two.'

On Sunday 1 July 2012, it would be Spain who scored four goals. And it could have been so many more that Iker Casillas, the Spanish captain, even asked the assistant referee to take pity and signal the end of the game out of respect for the Italians, closing the door on a match that had been nothing but a nightmare for the *Azzurri*. Mario Balotelli, who had played the full ninety minutes and not been one of the worst, burst into tears. Tears streamed down his face as Cesare Prandelli tried to console him with a hug. He had still scored three goals, won a runners-up medal and been given a spot in the Team of the Tournament alongside Cristiano Ronaldo and Ibrahimovic, but it was not enough to fulfil the dreams of a boy with a weakness for white chocolate.

Chapter 20

Balo is Back

In mid-November, he blurted out: 'I like Balotelli! Here I am!' In early December, he swore he was not spending his nights dreaming about him and that there were no negotiations taking place. In early January, he exclaimed that he was not convinced by Balotelli as a person. On 7 January, he used a fruit metaphor while being interviewed as a guest on the Antenna 3 TV Show *Lunedì di Rigore*. 'I'm sorry to say it, but a person's human side is very important at AC Milan. If you put a rotten apple into the dressing room, as they say, it might infect all the others. So, as I have to pass judgement on Balotelli the man, he's someone I would never accept within the Milan dressing room.' In late 2012 and early 2013, Silvio Berlusconi, honorary president of AC Milan and leader of the Polo delle Libertà political party, was prodded by journalists to have his say on Mario Balotelli time and time again. He weighed in heavily, then apologised, denying he was referring to Balotelli and that he had been speaking 'about the need for positive presence in the dressing room'. He added: 'I have never heard anything from anyone at my club about opening negotiations for Balotelli.' He reiterated this position on 24 January. When asked about the possible signing of Kaká and Balotelli, he replied curtly: 'Neither. It's not possible in the current climate.' Five days later, on 29 January 2013, AC Milan announced the signing of Mario Balotelli.

Whether motivated by football or politics – the Italian parliamentary elections were just around the corner on 24 and 25 February – Berlusconi backtracked. He also denied any investment in the election, although many maintained that the signing of Balotelli could lead to as much as a 2 per cent voting swing in favour of the Polo delle Libertà party. Berlusconi forgot that Balotelli did not convince him as a man or a person, a negative judgement that was most likely linked to his exploits off the pitch: namely, Raffaella Fico and Sara Tommasi. Fico, the Neapolitan showgirl and Mario's ex-girlfriend, attended the 'elegant dinners' held at Berlusconi's Arcore home and the former prime minister knew her personally. He also knew Sara Tommasi, another dancer who allegedly had a relationship with Balotelli. When the tantalising details of the evenings at Arcore first began to surface in the press, coining the term 'bunga bunga parties', Mario supposedly sent intercepted text messages to Sara Tommasi asking: 'Are you involved in the Berlusconi mess as well? If you are, I don't want you.'

It was water under the bridge. Any doubts the honorary president of AC Milan had about the national team striker seemed to vanish. He welcomed the club's new signing with the words: 'He is undoubtedly a quality player. He will be good for the team and AC Milan will be good for him.'

Super Mario landed at Milan Malpensa airport at 4.40 pm on 30 January 2013. Wearing jeans, a white hoodie and a black baseball cap on backwards, he walked down the steps of the private jet behind Adriano Galliani, vice president of AC Milan. They immediately tied a red and black scarf around his neck before taking his first pictures in the number 45 shirt. Mario said to the AC Milan TV channel: 'I've wanted to play for Milan for a long time. I was playing for other teams and I couldn't come here but now I had the chance and I ran.' Galliani, as it is customary to say on such occasions, confirmed: 'It's a dream come true, something we and the fans all wanted, with President Berlusconi at the forefront. We worked so hard and we've finally succeeded in signing him.'

It had been a complex, difficult and costly process: to see him in the famous red and black-striped shirt, the Milanese club would have to fork out €20 million plus €3 million in bonuses depending on the team's results, payable to Manchester City for the five years of his contract, due to expire on 30 June 2017. Mario would earn €4 million a season. The boy from Concesio's first day with AC Milan would be spent at medicals and shaking hands, before concluding with a dinner at the Da Giannino restaurant in the city centre. Five hundred fans were camped outside. The hardcore *Rossoneri* supporters unveiled a series of chants: 'If you jump up and down, Balotelli will score', 'He threw that shitty [Inter] shirt on the ground', 'Now you're at Milan, it's a dream come true for us', 'You score the best goals. We'll win with Mario Balotelli', and finally, 'If you don't jump up and down you're a *Nerazzurro*'. Super Mario came out to greet them and was submerged by chants and hugs. The celebrations got so out of hand that the police had to intervene to quell the riot that was threatening to break out on the pavement.

But it was not only AC Milan's fans that were happy. Milan had pulled off the return of the national team's striker; Italy's biggest footballing asset was back to enhance Serie A and the country's press, radio and TV channels were delighted. 'Balo is Back', read the title in the *Gazzetta dello Sport*. The only dissenting voice was that of *Il Manifesto*: the caption beneath a photo of Mario read: 'Kicked into Misery', followed by a comment that 'Berlusconi is playing a political card, buying Balotelli for 20 million while the figures betray about a 75 per cent cut in social policies.'

The official unveiling of the new signing took place with much jubilation in the San Siro's executive suite on 1 February 2013. Next to Galliani, wearing the club uniform of a black jacket, black tie, white shirt and the red and black crest, a timid Balotelli answered reporters' questions. 'Coming back to Milan was important to me, to be near my family and friends,' he explained. When a journalist from Rai 1 news asked him if he was offended by Berlusconi describing him as a rotten apple, he clarified: 'I didn't hear about it in England. I was only told about it after my agent had already talked about it and the president had already apologised so I'm not able to answer. I'm sorry.' Galliani took care of replying for him: 'The president did not apologise. The president explained that he had never said that.' 'I didn't know', Mario added. The Milan vice president gave him a friendly pat on the arm and continued: 'No, you don't know but I do. I'm older than you are and I understand the meaning of the questions.' He then turned to the journalist and insisted scornfully: 'Please address your questions to me, Madam. You'll see that I will answer them properly.'

Mario was on the receiving end of another question about Berlusconi: 'Have you ever voted?' 'I've never voted and I'm not interested in politics,' he replied. Inter was yet another controversial subject. The derby against Milan's blue and black cross-city rivals was scheduled for 24 February 2013. Would Mario celebrate if he scored? 'Yes, of course. The Inter fans will whistle at me of course, but it happens in football and I don't think they will still be angry with me …' They may not have been angry but there still seemed to be a bone of contention, judging by Inter president, Massimo Moratti's cutting comments on Milan's new signing: 'It's useful to Berlusconi for thousands of reasons. There are no regrets on our part. It's a good purchase but not one we could make because he had already been with us.'

Representatives from the British press curious to know whether Mario had any regrets about leaving England also livened up the press conference. No, he didn't have any. When it came to good memories, he mentioned his teammates, the Carrington ground, training sessions, the manager and fans. He said English football was wonderful, ahead of Italian football in terms of its stadiums, crowds and passion. Everything else was negative, starting with the press and continuing with the weather, food and driving on the left. There was no shortage of controversy when a journalist from the *Sun* asked him a question and he refused to answer: 'Your newspaper always talked badly about me,' he said drily.

At the San Siro, Mario said little about his nine hundred days in English football, but before leaving for Italy, he had given a long interview to the official Manchester City website: 'I said goodbye to everyone at the meal in London before the game at Queens Park Rangers. It was very emotional for me,' he confessed. 'I spoke with Roberto [Mancini] before I went to speak to the players. We spoke for some time about lots of things. He was sad and I was too. But it was a good conversation. I love Roberto, he has been very important for my career, and I will always thank him for having trust and faith in me. Being at City was an important part of my life and career. I needed to grow up like a player and as a person and it has been a very good experience for me. I think to win the Premier League was a very special moment, and I am proud to have been a part of that. I hope that City can win the league again this year and beat United. I think there are great players at the club and a great manager too. The club will be very successful in the future and that makes me happy.'

This came after 80 games in the light-blue shirt, 30 goals, FA Cup, Premier League and Community Shield trophies and a disastrous 2012–2013 season that had seen him score only one goal in fourteen Premier League appearances and two in six appearances in FA Cup and European games. And that was not counting all the arguments and polemics. Mario's final season at City had begun auspiciously enough. Everyone imagined that after his first 'shit season' and a reasonable second year, he would continue in the same vein as he had demonstrated in Euro 2012 in Poland and the Ukraine. Mancini was convinced Mario had turned a corner after his two goals against Germany. He was ready to turn from a good player into a great player. He reiterated: 'I really don't think he will leave even if lots of big clubs want him. This is a sign that he is a top player. The City fans love him and the club has never thought of depriving themselves of him.'

But things did not go as many had hoped. In July, Balo ended up on the front pages of the British tabloids. He was on holiday in Saint Tropez, snapped with his shirt off drinking champagne and smoking a hookah pipe while being massaged by a mystery blonde. The season began and Mario missed the Community Shield on 12 August. City dictated the play and beat Roberto di Matteo's Chelsea 3-2. On 15 August, he also missed the friendly between Italy and England. Both absences were down to a problem with his eyes that had been bothering him for a while. He had worn contact lenses for years but prolonged use had resulted in an allergy and painful conjunctivitis. On 4 September, he had laser surgery in Brescia to cure his short-sightedness. When he made his return against Stoke City on 15 September, all the newspapers could talk about was the €100,000 Porsche convertible Mario was said to have bought for his brother Enock. Few mentioned the racist insults he had received from a fan. Spotted by the TV cameras, the perpetrator, who called Mario a monkey, was fined and banned from all football grounds for three years. On 18 September, Mario was in the stands for the first Champions League game against Real Madrid at the Bernabéu. He was not fit and Mancini decided not to play him. He only played for five minutes against Arsenal in the Premier League on 23 September. On the way back to the dressing room, he asked for an explanation from the manager, who shoved him away. Mancini later said: 'I don't know what happened after the game. I don't know if he's asked me something but it's not important. Mario probably thinks it was important. I don't know. I'll ask him next time I see him.'

Balotelli's first goal of the season came two days later against Aston Villa in the third round of the League Cup. He opened the scoring in the 27th minute but Villa came back and went on to win 4-2 after extra time. The League Cup was not a priority for City but elimination in the early rounds was not good for morale. The second goal of the season for the Light Blues' number 45 came in the Champions League on 3 October in a first leg game against Jurgen Klopp's Borussia Dortmund. This time Mario's goal counted: he came on for Clichy nine minutes from time with City a goal down. In the 90th minute, he converted a penalty that earned his team a draw and a vital point. Along with Joe Hart, who had made a raft of saves, he was the hero of the night. The statistics would show that this had been his eleventh penalty in official competition and he had not missed a single one. It seemed as if he had been resurrected. It seemed as if the boy was back on track and fully aware of his duty: 'I realised I was throwing myself away. I have to work harder and sacrifice myself for others,' he confessed.

But it was an illusion. Mancini used him sparingly, he failed to score and the discontent increased. So much so that the manager and striker treated everyone to another sideshow on 5 November. In the 69th minute of the match against West Ham, Mancini called Mario back to the bench. Mario stared at him and, according to spies at the *Daily Star*, added some spice to his look with a 'F*** you'. The manager explained during the press conference: 'He was disappointed about the missed goal, not about the substitution.' Balo had made all sorts of mistakes. He finally hit the target on 28 November when he scored his first Premier League goal of the season against Wigan. This satisfaction was short-lived when City lost 1-0 to Borussia Dortmund on 4 December and were dumped out of Europe. Fourth in Group C with only three points and no wins from six games, they were eliminated from the Champions League and failed even to qualify for the Europa League. It was a harsh blow to Mancini & Co's dreams. Despite the titles, the Italian manager's bench was beginning to teeter. He needed to regain the Premier League to be sure of his job. He needed a win in the derby against United on 9 December. On this occasion, he did place his trust in Balotelli, from the first minute of the game. But the number 45 failed to take the bait. He had no bearing on the game and was taken off for Tévez at the start of the second half. Robin van Persie, the Dutch player Mancini was said to have wanted but who had eventually chosen to leave Arsenal for United, gave Sir Alex Ferguson the win in the 94th minute. The Red Devils opened up a six point lead over City at the top of the table. For City, it had been their first home defeat in the Premier League since the 2-1 loss to Everton in December 2010.

It was a rough time for the team and for Balotelli who, officially unwell, failed to make an appearance in the next four games. The boy still had plenty of fish to fry, both on and off the pitch. The British press were talking about an imminent farewell. They claimed that the heavyweights in the dressing room and some of the coaching team considered Balo's presence a disruptive influence. This said nothing of the club's executives, who found themselves faced with a legal action brought by the striker. Mario was suing City with regard to the huge €420,000 fine the club had imposed on him for his bad behaviour on and off the pitch during the previous season. On 19 December, when Mario withdrew the action and accepted the sanction, Mancini applauded: 'It's normal that when someone makes a mistake, they take responsibility and Mario has done that. He will have other opportunities.'

Personal affairs would not be resolved so easily. On 5 December, Raffaella Fico gave birth to Pia, a daughter from her relationship with Mario. A few weeks later, she did not hold back in an interview with the weekly *Chi* magazine that also came out on 19 December: 'Mario is irresponsible. At a certain point, he was no longer interested in anything, in me or our daughter,' she stated. She said: 'He hung up when I told him she'd been born', telling anyone who would listen that she would get a DNA test to prove to everyone that Pia was Mario's child, but that she would bring her up without help from her former flame. Balotelli took action, announcing in a statement that he had 'instructed his lawyers to take all appropriate legal action to defend my integrity against false statements made by Raffaella Fico'. Franco and Silvia Balotelli got involved in the saga with an open letter to Raffaella published in the *Gazzetta dello Sport* on 27 December 2012. Theirs was an impassioned plea that ended with: 'Mario, or anyone else in his position, would perhaps be by your side if you had understood in time that LOVE is worth much more than MONEY and FAME.'

Christmas and New Year were a busy time in the Balotelli household. On 3 January came another episode in the soap opera. This time it had a footballing flavour. During a rainy training session at the Carrington Centre, Mario went hard into a challenge on his teammate, Scott Sinclair. Mancini called him over and shouted at him to apologise. Mario shook his head. The manager, who had always had a fiery temper, lost his patience, walked over to him and grabbed him by his red bib. The disagreement worsened. Brian Kidd, a City staff member, separated the two adversaries and Angelo Gregucci, one of Mancini's assistants, led the player away. The scene ended up in all the papers with a series of photographs that spoke volumes. The English press blamed Mancini for the incident. The *Daily Mail* and the *Sun* dubbed him 'Madcini', while the *Star* called him a lunatic and added: 'You've gone too far this time boss.' Mario sped away from the Carrington Centre in his Bentley, not before – according to some eye witnesses – shouting: 'I'm done with City.' Two days later, Mancini tried to calm the waters, explaining: 'The photos made it look worse. I lost my temper for three or four seconds. This is what happened, nothing special. I will give Mario another 100 chances if I think he can change. He's 22 and he can make mistakes.' That chance arrived in an FA Cup game on 5 January against Gianfranco Zola's Watford. After a 27-day absence, Balotelli came on for Dzeko. He played the last twenty minutes, was applauded by the crowd, failed to score from a cross from Silva but played his part in the 3-0 result. It seemed as if Mancini and Balotelli had made peace. But the match against Watford was to be Mario's penultimate match in City colours. On 13 January, he came on in the last five minutes of the Premier League game against Arsenal, sporting a new look, platinum blonde hair. This was to be the end of his first adventure in England.

Just after touching down in Italy, the message from Mario was loud and clear: 'I didn't start the season well with City. I've come here to do well and reinvent myself as a key player.'

Chapter 21

Bye Bye Italy

Five hundred and sixty-eight days in a red and black shirt: 54 appearances and 30 goals but no titles before Super Mario boarded the plane back to England. A year and a half, one Confederation Cup and one World Cup before Mario regretted coming back to Italy and packed his bags again. These nineteen months were filled with goals, gossip, racism, Twitter, Instagram, controversy, red cards, great expectations and great disappointments. The period between February 2013 and August 2014 is best reviewed month by month.

February 2013

'Balotelli, You're Unique', 'Balotelli, the Cyclone', 'Record-breaking Balotelli', 'Balotelli Always Scores': the sports newspapers were running out of superlatives. The boy from Concesio scored four goals in his first three games for AC Milan. On 3 February, against Udinese at the San Siro, the 23rd league fixture of the season, he was supposed to start on the bench and come on mid-way through the game, but Giampaolo Pazzini picked up an injury during the warm-up and Mario had to step up. After 25 minutes, the number 45 scored with a left-footed shot to give Milan the lead. Udinese equalised but Mario secured the win from the spot a few minutes before the final whistle. A player had not scored twice on making his debut in a red and black shirt since 'The Panther', Giancarlo Danova, on 16 February 1958. Even

Berlusconi was excited by the performance of his former 'rotten apple'. Mario found the net in the next two matches against Cagliari and Parma, with a penalty in the Sardinian Sant'Elia ground and a rocket of a free kick against Parma's *Gialloblù*. He had the wind in his sails. It seemed as if Super Mario had finally found his niche in the team he had supported since boyhood, the team whose shirt he had tried on for size while at Inter, the team he had always dreamt of playing for. The fans were so devoted to him that in just three days Milan sold 2,000 shirts with his name on, more than those they had shifted on signing Ronaldo, Ronaldinho and Ibrahimovic. Having spent so much time on the bench at City, Mario reclaimed his first team place in a youthful strike force formed by Niang and El Shaarawy, with little more than sixty years of age between them. Milan were a team who had cleared out their old guard (Gattuso, Inzaghi, Pirlo, Nesta, Zambrotta and Seedorf), focusing instead on a renewal built on young talent. Managed by Massimiliano Allegri, the club had its sights set on third place and qualification for next season's Champions League. Twelve points behind Juventus, the Serie A title was a mirage.

Derby day fell on 24 February; Balo was to renew his acquaintance with his former club, teammates and the fans who had never forgotten that he had thrown his shirt on the pitch at the San Siro. The orchestrators of Inter *ultras* distributed leaflets asking supporters to whistle at the 'traitor' Balotelli, but to avoid any chanting or expressions that invoked racial discrimination. The fans in the Meazza took little notice. Two huge inflatable bananas appeared in the stands, accompanied by the usual boos. Not to mention banners displaying jibes such as: 'Balotelli, You're Just a Shitty *Milanista*'. Mario reacted, desperately trying to score a goal that he was denied by Samir Handanovic, the Inter keeper.

He then lifted his finger to his lips in a bid to silence the crowd and, at the end of the game, aimed a somewhat inelegant 'salute' in their direction. He was fined €10,000 for 'directing an insulting gesture towards supporters of the opposing team'. Inter received a considerably heavier sanction: €50,000 for the racist chanting and banners.

March 2013

On 21 March, Italy played Brazil in a glittering friendly in Geneva. Balotelli–Neymar was the most anticipated clash between two great players who got on well and were set to take centre stage at the forthcoming Confederation Cup and World Cup. On the night, the Italian won. At the end of the first half, Italy found themselves two goals down. Mario dragged them back to a draw. He scored the goal to make it 2-2 with a lob from outside the area and, if it had not been for Julio Cesar's prowess, he would also have got the winner. Balo hit a run of form in the league, scoring three goals in two games: a penalty against Genoa and two strikes against Palermo on 17 March. This increased to seven goals from six games, in which not only did he score but he was also the best player on the pitch. In less than two months, he had become one of Milan's leading players and was a happy boy. 'Am I in love? Yes, but I am not good at talking about it. I'm shy,' he confessed to *Vanity Fair*. He explained that he had met Fanny Neguesha – a 22-year-old model and dancer born in Vicenza to an Italian father and a mother who was half Congolese half Rwandan – in Brussels while he was still playing for City. 'Fanny is determined, confident and generous. In a short space of time, she found herself in sync with me. I could spend my whole life with someone like her. Thanks to Fanny, I have rediscovered the balance I needed in my work,' Mario admitted.

April 2013

Between Pope Francis, Mario Draghi – the President of the European Central Bank –Michelle Obama and LeBron James: Balotelli's name was there, one of the world's one hundred most influential people according to *Time Magazine*. Only Malala Yousafzai, the Pakistani activist, who survived being shot by the Taliban and future Nobel Prize winner, was younger than Mario. The news was officially announced on 18 April. For the American magazine, which had already dedicated a front cover to the boy from Concesio with the title 'The Meaning of Mario' in November 2012, he was an icon, a positive role model. Gianfranco Zola was asked to explain why the Milan number 45 was in the top one hundred, and he wrote: 'Mario has all the qualities to be a top player: power and athleticism, alongside a good understanding of the game – all positive. I worked with Mario for a short period with Italy's Under-21 side. I liked him straightaway. I liked the way he handled himself and his composure and calmness in situations. Mario could shrug off things happening around him. Only the big players have that calm. Mario can play the big games and handle the crucial moments, but he needs to keep control. That is vital for him. From afar, people may think he's a madman, but he isn't. Mario is a lovely guy, very humble and very funny. I can assure people he has always been a pleasure to deal with. He has returned to Italy from England and is the main man with lots of attention. Now he has to ensure he keeps control and keeps focus. Mario loves the pressure, but to succeed, it is about finding balance.' This was not easy given that he was often, all too often, targeted in Italian stadiums. It happened on 7 April in Florence with more racist chanting aimed at Mario and Kevin-Prince Boateng. After losing his rag, Mario pointed it out to the referee, Tagliavento, and threatened to walk off the pitch if it continued, but Tagliavento failed to intervene and cautioned him for protesting instead. That was not an end to the matter. After the final whistle, the number 45 had words with Emiliano Viviano, Fiorentina's goalkeeper. Doveri, the line judge, was watching the scene. Balotelli was far from happy and shouted 'What the f*** are you looking at, idiot?' It got him a three-match ban, which was later reduced to two. The *Rossoneri's* newest star missed the games against Napoli and Juventus. He made his return against Catania on 28 April but skipped the *Time* awards ceremony in New York to be there. He scored from the penalty spot but was also booked. After the game, he vented: 'Referees aren't fair on me. I always get fouled a hundred times and they don't whistle. If I protest, I get cautioned straight away.'

May 2013

The worst happened at the San Siro against Roma on Sunday 12 May. Roma's fans were relentless in their abuse of Milan's black players: Mario, Muntari and Boateng. They were so insistent with their chanting and ululating that, in the second minute of the second half, the referee, Gianluca Rocchi, suspended the match for a minute and a half. It was an unusual and brave decision that worked. The racists, who had mocked Mario's gestures for them to be quiet and repeatedly defied appeals from the loudspeaker, went silent. The sport's governing body punished Roma with a €50,000 fine while the referee's decision was a topic for discussion in all quarters. Cesare Prandelli, the Italy manager, maintained that Balotelli was not the problem, and urged referees to suspend matches to bring an end to these episodes. Allegri, the AC Milan coach, shared this opinion: 'To get rid of this stuff in our stadiums, you have to make big decisions. It may well penalise some people but in the long run it would help us to grow as a nation and become more civilised.' In an interview in English with CNN, Mario explained: 'I always said that if racism happened in the stadium, I will just do like, "nobody says nothing and I don't care". But this time I think I've changed my mind a little bit. If it's going to happen one more time, then I'm going to leave the pitch because it's so stupid.'

The final game of the season was played on 19 May: Milan were away to Siena. It was a crazy game that generated endless controversy over one penalty that was awarded and another that was denied, allowing Milan to grab third place and European qualification. Balotelli scored the equaliser from the penalty spot in the 37th minute to top off a positive assessment of his first fourth months as an AC Milan player: twelve goals in thirteen league games. Milan's celebrations on having accomplished their mission were marred by what happened after the match. At Florence's Campo di Marte station, thirty Fiorentina *ultras* lay in wait for the AC Milan coach on its way home from Siena, greeting it with shouts of 'Thieves!' This was of course accompanied by racist ululating aimed at Robinho and Balotelli. A furious Mario tried to react but he was restrained by AC Milan staff. He later wrote on Twitter: 'This rule about racist booing needs to be changed. If I walk off the pitch I'm going to leave my team with ten men. Please, it's inhuman.'

Matteo Renzi, Mayor of Florence at the time and now Prime Minister of Italy, phoned Mario to apologise for the offence caused by his fellow citizens. But this was not an end to the matter: on 20 May, while the league's outstanding fixtures were being completed elsewhere, Roma and Inter fans taunted Mario with insults even though he was not on the pitch. May was a month that ended in further controversy. Armando De Rosa, a former Neapolitan Camorra *mafioso* turned informant, claimed that as a joke Mario Balotelli had supposedly tried his hand at selling drugs in the city's run-down Scampia district during a stay in Naples in June 2010. An incensed Mario took to Twitter: 'Ah, so now I'm a drug dealer [...] You should be ashamed. You're using my name to publicise yourself.' He later deleted the message and told reporters at the national team training camp: 'I hate drugs and I have nothing to do with them. What this person said was an unbelievable lie. I understand that not everyone likes me but there's no need to exaggerate. I don't know how these people can get people into trouble. It shouldn't be allowed.'

June 2013

Mario had waited a year to play Spain. He had even written on his Facebook page that revenge was a dish best served cold, a reference to the humiliation the Spanish team had inflicted on the *Azzurri* in the final of Euro 2012. But when the time came, 27 June in the semi-final of the Confederations Cup, Mario was unable to play. He limped off the pitch after their 4-2 loss to Brazil. The medical report stated that he had pulled his left quadriceps. Sadly, Mario and his girlfriend Fanny left Fortaleza on 25 June and flew home. His Brazilian Confederation Cup had lasted only three games. Two wins (against Mexico and Japan) and a defeat to Neymar's Brazil. Two goals: one from the penalty spot against Mexico a second against Brazil.

July 2013

Mario went on holiday to Mykonos, alone, filling his days with the beach, pool and quad bikes. He had plenty of lady friends for company. The paparazzi snapped him on a lounger holding a cigarette; the gossip magazines alluded to a crisis between him and Fanny.

August 2013

On 16 May, Mario had launched his Twitter account *@final-lymario* with a 'Hey there! Here I am with Lucky', accompanied by a selfie with his dog, Lucky. In less than five hours he had 100,000 followers; by the end of his time at AC Milan, he would have 2.8 million. He had become a social media star who never stopped tweeting. On 9 August, he wrote: 'Finally my little pig has arrived. She's only two months old. She's a she but I've called her Super!' posted with a photo of his new piglet mascot asleep on his knee. On 12 August, he posted images of his house, including a life-size statue depicting him playing for Italy and a water feature with the letters MB 45 picked out in gold mosaic. On 14 August, he wrote 'Thank you Pope Francis with all my heart for those five minutes', posting a photo of him shaking the Pope's hand. Mario had a brief private meeting with the Holy Father as part of an audience alongside other Italy team members and Argentina players. Woe betide anyone who revealed the contents of their discussion: 'Journalists, don't try to guess or write about what I said to the Pope,' he added, also on Twitter. Mario did not figure in the Italy team that faced Argentina in a friendly at the Stadio Olimpico in Rome: he was still recovering from his injury. His 2013–2014 season began in Eindhoven on 20 August in a Champions League play-off against PSV. The game ended 1-1; Mario's form was not great but he was the best player on the pitch. He played his first league game four days later in Verona against Hellas. The city's Northern League mayor, Flavio Tosi, welcomed him with the words: 'If only Balotelli would be less provocative. He is very good at making himself disliked.' The number 45 replied with two tweets: 'People of Verona, I am a BRESCIAN!!! Please applaud.' When AC Milan asked him about the message that had added fuel to the fire, Mario simply replied: 'I did it because the rivalry means a lot to my friends.' He failed to score in the Bentegodi Stadium and Hellas Verona won 2-1. The number 45 regained his form in the second leg of the Champions League play-off on 28 August, scoring to help the *Rossoneri* to a 3-0 victory over PSV.

September 2013

In the second Serie A fixture of the season, Milan played Cagliari at the San Siro. A belter that flew in just beneath the crossbar was to be Mario's first league goal of the season. On 8 September, he made an unforgivable gaffe in Turin: he overslept and missed the national team's meeting with Cécile Kyenge, Minister for Integration, apologising afterwards by text. Two days later, on 10 September, he made a clutch of mistakes but scored the winning goal from the penalty spot in the World Cup qualifier against the Czech Republic. Italy qualified for Brazil with two games in hand. Still in Turin, he scored again, this time from eleven yards out against Torino. The positive run came to an end against Napoli at the San Siro on 22 September. Mario's penalty was saved by Pepe Reina, Napoli's Spanish goalkeeper (it was his first miss in 21 consecutive spot kicks). He scored a fantastic goal in injury time to pull one back but then got sent off as the game ended 2-1 to Napoli. When he saw the red card, he lost his head and threatened the referee, Luca Banti from Livorno. He received a three-match ban. AC Milan decided not to appeal. Allegri said: 'Balotelli has made a mistake. He has penalised everyone, the team, the club and the fans. Mario is not a child, he is 23-years-old and to be a champion you have to have a different attitude. Mario has to grow up. I hope for him he benefits from it and doesn't make any more mistakes in his career.' Four days later, like so many other times, the striker took responsibility. Mario told Sky

Sports: 'I'm sorry, particularly for my teammates. They train and work hard with me every day and I've left them alone. I'm also sorry to the fans and the club. I also apologise to the referee. There is one thing I don't get: if I commit a bad foul, I get punished but if someone else commits a bad foul on me, then he should also be punished. I don't need to apologise to everybody because it's not like I killed anybody.'

October 2013

His three-match league ban saw him miss games against Bologna, Sampdoria and Juventus but he did play in the Champions League against Ajax in Amsterdam on 1 October. Milan's saviour on the night, he won a non-existent penalty in the 94th minute and scored the equaliser. The 45,000 Dutch fans would not stop whistling. Frank de Boer, the Ajax manager, remarked: 'Balotelli delivered a knock-out blow.' In the next Champions League game against Barcelona, Mario failed to start. He had fitness issues and, after coming on as a substitute, made no impact on the final result, a draw that saw Milan advance to the second phase. Looking like a rapper, he went over to talk to his friend Neymar after the game. He was pilloried for wearing his own outfit instead of the club suit. Then came the push on a cameraman from an Italian sports TV channel for following him too closely as he arrived at Naples station with the national team; next a club charter flight that never arrived, leaving Mario incandescent with rage; then a car accident in Brescia, followed by criticism from various politicians and managers. Everything he did hit the headlines and every move he made saw him put his foot firmly in it. An angry Mario responded to this media bombardment with a tweet on 17 October: 'Stop talking and talking and talking. Live and let live! Live and let me live and you'll see the difference!' The papers got hold of a story that Milan had decided to provide Mario with a tutor. They wanted someone, a former policeman on this occasion, to help him sort out his head. In London, José Mourinho was enjoying every minute: 'Mario is a fantastic guy. I think a tutor would have nothing but fun with him. I don't know what his role would be but I'm sure he would never get bored with a lunatic like him.' Mino Raiola, Mario's agent, was quick to deny it: 'Mario is not getting a tutor. It's yet another media invention. The only things people talk about in Italy are politics and Balotelli. There was all this fuss in England too but it was more manageable. The news is always pumped up here. Perhaps we're all guilty and need to calm down a bit.' Mario also calmed down, according to the *Gazzetta dello Sport*, after a meeting with Adriano Galliani in which he signed what the Italian press referred to as the 'Milanello pact'. His good intentions were as follows: to ensure he would not arrive late at training, he agreed to leave his villa in Limido Comasco and move to Milan; he would change his Ferrari for a club car provided by their sponsor; he would wear the club suit and finally, he would cut off his mohican. After a month-long absence, he made his return against Parma with a completely shaved head and without the usual sparklers in his ears. This reappearance in the guise of a good guy did not really work. He played poorly, received a yellow card and, for the first time since he had signed for AC Milan, Allegri substituted him. Milan lost 3-2 and ended up tenth in the table, sixteen points behind the leaders, Roma.

November 2013

It was a rough time for Balotelli without his mohican. Like Samson, his strength had gone with his hair. If he had set everyone's hearts racing in the spring, now he failed to convince even the faithful. On Sunday 24 November, he wrote in a tweet: 'This is the end,' after a 1-1 draw at home against Genoa thanks to his miss from the penalty spot. The AC Milan fans in the Curva Sud fiercely criticised both the team and the management. Mario offered to go and negotiate with the *ultras*, but he was held back. The following morning he added: '*Forza Milan*, always and no matter what.' But the horse had bolted and a raft of interpretations was unleashed. The most popular focused on the number 45's next farewell: rumours were rife that, come January, he would join Mourinho at Chelsea.

December 2013

Balotelli's form returned at Catania with his first league goal in more than two months, his first since the match against Napoli on 22 September. Milan returned to winning ways in the league after 43 days. There was still plenty of controversy surrounding the number 45: after a midfield challenge, Mario pounced on Nicolás Spolli, accusing him of having called him a 'filthy n*****'. Nose to nose, the situation deteriorated and Kaká had to drag Mario away. Allegri substituted him to avoid disaster. Balotelli left the pitch with three fingers in the air, the goals Milan had scored that day. After reading the referee's report and watching the footage, the governing body decided not to punish the Argentine player for the alleged racist insult. 'Thank goodness there's justice in this country,' the boy from Concesio posted sarcastically on Twitter several days later. The newspapers said Balotelli was back the following week when Super Mario scored twice against Livorno. The first goal was a tap-in on the end of a cross from Montolivo, followed by an absolute screamer from 30 yards out that flew over the wall and into the top corner. It was too bad that another rocket, which would have given Milan a win rather than a draw, hit the crossbar. Balotelli was still happy and said: 'I've always been fine. There were never these big problems that were written about in the newspapers. I just wasn't scoring, that was all. I scored two today and it could have been three.' There was plenty to be hopeful about in the next Champions League game against Ajax. Down to ten men after Montolivo's sending off, Milan resisted the Dutch onslaught. Balo fought hard in the midfield to defend a 0-0 draw that saw the *Rossoneri* go through. After the match, Mario said with satisfaction: 'We are a good team. We'll get back to the top of the league.' But at the end of the month, rumours of a Balotelli departure became more and more insistent. Silvio Berlusconi was said to have demanded the striker be put up for sale during the winter transfer window. The club denied it.

January 2014

Massimiliano Allegri was sacked on 12 January. The 4-3 defeat to Sassuolo had cost him his job or more likely Milan's results during the first half of the season: five wins, seven draws, seven defeats, 22 points, eleventh in the table. The new manager, someone familiar to both European and Milanese football, arrived on 16 January: Clarence Seedorf. The Dutch manager's first game, against Verona, saw Balotelli score from the penalty spot in the 83rd minute, giving Milan the win. He dedicated the victory to Clarence. The manager explained: 'I've established an excellent understanding with Mario in just a few days. I'll try to help him grow because he has enormous potential. So many of the things said about him are exaggerated and not really true.'

February 2014

'Finally, the TRUTH :-) … Pia … Sweet child of mine!!! Your Dad.' Mario posted the above tweet on 5 February, announcing his paternity of little Pia, born to his ex-girlfriend

Raffaella Fico on 5 December 2012. Super Mario had undergone a DNA test before the judge had ordered him to do so. It was a happy ending to a story that had generated endless gossip, glossy covers and tabloid TV reports. The episode that had been discussed more than Maradona's antics had ended up in court. The final curtain had fallen the night before Milan's game against Napoli, the city in which Pia lived with her mother. Mario dreamt of scoring a goal to dedicate to his daughter, but by the 73rd minute, he had failed to create anything and Seedorf called him back to the bench. Mario lifted up his black jacket over his face. When he pulled it down again, his face was streaked with tears. Not only had he failed to score, he had lost the head-to-head with Gonzalo Higuaín, who had scored twice. Payback came on Valentine's Day when Balo hit the target from 35 yards out against Bologna at the San Siro. There were no celebrations. Seedorf was full of applause: the boy had taken the heat off him.

March 2014

Clarence Seedorf declared: 'Who cares if he plays ping pong? The sad thing is that this is a news story in Italy.' And yet everyone was talking about it. Out for two weeks with a shoulder injury, on 5 March, Mario tweeted a photo of himself at home with his shirt off, standing by a table tennis table holding two bats with a ball in his mouth. The caption read: 'Good night everyone. If anyone thinks they can beat me, just let me know. I've never lost!' The following morning, Milan's management expressed their disappointment. Mario countered: 'Milan doesn't like it? What? Ping pong? Ahahh Ahahhhh! I didn't play and even if I had, I'm left-handed.' He then posted a photo of himself undergoing physiotherapy on his injured shoulder.

Once the ping pong crisis had blown over and the injured shoulder had healed, Mario made his return with three goals against Parma, Fiorentina and Chievo. With thirteen goals behind him, he had exceeded the previous season's tally, although he had only played thirteen league games that year. Seedorf reported a marked improvement, adding that Mario was growing up and behaving in an exemplary way, both as a player and a person.

April 2014

An argument on live TV occurred after tension had arisen with Seedorf following Mario's substitution during Milan's resounding 2-0 loss to Roma. Three retired players were offering their expert opinions in the studio: Giancarlo Marocchi (formerly of Juventus), Zvonimir Boban (Milan) and Christian Panucci (Roma). Marocchi pointed out: 'My criticism is that you don't move around the pitch very much.' Super Mario replied, with a hard stare: 'Who's speaking? I don't think you know anything about football.' Boban then asked him: 'Do you really think you're a world-class player?' 'I don't think I'm a world-class player. I think I'm a normal player. I've never said that, you're the ones who talk about that.' Of course, that was not the end of it: the Milan number 45 let loose on Twitter at 4 am: '*Mamma mia*, I split Italy into two! While almost everyone everywhere else is on my side. What a strange game.' Mario went on the attack to defend himself and criticism rained down on him from all quarters. AC Milan were unhappy and there was already talk of a summer departure to Monaco or the Premier League. The national team staff were worried: the boy had not grown up, he was invisible in important matches and his performance as a striker was not worthy of the World Cup in Brazil.

May 2014

Derby time. This was to be Mario's 100th performance in Serie A. He had scored 46 goals. The Inter fans targeted him with racist chanting before turning on all Neapolitans. Mario failed to score but the winning goal came from a free kick awarded for a foul against him. Nigel de Jong found himself on the receiving end of a cross from the right before heading it past Handanovic. The *Rossoneri* had beaten the *Nerazzurri* for the first time in three years. Attention turned away from football to Mario's adventures off the pitch. Firstly, he went after a thief: while they were leaving a nightclub, Super Mario and his brother Enock gave chase in pursuit of a scoundrel who had apparently stolen his mobile phone. They caught him and, according to Italian celeb magazine *Diva e Donna*, a scuffle ensued. Then came a burglary at Mario's Limido Comasco villa. Thieves ransacked the house, stole jewellery and watches and drove off in his rented Porsche Carrera, which was found abandoned several hours later. Tucked up in the garage, the Ferrari was safe and sound. The final Serie A game of the season, between Milan and Sassuolo, was played on 18 May. Balotelli was on the bench because he had arrived an hour and a half late for a training session during the week. The theft had resulted in some difficult days. He came on in the 73rd minute, just enough time to show off the new boots he would be wearing at the World Cup. Milan won 2-1. They finished eighth in the table with 57 points, compared with the 102 points earned by Juventus to win the league. They were knocked out of the Champions League in the second round by Atlético Madrid. They lost in the quarter-final of the Coppa Italia against Udinese. After sixteen years, they would not take part in European competition of any kind. Balotelli ended his run with fourteen league goals and four in the Coppa Italia and Champions League combined. He was the team's top scorer but his stats were a long way from those of Serie A's top scorer, Ciro Immobile, who had scored 22. They were also light years away from the 31 scored by both Cristiano Ronaldo and Luis Suárez, the top scorers in Europe's other leagues. In short, Balo's first full season with AC Milan had been a fiasco. Luckily, there was the World Cup in Brazil to look forward to, the one Mario had been dreaming about since he was a boy. Things got off to a bad start at the Coverciano training camp. At 11 am on 21 May, Balotelli, Cassano, Marchisio and De Rossi were training on a side pitch when someone shouted from outside the fence: 'Filthy n*****'. Mario did not notice at first but then got angry: 'You only get these idiots in Rome and Florence,' he told his teammates.

June 2014

'She said yes ... The most important yes in my life.' Mario made the announcement in English on his Instagram page on 10 June: he had asked his girlfriend, Fanny Neguesha, to marry him. He added, alongside a stream of photos: 'That was the place of my question [Ipanema Beach]. I love you and happy birthday too! Je t'aime my WIFE.' His teammates showered the future groom with applause and hugs at the Mangaratiba training camp. It was to be a moment of romance before the serious work started. There were only four days left until Italy were scheduled to begin their assault on the World Cup in their opening game against England on 14 June.

'Balotelli condemns brave England to defeat' (*The Telegraph*). 'Balotelli rises to wreck England's ambitions after sign of promise in Manaus' (*The Independent*). 'Ex-Man City man Mario Balotelli fires Italy to victory against England' (*Daily Star*). 'Italy's Mario Balotelli leaves England's Group D hopes in the balance' (*The Guardian*). The following day, Super Mario appeared on the front page of every newspaper in England. He was behind the *Azzurri*'s 2-1 win over the Three Lions. Antonio Candreva got past Leighton Baines on the right and crossed the ball into the box, where the number 9 jumped onto the shoulders of Gary Cahill and headed the ball into the back of the net, past his former teammate, Joe Hart. He had scored and dedicated his goal to his future wife, Fanny, who was watching in the stands. At the end of the match, Chiellini was the first to hug him, telling him: 'Laugh, Mario, laugh!' This time, the player who never celebrates broke into a huge smile. Balo and Andrea Pirlo, who almost made it 3-1 with a free kick that grazed the crossbar, were the players who made the difference. Italy was back to winning ways after stalling for nine months.

Back home, people played along. On Instagram and Twitter, Mario showed how happy he was with idyllic photos, videos of his fiancée and dedications to his younger sister. At a press conference on 19 June, the day before the second Group B game against Costa Rica, he showed just how impassioned he was. They asked him: 'Neymar, Balotelli … Who will be the star of this World Cup?' 'I hope Italy will be the star. Not Balotelli. My aim is to help Italy win the World Cup.' 'How keen are you to win the Golden Boot?' 'The Golden Boot is an honour, but at the moment I'm not interested in it. I'm interested in the World Cup, which is more important than a league title, a Golden Boot or the Champions League.' He refused to talk about his future: 'At the moment, I'm only thinking about playing in an Italy shirt.'

He appeared a hundred times in an Italy shirt in his own special Panini sticker album. Mario posted a photo on Facebook, where he has more than seven million fans, of a page from a Panini sticker book filled only with stickers of himself, accompanied by the caption, 'Why Always Me?' At the press conference, he added: 'It will be tough to beat Costa Rica. We'll have to give 200 per cent.' A few hours before the match, after England had lost to Luis Suárez's Uruguay, he tweeted in English: 'If we beat Costa Rica, I want a kiss, obviously on the cheek, from the UK Queen.' Balotelli had done his calculations and he knew that England's qualification depended on the *Azzurri* beating Costa Rica and Uruguay. The kiss from the Queen was not to be. Instead came a resounding slap in the face dished out by Bryan Ruiz, the Costa Rica captain. Italy lost 1-0 to Costa Rica in Recife on 20 June. The number 9, who hid his face in his blue shirt, was a picture of disappointment, of embarrassment, of failure, as the press would report. Italy had missed their chance and Mario had missed a sitter in the 31st minute. A clever pass from Pirlo bypassed the defence but Mario's first touch was poor. He tried to make up for it by running after the ball. He had the advantage over Keylor Navas, the Costa Rica keeper, who stayed on his feet. Mario tried to lob it past him but kicked it into touch. 'Ah, if only Mario had scored that goal,' Prandelli was later heard to say. All was not lost though: Italy needed a win or a draw in the last game against Uruguay to qualify.

Meanwhile, in Genoa, Barbara Berlusconi, Silvio's daughter and vice president of AC Milan, was about to set sail on the club's *Rossonero* Cruise. She commented: 'Mario is a great player and a real Italian talent and I would like to see him stay with us. But nobody is irreplaceable. We'll see what happens.' It was clear she was open to selling the number 45. Transfer market hearsay reported that Arsenal were prepared to pay as much as €32 million for the player.

On 24 June, Italy said farewell to the Brazil World Cup

at the Das Dunas Stadium in Natal. Diego Godín, the man who won La Liga and almost the Champions League for Atlético Madrid, took the Uruguayans through to the knockout phase with a header that came off his shoulder. Mario's display was barely watchable: he received a yellow card, failed to stop the ball twice and attempted a woeful shot. He was substituted for Marco Parolo at the beginning of the second half. The match would go down in history for Luis Suárez's bite on Giorgio Chiellini and the turmoil it caused within the Italian team. Insults flew around the dressing room and Balotelli was the number one culprit. Veteran players, Gianluigi Buffon and Daniele De Rossi did not hold back when it came to their teammate. He was accused of thinking more about himself than the team. Mario gave as good as he got and then sat on the team bus on his own before being asked to return to pay tribute to Andrea Pirlo, who was retiring from international football. Cesare Prandelli assumed all responsibility for the defeat and announced his irrevocable resignation, as did Giancarlo Abete, the president of the Italian Football Federation. But before he left, Prandelli took a shot at Mario: 'You can never tell whether he's calm or stressed. I took him off because he'd already been booked and I was afraid we'd end up with ten men.' He also intimated that he had made a mistake by focusing on the AC Milan player.

Italy's hero in Germany 2012, he had become a scapegoat, ostracised as the guilty party in the defeat. Accusations of all kinds came thick and fast, such as one fan who made a video insulting Mario, telling him: 'Mario, you're not really Italian.' Balotelli's response was immediate. It came on Instagram: 'I didn't choose to be Italian. I strongly wanted to be because I was born in ITALY and have always lived in ITALY. I was really motivated for this World Cup and I'm sad, angry and disappointed with myself. Sure, maybe I could have scored against Costa Rica. You're right but so what? Is this what you meant to say? I'm not going to allow the blame to be placed only on me this time because Mario Balotelli gave his all for the national team and didn't do anything wrong (character-wise). So look for another excuse because Mario Balotelli is prepared to move forward stronger than before with his head held high. Honoured to have given his all for his country. Or maybe, like you say, I'm not Italian. Africans would never cast aside one of their "brothers". NEVER. In this, us n******, as you call us, are light years ahead of you. Missing a goal or running around a little or a lot is not SHAMEFUL. These comments are SHAMEFUL. Real Italians! Really?'

Mario shouted about injustice for all the world to hear but few people listened and other problems that were not to do with race soon came to the fore. According to Emanuela Audisio in *La Repubblica*: 'Samuel Beckett waited forty years for Godot. The result was an absurd work about waiting for an eternity. The leaves fall and days pass. Maybe tomorrow. In Italy's story, no one is waiting for Balotelli any more. Not even now that he's taken on the guise of Black Power, shouting: "You're treating me like a n*****." Everyone has grown tired of it: Prandelli, who has gone, the national team, which has changed its mind, his teammates, who have dismissed him, the country that has been misled and hoped for more [...] He had everything it takes to be happy: a woman, a team that told him to laugh more, a manager who always defended and protected him and a world ready and waiting to welcome his talent. He is at an age, 24, that offered much as an investment in future World Cups. But now everything has gone up in smoke. His tweet is that of a boy who is incapable of even a crumb of conscience. The impression is that he imploded under the tension and expectation. It was all too much for him. The genuine and unfortunate provocation he has received in stadiums across Italy, as well as that which has been self-inflicted, has condemned him to stay holed-up in a desperate burrow instead of coming out to share what life has to offer. The World Cup has shrunk and reshaped him. He is not a champion or a star; he is not a great leader but a good player. And not because of the colour of his skin, because he was not on the receiving end of any boos in Brazil, only of applause.'

July 2014

After coming back to Italy, Fanny and Mario flew to the beaches of Miami for an early honeymoon, which was documented in detail on social media. On 11 July, Super Mario started talking about himself again: this time with a rifle pointing down the lens. The photo was accompanied by the caption: 'Big kiss to all the haters.' The picture was removed immediately and replaced with a calmer image and message: 'The wing structure of the bumble bee, in relation to its weight, is not suitable for flight, but it does not know that and flies anyway.'

Fanny posted another snapshot with Mario in front of the Arsenal store in New York. The Gunners fans were keen, telling Mario to 'Come to us'. If transfer market rumours were to be believed, Adriano Galliani seemed about to offer Arsène Wenger an exchange: €15 million plus Joel Campbell, the Costa Rica centre forward, for Mario. The deal did not go through. Perhaps because, as Silvio Berlusconi said at a meeting of his Forza Italia political party leaders: 'It wasn't Italy who lost the World Cup, it was me. I was about to sell Balotelli but who will want him now?'

On 22 July, AC Milan set off for New York to take part in the Guinness Cup, a summer tournament for Europe's biggest teams. Balo joined the group in the Big Apple. Pippo Inzaghi, former *Rossonero* striker and Under-20 coach, had taken over from Clarence Seedorf. Before boarding his transatlantic flight, he said the following about Mario: 'I will forget everything I have heard about him, for better or for worse, as I've done with the other players. Mario is a talented guy and I will try to get the best out of him.' But he would not be drawn on the number 45's future: 'Is he untransferable? That's a decision for the club.'

The first game in the Guinness Cup was against Olympiakos in Toronto on 24 July. The Greeks won 3-0. The second match was against Manchester City on 28 July. Manuel Pellegrini's team won 5-1. Balotelli discovered he was also popular in the US, as was demonstrated in Pittsburgh: two fans wearing Milan shirts invaded the pitch during the warm-up just to have their picture taken with Super Mario.

August 2014

The final Guinness Cup game was played against Liverpool in Charlotte on 2 August. It ended in a 2-0 win for the English team. Brendan Rodgers, the Liverpool manager, talked about Balotelli in the press conference the day before the game: 'He's got all the qualities. He's 6 ft 3 ins, he's quick, his touch is terrific and he can score goals. I saw that in his time at Inter Milan as a young player and obviously going to Manchester City when we had a real close eye on him there. He's a big talent. He went back to Italy to play and he's still young. If his focus is right, his concentration is right and he leads the lifestyle of a top player then he can play for any team in the world.'

Twenty days later, Mario ended up at Liverpool.

Chapter 22

Flop

He buries the past with a single, curt phrase: 'It was a mistake to go back to Italy.' And for those who still had not quite got it: 'Leaving England was the wrong thing to do.' Excited about the present, Mario says: 'I'm happy to be back in England. English football is beautiful. Liverpool are one of the best teams in England and the football is very good here. It's a great team with young players and that's why I came here. I maybe have a little bit more experience than other players. If I can help them, I'm happy to. I didn't expect this kind of welcome because I've always been playing against Liverpool. Whenever I played against Liverpool, the fans we're not nice with me. But that's normal, it's football! Now that I play for Liverpool, I can see the expectation in people. They're delighted and that makes me very happy at the same time. Playing on the pitch at Anfield will be special. I'm excited about playing here.'

In his first interview with the club's TV channel as a Reds player, Mario Balotelli seemed very ambitious and was oozing happiness from every pore. He continued: 'I always start a competition wanting to go as far as possible. I want to take Liverpool to the Champions League. I want to win another one [after winning once with Inter]. I was in a team but it wasn't all mine.'

It was 25 August 2014 when the former AC Milan player arrived in Liverpool. He signed a contract that would keep him at Anfield until 2019. He would earn £5.7 million a year; his signing cost Liverpool £16 million. He posed for the customary photos in his number 45 red shirt. He told the English reporters: 'When I was young, I first played three or four games with Inter Milan in the number 45 because the numbers for young players went from 36 to 50. I took number 45 because I was joking that four plus five is nine and I scored in every one of those four games. It brings me luck and that's why I've always kept number 45. I hope it brings me luck here too.' He then laced up his boots, pink for the right foot and blue for the left, before being put through his paces by one of the Reds coaches, Ryland Morgans, in a brief training session.

He was straight off to Manchester, where Liverpool were due to play their second Premier League game against Manuel Pellegrini's City. Dressed in black, Balotelli caught up with some of his former teammates at the Etihad, including Pablo Zabaleta, before settling into the directors' box to watch the match. He was mocked by City's supporters and applauded by the Liverpool fans. It was a shame the Reds took a beating that day: they lost 3-1, leaving Balotelli with a worried look on his face. It was worse for Brendan Rodgers, the manager, who had very little time to get the best out of a whole new team. The £75 million banked for the sale of Luis Suárez to Barcelona had unleashed an extravagant purchasing campaign that saw the arrival of nine new players, including Adam Lallana, Dejan Lovren, Lazar Markovic, Alberto Moreno and Divock Origi. The Northern Irish manager was well aware of the work he had ahead of him. In the post-match press conference, he was clear about just how much needed to be done. He did not hold back on discussing the arrival of Mario. He was asked whether signing him had been a calculated risk. He said: 'We will see but when I talked to him about it, he seemed to see the transfer as a great opportunity. There's no doubting Mario's ability. He is a world-class talent and someone who, for such a young age, has vast experience of playing at the very highest level with Inter, City and AC Milan. We can improve him as a player and help him mature. He's a very bright boy. He is very clever. He understands where he's at, at this stage of his career, and he knows himself that this is probably his last chance.'

Strangely, this was also what had been said by Mino Raiola on closing the deal between AC Milan and Liverpool. Balo's agent clearly thought Liverpool was his client's last resort at the highest level. 'It's all or nothing. Mario is 24. He can no longer use his age as an excuse.' Raiola went on to say: 'I tried to find him a team where he can be an important player without being asked to lead. Liverpool have Gerrard so Mario will be protected and there he will be at his best. Now it's up to him. Another flop is not recommended ...' Raiola did not mince words when it came to Mario's time at AC Milan: 'I have always wanted to satisfy my players. With others I have always gone with my own mind but with him no. He said: "I need my mum, my friends, Italy." Being a dad and wanting to make him happy, I brought him back to Italy from City. It was one of the biggest mistakes of my career.'

Speaking of Italy, it is fair to say that the internet went crazy as soon as Liverpool's signing of Balotelli was announced. There was irony (Mario's Ferrari was mocked up on the pedestrian crossing at Abbey Road behind the Fab Four), teasing ('he'll teach the English how to use Twitter and Instagram as that's the only thing he knows how to do'), regret ('the loss of a talent without whom things will not get better') but also relief that the classic torment of the football fan, the eternal swing between hope and disappointment, was now over.

Italy's press welcomed Mario's departure with resignation.

The comments were disenchanted and tinged with a touch of bitterness. The *Corriere della Sera* ran with the front page headline 'The (Failed) Fable of Balotelli'. Mario Sconcerti went on to write: 'Balotelli has an unusual talent for making people happy when he arrives and even happier when he leaves. He is someone who gets tired quickly because he promises much but cannot sustain it.' Gabriele Romaglioli wrote in *La Repubblica*: 'The boy with his suitcase in his hand cannot find a home when it comes to football. Balotelli found an adoptive family but no shirt or flag to represent. When the comings and goings mount up, the route begins to lose meaning and future.' The analysis in the *Gazzetta dello Sport* opened with the headline: 'Another Failure But We Won't Miss Him.' Luigi Garlando proclaimed Balotelli was 'condemned to chase a rainbow he will never reach. He is Ulysses without Ithaca. The suspicion at this point is that he will always be known as an errant striker. Not even the club he has loved for a lifetime could make him feel at home. The odyssey continues.' In short, it was a sad and melancholy farewell.

Luckily, in Merseyside, his arrival was seen in a good light by the Reds fans. A survey sponsored by the *Liverpool Echo* found that 85 per cent of those interviewed were happy to see Super Mario come to their city. They hoped he would bring back the goals that had vanished with Suárez, convinced that Rodgers could get a handle on the Italian's unusual talent, believing he could form a fantastic strike force alongside Sterling and Sturridge. It did not stop debate between former players bubbling up on the banks of the Mersey. There were those who, like Mark Lawrenson, claimed Mario's price tag had not been that high and his mistakes were a thing of the past, while others, like Gary Gillespie, were convinced that Liverpool were taking a big risk. His reputation preceded him. There were also those who, as described by the *Guardian*, saw Balo 'as a sort of footballing version of Bardarbunga, the volcano currently active in Iceland: fascinating to watch and likely to blow at any time, potentially engulfing his club in a dense cloud of chaos'.

As Rodgers said, time would tell.

Five thirty in the afternoon on 31 August 2014 and the final whistle of Tottenham–Liverpool had not long blown.

The Reds had won 3-0 and Mario tweeted: 'Great win! Wonderful experience to play my first match in Liverpool FC shirt #Honour Fans were fantastic travel safe back home #LFC #YNWA [You Never Walk Alone].'

Mario had played his first game in his new red shirt: after an hour on the pitch, when Liverpool's mission had already been accomplished, he was substituted for Lazar Markovic. Super Mario may have missed three sitters and failed to score his first goal for the Reds, but every comment had been positive. It was enough just to listen to what Gerrard, the captain, had said after the match: 'What impressed me was that all eyes were on him with people asking: "Is he going to work hard for the team or is he going to play like a spoilt kid?" Everyone was waiting to criticise him, but I thought he was a terrific team player. He did a lot of ugly work for the team and showed some great touches.' Even his manager was surprised by his new signing's defensive work and explained during the press conference: 'For the first time in his life he marked at a corner. Seriously. An international player who has won three titles and the Champions League and we were training during the week and he said to me, "I don't mark at corners." I said: "You do now." And he went in and did it great.'

It really did seem as if Mario had immediately understood what was expected of him: hard work, commitment on all fronts, sacrifices for the good of the team and of course, goals. His debut had gone well, his first home match, not so much. On 13 September, Liverpool lost 1-0 against Aston Villa at Anfield and the *Daily Mail* asked: 'Did Mario Balotelli really get a standing ovation from Liverpool fans after doing the square root of nothing for 71 minutes?' Of course, opinions can be volatile in football. Just three days later, the tune had changed entirely. This time the *Daily Mail* wrote 'Liverpool fans ready to fall in love with Mario Balotelli', while the *Guardian* maintained that 'Mario Balotelli shows why he was a risk worth taking for Liverpool'. The *Express* echoed a phrase Rodgers had used the week before ('this season will not become "the Balotelli show"'), claiming that in fact the manager 'was thankful the Italian took to centre stage'. All this because Super Mario had scored at Anfield in the first Champions League Group B game against the Bulgarian team, Ludogorets. In football, one goal can change everything. There were only eight minutes remaining when, thanks to a mix-up between two Bulgarian defenders and Mario's tenacious defence of the ball, an outside foot gave him the first goal of his Liverpool career. He celebrated aggressively. It was 1-0 for the home team, who, incredibly, allowed themselves to be caught in the 91st minute on the counterattack following a mistake by Sterling. It was Steven Gerrard who, four minutes into stoppage time, gave Liverpool the victory by converting a penalty against a goalkeeper whose name just happened to be Milan. The captain was the hero of the night, but yet again he complimented the former boy from Concesio: 'You have to give Mario credit. When you are trying to find a breakthrough you keep going and he did. Great strikers need only one chance and he took it,' Gerrard said. He maintained that Balo could become a Reds Legend and had a selfie taken with him. Not only did he have the trust of the captain but also that of the fans, who hoisted a banner, written in Italian, with the words: 'I have nothing to declare except my genius', one of Oscar Wilde's most famous quotes. And there was more. The stands echoed with the chant: 'Mario *fantastico*! Mario *magnifico*! Ole, ole! Ole, ole!'

It was love at first sight, or at least so it seemed. But foot-balling love, like all kinds of love, needs to be fed and nur-tured. With dedication, and goals in the case of a striker. But the goals failed to come. It would be more than two months until the number 45 could find the target again. In the meantime, there was gossip, rumours, criticism, contro-versy and social media warnings. In September, the usual suspects among the British tabloids, namely the *Sun* and the *Daily Star*, insinuated that Mario and Fanny were no longer together. The rumour was soon confirmed. Fanny Neguesha would explain the break-up several months later during an interview for *Verissimo*, a TV talk show on Italy's Canale 5: 'We had a great time together. I dreamt of starting a fam-ily with Mario but there were some things we didn't agree on. I wanted to keep working but he didn't want me to. He didn't want me to keep dancing, singing or appearing on the front pages of the newspapers. I tried to convince him but he's stubborn.' She said that when their love story had come to its conclusion, she gave him back her engagement ring. 'I didn't want him to think I was with him for his money. Although it's over, we still speak to each other every now and then. We're still fond of each other.'

The papers were full of one of many rumours in early October. According to the *Sunday People*, Liverpool had hired a bodyguard for the Italian striker. He was supposedly tasked with accompanying the player everywhere, living with him in his £1.8 million mansion in the north of the city and following

Mario's every move in his Ferrari. The measure was intended to avoid any unfortunate mishaps. The news was supported by photos of the former Milan and Inter player shopping in the city flanked by the man employed by the club. It was nothing new; there had been talk of a bodyguard while Mario was in Milan, a story that was regularly denied. Once again, the existence of the British bodyguard was not confirmed. What was certain was that during the negotiation between AC Milan and Liverpool, there had been a lengthy discussion about a good behaviour clause that the British club wanted to include in the contract at all costs. It was eventually linked to the footballer's salary. If Balo behaved inappropriately, it would hit him straight in the wallet. Something that happened regularly. Mario got up to his old tricks in the Champions League game against Real Madrid with a gesture that turned out to be anything but popular in English football. It was sacrilegious. At the end of the first half, with the Reds 3-0 down, he swapped shirts with Pepe, the Real defender, on the way into the tunnel. Rodgers immediately sent him for an early bath and substituted him for Lallana. Widespread indignation followed. The *Daily Mail* described Mario as a 'Real Idiot', while the *Liverpool Echo* launched a campaign entitled: 'Why Balotelli has to say sorry to the Liverpool fans.' Former Reds players were incensed. Jamie Redknapp declared: 'I don't blame Balotelli. I blame Brendan Rodgers for bringing him here. How could he have thought he could turn around a player who Mourinho, Mancini and Prandelli have all washed their hands of?' Phil Neville, the former Manchester and England player, was unequivocal: 'There are some things you don't do when you're 3-0 down in the Champions League. You don't go swapping shirts in full view.' Former Liverpool captain Jamie Carragher held forth: 'I'd be surprised to see him here next season.'

Quite apart from next season, many were saying and writing that Liverpool were already preparing to see the number 45 leave, claiming he would be put up for sale during the winter transfer window, with the possibility of going to Rafa Benitez's Napoli. Such a decision was put down to the fact that Mario had not even come close to what had been expected from him. He was not a perfect replacement for Suárez. He had not become part of the group nor made an effort to adapt to new strategies and tactics; he had not studied the history of the club nor fallen into step with the city and its footballing culture, so the detractors claimed. Ian Rush, the Liverpool legend, defended him saying that the Reds fans 'are some of the most patient, but he has to realise he's playing at Liverpool Football Club, not just any other club'. The fans were not all that patient as it turned out. On Saturday 25 October, the jokers at Paddy Power set up a stand right beneath the Kop before the match against Hull City. In big yellow letters, a sign read 'Swap Your Balotelli Shirt Here', giving fans the opportunity to exchange their Balotelli shirts for those of any other player. The queue was far from short. On the pitch, Mario tried desperately to score but the match ended in a miserable draw. Everything changed three days later in a home game against Swansea in the fourth round of the Capital One Cup. In 15 minutes exactly, the number 45 was back on top, turning from a 'Real Idiot' into 'Magic Mario'. He came on in the 79th minute with the Reds 1-0 down. Six minutes later, he sped onto the end of a cross from Fabio Borini coming in from the right and fired it into the net with his left foot. The strike saw Liverpool equalise (the winning goal came in the 96th minute courtesy of Dejan Lovren). The praise kept coming and coming. Everyone said that, for once, the enigmatic striker had come off the bench and saved Brendan Rodgers's skin, leading the comeback and putting himself in the right place at the right time. There was, of course, a hint of controversy thanks to Mario's clash with Shelvey at the end of the game, but it mattered little. The curse had been broken and a delighted Mario tweeted: 'FINALLY' with an emoticon that was crying with laughter. The happiness was incredibly short-lived. On 1 November, he played 90 minutes against Newcastle (1-0 to the Magpies) without finding the goal. It was to be the last full game he would play for a while. On 8 November, he started against Chelsea (2-1 to Mourinho's team) but was substituted in the 79th minute for Lambert. It would be another five and a half months before he would find himself in the starting eleven in a league game again. He spent the intervening period on the bench or in the stands.

There was also bad news where the Italian national team was concerned. One hundred and forty days after the drama of Italy-Uruguay, after being banished by the *Azzurri* old guard, after being discharged by Prandelli, and after being crucified by the press, Mario was called up by Antonio Conte on 9 November for the Euro 2016 qualifier against Croatia and the friendly against Albania. The new manager had not considered him for the team's matches during September and October, but this time, perhaps under pressure from the sponsors, Conte decided to select him. But he immediately made it clear that Mario was under special surveillance. Conte said: 'I've heard a lot about him, but I don't like hearsay. In seven to nine days, he has to give me the right answers in terms of technique and character. He has to show me what I need to see. To me, he's just anyone. He might end up on the pitch, on the bench or in the stands. He's starting at a disadvantage: Immobile, Zaza, Giovinco and Pellè have already worked with me.' In a nutshell, the former

Italy number 9 was about to undergo a thorough examination. One that he failed, without the option to re-sit. Or
rather, thanks to muscle fatigue and the usual groin strain,
he left Coverciano and went home. This was the official version. Behind-the-scenes rumours maintained that Conte had
invaded the pitch during a friendly against the Under-18
team, shouting 'Run, run' at Mario, who was ambling around
the pitch seemingly in protest. A dispute between the pair
proved difficult to resolve and Mario left the following day
with a medical certificate. In an interview with Rai Sport,
Conte tore the Liverpool number 45 to shreds: 'I'm not so
arrogant as to claim that I'm different to the great coaches
who have failed to change Balotelli. I don't have much time
available.' It was hard to imagine Mario returning to the
team, at least while Conte remained at the helm.

Several days later, Mario responded to the national team
coach in an interview with Fox Sport Australia: 'I don't need
people to believe in me as long as I have faith in myself. For
me, it's my family and a few close friends that are important.'
He also had something to say about his performance in a
Liverpool shirt: 'Even if some think that because I didn't start
this season very well I can't be a top player or a really good
player for this team, it's their business. I don't care about
the stories because I know they are lies. I would give myself
a seven out of ten for how I'm playing because I'm running
more than before. Goals, they will come. It is something
that is not coming at the moment but it's not something
that has gone.'

Unfortunately, the goals would take months to arrive while
Mario continued to get himself into trouble. The FA handed
him a one-match ban and a £25,000 fine, ordering him to
attend a re-education programme for posting an image on
Instagram in early September. 'Don't be racist! Be like Mario.

He's an Italian plumber created by Japanese people, who speaks English and looks like a Mexican … jumps like a black man and grabs coins like a Jew', Mario had written to accompany an image of Super Mario, the Nintendo video game star. The Football Association adjudged the message to be 'abusive and/or insulting and/or improper', including references to 'ethnic origin and/or colour and/or race and/or nationality and/or religion or belief'. That the message was immediately removed and Mario wrote 'not all Jewish people love money' and 'my mum is Jewish' made no difference.

Whatever the case, it was coming to something when a symbol of the struggle against racism was reprimanded for a racist post. Mario apologised: 'I made a mistake, I deserve the ban, I won't do it again.' His repentance failed to stop the onslaught of adjectives (stupid and immature) that rained down on him for the anti-Semitic reference. Not to mention the criticism of his conduct on the pitch. Everyone was taking a shot at him. Even an old judgement made by Rio Ferdinand after a Manchester derby was dusted off: 'Balotelli? Half the Premier League hates him. He doesn't know the rules, whether they're written down or not and the fans know that.' Commentators, former players, pundits and ex-teammates let rip, making Mario the scapegoat for a Liverpool that had failed to get to grips with its summer signings.

Thanks to a draw at home against FC Basel on 9 December, the Reds could not get out of the Champions League group stage. They ended 2014 in a paltry eighth place in the Premier League with only 28 points, eighteen points adrift of the leaders, Chelsea. Brendan Rodgers, who was getting it in the neck from all sides for bringing Balotelli to Anfield, began to distance himself from the number 45. He realised he was not suited to Liverpool's style of play and that aggression and the pressing game were not for him. In short, he would have to adapt and get used to being on the bench, on standby to give his all when the team needed him.

It looked like a green light for putting the unsuitable striker up for sale in the January transfer window. Sampdoria were being touted as possible buyers, with talk of an exchange for Sergio Romero, the Genoese team's Argentine goalkeeper. However, in Genoa, the story was soon archived as idle market gossip. There was also talk of Parma as an option, or a return to Roberto Mancini's Inter. In an interview with *Corriere della Sera*, Mario's father figure was questioned about the player he had given his Serie A debut. They asked him: 'Are you disappointed he is the greatest Italian player to have imploded?' Mancini replied: 'I am extremely regretful of that. Mario used to go out with my sons, and the fact that they were more or less the same age was something that helped me build a relationship with him. As a person, I feel a strong affection towards him. He is a good person, someone who acts with his heart. I think he's doing his very best at Liverpool. It's all up to him. He is still young and he has the strength to get back up. After leaving City, he became weaker in every aspect of his game. I was convinced he could do well in Milan, but that was not the case … He risks ending up like Adriano, maybe for different reasons but that's what he could end up like. I hope he wakes up one morning and realises he is wasting everything. I have no clue what the right medicine could be, but anyone coaching him should be paid double – a Balotelli indemnity.'

Brendan Rodgers paid careful attention to what Mancini had to say and agreed: 'Mancini's right. I should be paid double for working with Mario!' The joke was followed by a denial of the transfer rumours. The Liverpool manager told anyone who would listen that Mario was not for sale and that he would not be leaving Liverpool in January. His adventure with the Reds was far from over. Rodgers explained: 'He has come in here and not scored the goals he wanted. He has had a difficult time but we will help him to improve.'

10 February 2015, the 25th league fixture of the season, saw the start of Mario Balotelli's rehabilitation. He scored his first Premier League goal. It was a very easy goal just a yard out on the end of a low cross from Lallana, but it was extremely important because it gave Liverpool a 3-2 win over Tottenham, their rivals in the race for a top four finish. Super Mario, who was sporting a new look complete with moustache, had ended a drought of three and a half months. It had taken him 170 days, thirteen matches, 769 minutes and 48 shots to get his first league goal. He celebrated the goal in restrained fashion, with hugs from his teammates, applause for Lallana and a thumb raised up towards the bench. Nothing more, even if he did post a smiling selfie on Instagram, alongside the words: 'Great game guys!!! This smile is ONLY for those that always believe and support me. Thank you, ♥ and Forza Liverpool👍. But now head down and keep working hard. Tonight is past.'

The wind seemed to have changed; the spell of injuries (muscle problems, groin strains and flu), benches and stands seemed to be over. Or at least, that was what the press hoped for with 'Balo Kop Hero', something the fans craved. Even those who were convinced Mario was a waste of space allowed themselves to believe that this goal had broken the number 45's curse once and for all.

It certainly seemed that way when Super Mario scored again nine days later. This time it was on his own terms in the first leg of the Europa League knockout phase against the Turkish team, Besiktas. As usual, he started on the bench and came on for Coutinho in the 63rd minute. It took him

22 minutes to find the goal, or rather to take the goal. Jordan Ibe was brought down in the Turkish area by Ramon Motta. In the absence of Gerrard, the designated penalty taker was Joe Henderson, but Mario stole the ball out of his hands and, despite insistence from Sturridge that he should give it back, put the ball down on the spot. He struck it with his usual coolness, wrong-footed the keeper, Gonen, and scored. It was the 27th successful spot kick from 29 penalties. He then went over and hugged Henderson. The pair smiled: all's well that ends well. The captain, who was not altogether delighted about the mutiny, commented: 'Mario showed a lack of respect towards Joe and the club's codes.' Despite this, Mario was effusive in his thanks to his teammate, posting: 'Thank you Hendo for letting me take the penalty ... Stop drama now. We won and that's what counts. We are a team and especially we are Liverpool. Come on guys.'

And with that Super Mario closed his account. The hijacked penalty is still his last official goal in a red shirt.

Stoke-on-Trent, 24 May 2015, final day of the Premier League season. On a sunny afternoon in the Britannia Stadium, Liverpool were punished six times by the Potters. It was the Reds' worst defeat since the 7-2 loss at the hands of Tottenham, as long ago as 1962. Their only salvation was Steven Gerrard, about to depart for Los Angeles Galaxy, who pulled one back to save face. Rodgers's team had finished sixth in the table with 62 points, compared with the 87 points scored by Chelsea to take the title. They were out of the Champions League and had only just managed to nab a spot in the Europa League by the skin of their teeth. It had been a disastrous year, demonstrated by their elimination from the Europa League at the hands of Besiktas in the knockout phase, by Chelsea in the semi-final of the League Cup and by Aston Villa in the semi-final of the FA Cup. The team that had missed out on the Premier League title by a whisker the season before, scoring 101 goals, had only scored a total of 52.

What about Balotelli? As was by now the custom, he watched the last match of the season from the stands. The last time he had set foot on the pitch was 28 April: 65 minutes against Hull City in the 33rd match of the season. It was a decidedly uninteresting appearance … as was the figure he cut as a player. He seemed to have disappeared. Super Mario had not played much in March, April and May and done little to get himself talked about for his footballing skills. One happy Sunday he scored with a rocket from outside the area in the All-Star charity game at Anfield on 29 March. He played in Carragher's team against Gerrard's team and had a selfie taken with Didier Drogba and Thierry Henry after the match. In the FA Cup semi-final against Aston Villa on 19 April, he had a legitimate goal disallowed for offside. It was a goal that would have seen Liverpool equalise and earn a glimmer of hope in extra time. Complete with a picture, Mario posted on Instagram: 'No words. This picture says it all. Congratulations to Aston Villa anyway … And guys, HEADS UP. We are Liverpool and YNWA especially when we lose.' For the first time since 8 November 2014, he started the match against West Brom on 25 April. He was eventually substituted for Borini in the 75th minute after a lacklustre performance in a game that finished in a 0-0 draw. According to the English media, Brendan Rodgers had had enough of Mario by this point and couldn't wait to get rid of him. His departure was taken for granted, giving rise to a plethora of rumours about the striker's possible destination. These ranged from Fiorentina to Sampdoria, where the melodramatic president Massimo Ferrero had already said he would welcome him with open arms. There was no shortage of theories, even America, Orlando City to be precise.

In addition to the rumours and profiles of possible buyers, there was little else to mention apart from the letter Mario wrote to Steven Gerrard on 16 May, the day of the Reds captain's departure from Anfield. 'I have the honour to play with you, not for long but still an amazing and unforgettable experience for me. You are a great man and a cool captain! It's a pleasure to leave free kicks and penalties to you. I wish all the best for your next venture and your family. You deserve the best. Good luck my friend. Mario Balotelli.'

There was more news about Super Mario when it came to social media. He posted an angry video on Instagram: 'Do you know me? Did you ever talk to me, personally? Do you know what I've been through in my life? You just saw me play football on the pitch. Man, shut up!' He posted an anti-United tweet in celebration of the goal scored by his former teammate Agüero in the Manchester derby, but he was too quick off the mark and City were bulldozed 4-2 by the team from Old Trafford. According to Kick It Out's report on racism, Balotelli was the most abused Premier League player on social media. He had been the target of 8,000 abusive posts, just over half of which were racist in nature. Where gossip was concerned, he was nabbed by the usual paparazzi in a Manchester nightclub after bailing on the match against Arsenal due to a knee injury picked up in training. On 14 May, he was given an £800 fine and a 28-day driving ban: on 3 December he had been stopped for speeding (109 mph) on the M62 in Merseyside. Gossip in Italy centred on the supposed rekindling of his romance with Fanny. They had been spotted at a hotel in Milan. Mario's apparent disappearance over the previous few months had led to zero tolerance when it came to gossip and harsh criticism of his first year at Liverpool. The *Daily Mail* decided to question

Liverpool's finances, investigating the millions spent on signing Mario and his performance in the Premier League. It was
a merciless analysis of costs and benefits: £962,000 for every
shot on goal; almost £2 million for every chance created;
£79,834 for every pass and £19.24 million for every goal. He
had scored only once.

With the end of the season came the final reckoning:
sixteen matches played in the Premier League for a total of
939 minutes, ten matches started, six substituted and one
goal; twelve appearances in the FA Cup, League Cup and
European cups, with three goals in total. Numbers can never
be discounted and they speak for themselves. The *Telegraph*
ranked Super Mario second in the list of Premier League
flops, just behind Angel Di Maria and ahead of Falcao. He
was given four out of ten and the newspaper maintained
that bringing him in to fill the hole left by Suárez 'was like
replacing a Ferrari with a tuk-tuk'. It could not get any worse.

It had been another flop. A fairy tale without a happy ending. A great player drowned in nothingness. A talented boy
called to be a star of world football who had got lost *en route*.
That's how many people see it. But not Mario. On 24 May, he
posted a picture on Instagram. The photograph shows him
from the back wearing a Liverpool shirt with chains around
his wrists. He looks off into the distance towards the Anfield
pitch, beyond the walls of an amphitheatre. A handful of
words accompanied the image: 'Thanks to Liverpool fans for
this year … I'm loading for next season.' Like a Rorschach
inkblot test, the montage has plenty of different interpretations: Does he want to get back onto the pitch after spending so much time in the stands? Does he want to play for
Liverpool? Does he want to leave Merseyside? Who knows …?

The only certain thing that can be said is: Let him have
his freedom! Once and for all!

A Career in Figures

Name: Mario Balotelli, born Mario Barwuah
Nicknames: Super Mario, Turbo Mario
Date of birth: 12 August 1990
Place of birth: Palermo, Italy
Nationality: Italian
Biological parents: Thomas and Rose Barwuah
Adoptive parents: Franco and Silvia Balotelli
Biological sisters: Abigail Barwuah, Angel Barwuah
Adoptive sister: Cristina Balotelli
Biological brother: Enock Barwuah
Adoptive brothers: Corrado and Giovanni Balotelli
Daughter: Pia
Height: 189 cm, 6 ft 2 in
Weight: 86 kg, 13 st 7 lb
Position: Striker
Number: 45

Youth Teams
Unione Sportiva Oratorio San Bartolomeo (1996)
Unione Sportiva Oratorio Mompiano (1997–2000)
Gruppo Sportivo Pavoniana Calcio (2000–2001)
Associazione Calcio Lumezzane (2001–2005)
Football Club Internazionale Milano (2006–2007)

Club Teams
AC Lumezzane (2005)
FC Inter (2007–2010)
Manchester City FC (2010–2013)
AC Milan (2013–2014)
Liverpool FC (2014–currently)

Lumezzane

Serie C1 debut: 2 April 2006 against Padova

Appearances:

C1: 2   Goals: 0

Inter Milan

Debut: 16 December 2007 against Cagliari, Serie A
First goal: 19 December 2007 two goals in the Coppa Italia
against Reggina

Appearances:

Serie A: 59   Goals: 20
National cups: 13   Goals: 5
Europe: 16   Goals: 3

Manchester City

Debut: 19 August 2010 against Timisoara, Europa League
First goal: 19 August 2010 against Timisoara, Europa League

Appearances:

Premier League: 54   Goals: 20
National cups: 9   Goals: 3
Europe: 17   Goals: 7

AC Milan

Debut: 3 February 2013 against Udinese, Serie A
First goal: 3 February 2013 two goals against Udinese, Serie A

Appearances:

Serie A: 43	Goals: 26
National cups: 1	Goals: 1
Europe: 10	Goals: 3

Liverpool

Debut: 31 August 2014 against Tottenham, Premier League
First goal: 16 September 2014 against Ludgorets,
Champions League

Appearances:

Premier League: 16	Goals: 1
National cups: 7	Goals: 1
Europe: 5	Goals: 2

Italian National Team

Debut: 10 August 2010, friendly against Ivory Coast
First goal: 11 November 2011, friendly against Poland
Appearances: 33   Goals: 13

Tournaments:

Euro 2012
Confederation Cup 2013
World Cup 2014

Trophies

Inter Milan
Serie A Championship: 2007–2008, 2008–2009, 2009–2010
Coppa Italia: 2009–2010

Italian Super Cup: 2008
Champions League: 2009–2010

Manchester City
FA Cup: 2010–2011
Premier League: 2011–2012
Community Shield: 2012

Bibliography

Books

Federico Bertone, *Tutti pazzi per Mario: Il fenomeno Balotelli* (Florence, Firstonline goWare, 2013)

Simonctta Bisi and Eva Pföstl, *Non solo Balotelli: Le seconde generazioni in Italia* (Rome, Bordeaux Edizioni, 2013)

Andy Buckley, *The Pocket Book of Man City* (Kingston upon Thames, Vision Sports Publishing, 2010)

David Clayton, *The Man City Miscellany* (Brimscombe Port, The History Press, 2011)

Concita De Gregorio, *Io vi maledico* (Turin, Einaudi, 2013)

John Foot, *Calcio 1898-2010 Storia dello sport che ha fatto l'Italia* (Milan, RCS Libri, 2010)

Luigi Garlando, *Buuu* (Turin, Einaudi, 2010)

Laura Grandi and Stefano Tettamanti, ed. *La partita di Pallone. Storie di calcio* (Palermo, Selleria Editore, 2014)

Luigi Guelpa, *Super Mario Balotelli* (Siena, Barbera Editore, 2013)

Gianni Mura, *Tanti amori, Conversazioni con Marco Manzoni* (Milan, Feltrinelli, 2013)

Raffaele Panizza, *Mario Balotelli Negrazzurro* (Reggio Emilia, Aliberti, 2010)

Raffaele Panizza Raffaele and Gabriele Parpiglia, *Balotelli. A cresta alta* (Bergamo, Roberto Maggi Editore 2013)

Fabio Ravera, *Oro nero Balotelli e la sua generazione* (Arezzo, Limina, 2009)

Andrea Santacaterina, *Il significato di Mario Fenomenologia di Balotelli, Centravanti di cambiamento* (Rome, Ultra Sport, 2013)

Guillermo García Uzquiano and Aritz Gabilondo, *Sueños de gol. El origen de las estrellas* (Madrid, Aguilar, 2014)

Mauro Valeri, *Mario Balotelli, Vincitore nel pallone* (Rome, Fazi Editore, 2014)

Bruno Vincent, *The Secret Diary of Mario Balotelli,* (London, Sphere, 2012)

John Williams, *Red Men: Liverpool Football Club – The Biography,* (Edinburgh and London, Mainstream Publishing, 2010)

Frank Worrall, *Why Always Me? The Biography of Mario Balotelli: City's Legendary Striker* (London, John Blake Publishing, 2013)

Magazines

FourFourTwo, London
France Football, Paris
So Foot, Paris
Guerin Sportivo, Bologna
SportWeek, Milan
Vanity Fair Italia
GQ Italia
Panenka, Madrid
Time Magazine, USA
Sports Illustrated, USA
Chi
Diva e Donna

Newspapers
Italy:
Corriere della Sera
La Repubblica

La Stampa
La Gazzetta dello Sport
Corriere dello Sport-Stadio
Tuttosport
Il Manifesto
Bresciaoggi

UK:
The Times
Guardian
Independent
Daily Mirror
Daily Mail
Daily Star
Daily Telegraph
The Sun
Manchester Evening News
Financial Times
News of the World
Sunday People

TV Channels
Italy:
Rai 1
Rai 2
La Sette
Italia 1
Canale 5
Rete 4

UK:
BBC
Sky Sports

USA:
CNN

Australia:
Fox Sport

Websites
www.mariobalotelli.it
www.usosanbartolomeo.com
www.usomompiano.com
www.aclumezzane.it
www.inter.it
www.mcfc.co.uk
www.acmilan.com/it
www.liverpoolfc.com
www.fifa.com
www.uefa.com
Mario Balotelli @FinallyMario
Mario Balotelli @mb459

Acknowledgements

I would like to thank: Maria Brai, Manlio Lo Cascio, Alberto Armanini, Marco Duina, Gianfranco Lenza, Giuseppe Magnani, Mauro Tonolini, Lino Fasani, Don Guglielmo, Giovanni Valenti, Andrea Ferrarese, Tiziana Gatti, Renzo Cavagna, Giorgio Cavagna, Disma Bossini, Anna Bertolina, Dario Lazzarìn, Massimo Boninsegna, Michele Cavalli, Marco Pedretti, Andrea Bravin, Adama Fofana, Marco Martina Rini, Sergio Viotti, Ezio Chinelli, Valter Salvioni, Vincenzo Esposito, Santiago Solari, Duncan Heath, Philip Cotterell, Arend Hosman, Michael Sells, Pieter van der Drift, Laura Bennett, Laure Merle d'Aubigné and Roberto Domínguez.

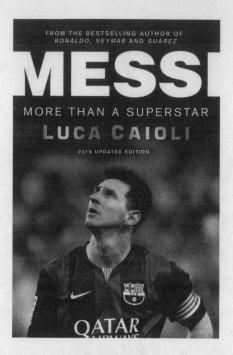

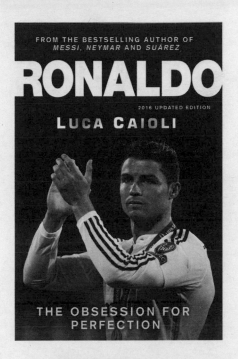

RONALDO

Season after season, Cristiano Ronaldo continues to prove that he is one of football's true greats. A three-time winner of the FIFA Ballon d'Or and the man whose astonishing goalscoring feats have fired much of Real Madrid's recent success, he is driven by an insatiable desire to succeed and to improve himself year after year.

Here Madrid-based journalist Luca Caioli tells the inside story of the global superstar, featuring insights from those who know him best: coaches, teammates, girlfriends and even the man himself. Updated to include all the action from 2014/15 – a campaign in which he claimed the European Golden Shoe for a record fourth time – *Ronaldo* lays bare the career of a modern footballing icon.

ISBN 978-190685-093-7 (paperback) / 978-190685-094-4 (ebook)

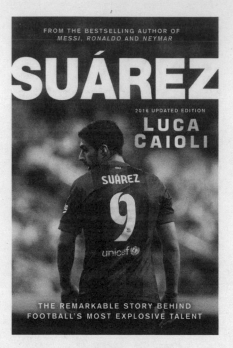

FROM THE BESTSELLING AUTHOR OF
MESSI, RONALDO AND NEYMAR

SUÁREZ

2016 UPDATED EDITION

LUCA CAIOLI

SUÁREZ

9

unicef

THE REMARKABLE STORY BEHIND
FOOTBALL'S MOST EXPLOSIVE TALENT

SUÁREZ

Luis Suárez is one of the most brilliant and controversial
players in world football. Signed by Barcelona in 2014 despite
a lengthy ban for biting an opponent, he quickly became a
central figure in their sensational treble-winning campaign,
setting the seal on it with the decisive goal in the Champions
League final. However, a history of violent on-pitch incidents
has left supporters wondering whether the maverick centre
forward can ever completely conquer his demons.

This updated biography, featuring exclusive interviews with those who
have known and worked with him, offers a unique behind-the-scenes
look at the life and career of one of football's most enigmatic stars.

ISBN 978-190685-097-5 (paperback) / 978-190685-098-2 (ebook)